KiTCHEN COACH

COACH

WEEKEND COOKING

KiTCHEN COACH

WEEKEND COOKING

JENNIFER BUSHMAN
and SALLIE Y. WILLIAMS

WILEY

Wiley Publishing, Inc.

Published by John Wiley & Sons, Inc., Hoboken, New Jersey

Published simultaneously in Canada

For general information on our other products and services or for technical support, please contact our Customer Care Department within the United States at 800-762-2974, outside the United States at (317) 572-3993 or fax (317) 572-4002.

Wiley also publishes its books in a variety of electronic formats. Some content that appears in print may not be available in electronic books. For more information about Wiley products, visit our website at www.wiley.com.

Library of Congress Cataloging-in-Publication Data:

Bushman, Jennifer, 1967–
     Kitchen coach : weekend cooking / Jennifer Bushman and Sallie Williams.
          p. cm.
     ISBN 0-7645-4313-X (paper)
1. Cookery. I. Williams, Sallie Y II. Title.
     TX714.B88 2005
     641.5—dc22   2004016044

Printed in the United States of America

10 9 8 7 6 5 4 3 2 1

Contents

Acknowledgments

I have had many supporters in my journey to bring this book to life. First of all, I thank my editor Linda Ingroia and assistant editor Rachel Bartlett for their invaluable assistance. I also appreciate the efforts of other dedicated Wiley staff including Shannon Egan, the production editor, Jeff Faust and Holly Wittenberg, the cover and interior designers, and Gypsy Lovett and Michele Sewell in publicity. Thank you, Jeffrey Dow, for your great photographs that brought my food to life. Thanks so much to Chad Boyd and the entire team at Patrick Davis for helping me to share my passion with the rest of the world. To my cowriter, Sallie Williams: Your support and guidance have made this entire project possible. Thanks to everyone at Nothing to It! Culinary Center, as none of this would have been possible without you. You have supported me in so many ways as I have taken my mission out into the world. Great thanks must also go to Jonathan, Brooke, Kenneth, Mom and Dad, for without your help I could not ever have made it this far. And finally, to my loving husband Jay and my dearest Matt B., words cannot express the importance you have played in my life. The spirit of family lives in my kitchen every day because of the life that we have built together.

Jennifer Bushman

Introduction

Here's the truth: I love to cook—and weekends, with the extra time available to produce something special for my family—are my favorite times in the kitchen. Of course, it's very simple to pick up some ready-cooked foods or go out to eat, but instead, I remind myself of why I love to cook—and why it simply makes good sense.

The sights, smells, and sounds of cooking can be a source of true pleasure. The methodical rituals of cooking—chopping tomatoes, stirring pasta, rolling pastry—are a good way to unwind; even while working, my mind and body are both relaxing from the tensions of the week. Cooking also offers a creative challenge: I may start by thinking, what can I create with what's already in my kitchen? Or I sit down with a cup of coffee and plan something, taking time to make a list and go to the store for ingredients that aren't on hand. When it turns out that, with a little effort, I've actually outdone my own expectations, I get a real feeling of accomplishment and pleasure. From baking a beautiful chocolate cake, to grilling fresh vegetables for a simple salad, to even taking a slow-cooked pot roast and vegetables from oven to table, creating a delicious meal makes me glad I cooked at all.

I bring my love for—and sense of fun with—food to all the cooking classes I teach. My students have found that learning a few versatile techniques and adaptable recipes can make anyone a more comfortable, efficient, confident cook. As my students' "kitchen coach," I go one step further and inspire and motivate them to want to cook—to enjoy the process of cooking, not just the results, to dare to tackle something new. In *Kitchen Coach: Weekend Cooking*, I aim to get you in on the fun, too. I bring you recipes for more leisurely cooking, when there is time to enjoy making dishes that require a little more time or a few more steps than you can cope with during the weeknight rush.

This book is meant to help you go from weekday "warp speed" to the more manageable weekend mode, which gives us an opportunity to appreciate cooking for both its real, as well as its less tangible, benefits. There's no getting around the fact that preparing a meal usually takes more time than you spend eating it. The usual weeknight focus is on getting the food on the table as quickly as possible. But weekends offer an opportunity to develop a sense of pleasure and fulfillment while working in the kitchen. It's this sense of pleasure and the accomplishment that goes with it that can take the "chore" factor out of cooking.

I have found that people usually don't hate cooking; they dislike wasting time in the kitchen. You'll find that I emphasize time management and organization in my recipes. Even though this sounds as if you'll have to follow unpleasantly rigid practices, in fact, organization boils down to some simple principles, beginning with the French culinary concept of *"mise en place"* or "everything in its place." Being organized really does simplify preparing a meal. Simpler means less stressful, which means more enjoyable. By organizing your ingredients, equipment, and utensils, and properly anticipating the time a task will take, you set the mental boundaries needed to fully focus on the experience.

Cooking can also be more manageable and fun when you target it to the specific needs of your day. Even on weekends you are sometimes tired and overbooked. Other times your family simply wants a favorite dish, like pizza—again; or your kids and spouse have crazy schedules and you need food that can travel, that will keep, or that can be easily reheated.

In the chapter "Why Cook on the Weekend?" you'll find a simple chart to help you decide what to prepare for dinner. I'll give you suggestions for types of dishes or meals—like backyard barbecues, slow-cooked comfort foods, hearty soups, or birthday buffets and family feasts—and you decide what will work for your family, or just what you're in the mood to cook. You might refer to this chart a few times, but soon it will become an automatic trigger, an easy checklist to think about before you plan any meal, or series of meals. It takes the pressure off and gets you on the right path.

Kitchen Coach: Weekend Cooking will be your guide to weekend cooking success. Success might mean you know the whole family is eating fresh, healthful, tasty food, or maybe that a family celebration became a big hit with your food taking center stage. Cooking isn't magic, but it gives you an opportunity to exercise your creativity, all the while bringing your family a little closer together. I'll give you the tools and the ideas you need to get the most out of cooking no matter what your weekend schedule is like. These recipes will let you stretch your culinary experience to include some truly memorable dishes. So figure out what you want to cook, pick out a recipe, and enjoy!

Why Cook on the Weekend?

You've just finished the weekday crunch—fitting in as much work and as many school activities, household chores, and social activities as you can manage. On the weekends, perhaps you just want to relax and not think about cooking; or maybe your weekends are just as action-packed as your weekdays and you just can't seem to find the time for cooking.

There are so many alternatives to cooking as well: going to restaurants, stopping for takeout, picking up a prepackaged heat-and-serve "meal" (even gourmet meals are readily available these days) at the market; you can get adequate nutrition almost without dirtying a dish or breaking the bank. So why, even on days off, go to the trouble and time to cook when it can be done for you so conveniently?

Because weekend cooking can be a fun experiment, a creative outlet to unwind from the week, or a chance for you to connect with your family. You can cook a dish that uses exotic ingredients or that might involve a technique you've been wanting to learn, such as Braised Salmon with Caramelized Fennel and Wasabi Mashed Potatoes. Or you can prepare foods that are classic favorites but just take a little time and effort. Who doesn't love serving a rich, filling stew in the winter or surprising someone with a knockout cake for a special meal? With these dishes, both the creating and the eating are rewarding. And if you are sharing the meal with your family—wow, everyone's actually at the table at the same time—or with friends you don't get to see often enough, the meal is the bonus to the gift of quality time with people you care about.

So where do you stand on weekend cooking? Ask yourself a few questions:

1. Do you feel you are spending too much time and money eating out?

2. At the end of a busy week, do you think you are too exhausted to plan and cook something good for your family?

3. Do you feel you and your family could be eating better quality and more healthful food than you are?

4. Do you find yourself dreading the time spent in the kitchen?

5. Would your family benefit from sitting down together for dinner a bit more often?

6. Would you like to invite friends over more often but planning a party or special dinner seems too overwhelming a task?

If you answered yes to any one of these questions, this book is for you. Cooking can give you a great return for your time invested. When the meal is done, I bet you'll be happier that you cooked. Sounds simple, but with the amazing variety of activities you could enjoy in the modern world, the age-old activity of cooking fulfills both basic human requirements—the need to be fed (actually, the need to be well-fed), the need for sensory stimulation—and the grander goals that you may not think about all the time, like the need to learn, achieve, and contribute.

How? Here's a scenario: It's Saturday afternoon, raining cats and dogs, and everyone is suffering from cabin fever. You need something good for dinner that will perk up attitudes as well as appetites. Chili is just the thing. You have some good ground beef in the freezer, bacon in the fridge; everything else is in the pantry. The sizzle of the bacon and the combined aroma of cooking onions and garlic drifts throughout the house and heads begin to pop into the kitchen, accompanied by queries of "What's for dinner?" Add the tomatoes and fresh herbs, along with the heat of some good chiles and the complex fragrance wakes up the senses. The process of adding a little more of an ingredient you like, a little less of something else, gives this chili a personal touch and gives you the satisfaction of being involved not just in combining ingredients together, but of creatively developing it. Gather together the add-ons like grated cheese, sour cream, chopped green onions, and lots of steaming hot tortillas, and you will have turned what could have been a dismal weekend into something a lot more fun.

Your result is something simple yet different, terrifically flavored, filling, and fairly cheap to make—quite an achievement. In fact, it's a small but personal triumph. To top it off, your family is so happy you cooked this homemade meal that they finish off the entire pot of chili. That's a lot of good stuff happening and it's just from making a little dinner.

Okay, so maybe dinner at your house won't be like that every weekend, but it's worth striving for. Take some satisfaction that by accomplishing the smaller, mostly unacknowledged steps of cooking, you benefit. A tasty pasta dish one night, a slow-cook braise another night, or a comfortable brunch for friends on a Sunday—these are little perks in your life, and they add up to keep you going, to help you face the rigors of the week to come.

For many people, including me, cooking is also part of "the good life." The time we put into cooking is valuable time, not wasted time. Many culinary experiences last well beyond the food and flavors of the moment. Every time you cook, what you bought, how you cooked it, and how you and your family responded register in your mind, giving you a bank of ideas for future reference—about how to cook more efficiently, more creatively, and more precisely, just for starters.

Also, good food, good meals—especially weekend meals—can become lasting memories. Even if your own family didn't cook much, you may still be nostalgic for the fried eggs on Sunday ritual, or the coconut cake your mom made. For me, there are plenty of great memories: my grandmother's latkes, my grandfather's weekend morning pancakes, my mother's melt-in-your-mouth cookies.

Our life experience is the sum of all the good and bad we take in. Cooking allows us to stack the deck in our favor. Knowing there's something to look forward to at the end of the week makes life's ride a little easier, whether you are thinking about the delicious steak you're going to make for dinner or anticipating your child's reaction when you make his favorite dessert. To me, the good life is about pleasurable experiences. The more of these experiences you create in the kitchen, the happier you and your family will be.

Enjoying the Journey

You have likely heard the expression, "Life is about the journey, not the destination." In the same way, you could also say, "Cooking is about the process, not what's on the plate." My guess is that if you've picked up this book and are still reading, you probably do love food, or can imagine that you might, if only you knew some of the techniques needed to cook well. To help you enjoy the process of cooking, you first have to downshift your brain from autopilot (often needed to handle your busy everyday life) to manual, in order to appreciate what's happening when you cook. Going back to the example of making chili, there was the sound and aroma of the bacon and garlic cooking in the pan. Making other sensory connections to food and cooking means paying attention, being curious, and being adventurous: knowing how to pick the most fragrant melon; trying new vegetables just to see how they taste; grinding your own spices to release maximum fragrance and taste. Actually, tasting, in particular, is an essential thing to do all through your cooking (except with potentially unsafe foods, like raw poultry, of course). Tasting tells you if your cooking is going in a direction you like or if alternative action is needed. And if the result is good, you'll be quite pleased with yourself!

Fit Cooking into Your Life

In my years of working with home cooks, I've heard just about every reason for not cooking, including no time, hectic schedules, the ease of having restaurants on every street corner, and the availability of takeout and delivered meals.

First, let me be clear that I am not a proponent of cooking every meal. It's fun to get out and try new restaurants or frequent old favorites. And if you want or need to bring home takeout on occasion, or have something delivered to the door, do it by all means. But because there are so many benefits from cooking, the scale should be tipped well in favor of cooking at home.

I've found that teaching someone how to cook is not the tricky part. It's helping him or her fit cooking into his or her life that isn't easy. That often takes a little outside-the-box thinking and creativity. But fitting cooking into your weekend life is really no different from fitting in other things that you want and need to do. You just have to make the time.

Advance planning really does work. I urge you to spend some time looking at your calendar and giving some thought to what you are doing with your time. There might be one little change you can make or one thing you might say "no" to that will free up enough time for you to cook. If cooking is a priority, the time appears somehow. Try not to fall into a rut of thinking you have "no time." Yes, you need to do the bigger weekend chores like clean the house, mow the lawn, or possibly redecorate a room, plus fit in shepherding your children to friends' homes, the mall, or other activities, and you want to rest somewhere between Friday evening and Monday morning. But, if you take away that edge of stress normally associated with cooking fast on weeknights and imagine that cooking can be a fun, social (if you get your family and friends in on the act), even cathartic activity, it can be something anticipated, rather than dreaded.

Once you find the time, you need to think about planning the details. Spend 10 to 15 minutes planning the shopping and cooking in advance, visualizing how you are going to get it done. Which store has what you need? Do you need to check that any necessary equipment—like cake pans, the grill, or a fondue pot—is available? Ask yourself what's the first thing you should do to get started? Just a little fore-thought can make everything go more smoothly once you are ready to cook. It's okay to wing it now and then, but cooking almost always turns out better when you put a bit of thought into it. As great athletes will attest, visualizing the task (or at least thinking it through) before starting really improves performance.

Another reason people don't cook is that they feel apprehensive about even the idea of cooking. Few want to admit it, but they are a bit scared of cooking because they never really learned how. Part of it may be because the traditions and legacy of cooking stopped in their parents' generation. Their mothers (the family cooks for the most part) weren't in the kitchen every day, sharing their culinary skills. So, today, they may know how to get by in the kitchen—program the microwave, turn on the stove, or follow the directions on the back of a box—but there's no comfort, pleasure, or confidence in cooking. (So, keep in mind that your cooking in your own kitchen, making it an integral part of family life will actually help you develop more self-reliant children.)

If this represents your situation, and you think you want to get past rudimentary skills and the fear of failure, first you have to tell yourself, "I can be a good cook," and "I can enjoy this—mistakes and all." Remember, it's just food. If it doesn't turn out the way you want, you'll have another chance very soon to do it right. You have to eat every day, don't you? My goal in this book is to help you address what your cooking issues are—fear of cooking, lack of skills, lack of time, lack of ideas—and help you cook foods that work within your world. I'll also help you shore up your cooking ability and confidence so that weekend cooking doesn't feel like a chore, a bother, or an insurmountable challenge.

The key to good cooking lies in a simple equation: Good Ingredients + Good Techniques = Good Food. It's really that simple.

So, let's get started.

Defining and Dealing with Cooking Challenges

There are 150 recipes and lots of cooking information in this book, and you can use this any way you like. Pick your three favorite recipes and make only those until they are your specialty. Or, look in the index for an ingredient you might already have in the kitchen in order to make a spur-of-the-moment meal. Or, try all the recipes—one at a time. They are all simple-to-make and tasty and the majority of the recipes can be prepared in an hour or two—less, once you have made them a few times.

Make a list of things you and your family like to eat. If you like, make a computer file with the list, so you can print it out and use it as a shopping list, adding to it the things you might need for particular recipes. Keep a copy by the refrigerator and take it with you when you shop.

(continues on page 5)

What to Cook

The Situation	Type of Recipe Needed	Recipe Suggestions
1. It's Saturday afternoon and your neighbors are coming for dinner.	You need something interesting that doesn't need a lot of last-minute attention.	Try Maryland Crab Cakes with Chipotle Aioli Sauce (page 34), Three-Cheese and Herb Lasagna (page 78), or Country Pot Roast with Potatoes and Green Onions (page 116).
2. The budget has taken a real hit because the hot-water heater died, but you have a family celebration coming up.	You need good food that you can do on a shoestring.	Try Minestrone (page 65), Meatloaf Burgers with Italian Tomato Jam (page 98), or Brined Herb Pork Chops with Grilled Polenta (page 107).
3. Your son's birthday party is on Saturday and you have ten 8-year-olds on the invitation list.	You need easy but tasty fare for party-fueled appetites.	Try Mrs. Sarrett's Chocolate Cake (page 207), vanilla ice cream (page 175), or any of the pizzas from the Adventures in Pizza chapter (page 66).
4. You and your family will be out all day, involved in your favorite sports. Appetites will be hearty and time short.	You need rib-sticking food ready when you are.	Try anything from the Cooking for the Week Ahead chapter (page 165), or Three-Cheese and Herb Lasagna (page 78), or big bowls of Ribbolita (page 61).
5. Bathing suit time is coming.	You need weekend food that's good for you and tastes good, too.	Try Marinated Shrimp on a Stick (page 32), Franny's Granola (page 21), Green Bean and Herb Salad (page 42), Minestrone (page 65), or Sage and Shrimp White Bean Chili (page 138).
6. Your bridge buddies are coming Saturday evening.	You need something wonderful to serve with coffee.	Try anything from the Bake the Cake chapter (page 202), or make some Chocolate Chip Mousse Brownies (page 187), or a Chocolate Ice Cream Roll Cake (page 210), or even Mom's Fruit Pizza (page 73).
7. It's your turn to have the neighbors over for cocktails.	You need terrific simple finger foods and dishes you can make ahead.	Try several recipes from the Finger Foods chapter (page 27), or Herb-Cured Salmon with Rye Bread and Sour Cream Dressing (page 53), or wedges of Endive, Pancetta, and Fontina Pizza (page 72).
8. You want to bring the kids into the kitchen with you.	You need appealing but easy recipes you can do together.	Try any of the pizzas in the Adventures in Pizza chapter (page 66), or the Hot and Spicy Chili with Beans (page 134), or Mahogany Chicken Wings with Crumbled Blue Cheese Sauce (page 149), or bring out the ice-cream machine for Peach Ice Cream (page 177).
9. Weekend breakfast is a family tradition.	You need some new ideas.	Try any of the scone recipes (pages 23–25), or make a Country Frittata (page 20), or Papa's Pancakes (page 19), or even Stuffed Bread Pizza (page 70).

Add a line that says "Foods to Try" and on a regular basis jot down one or two items—like arugula or panko bread crumbs—so you remember to look for them in the supermarket or figure out where there's a specialty food store nearby that might have them. Trying a new food from time to time will keep cooking interesting and creative.

Next, and most important, make a list of things that you consider challenges to your weekend cooking. I've done this for myself and with cooking students and we have all found it helpful in making cooking regularly more manageable.

Maybe you are stressed from the week's work, or too tired catching up on chores to cook, or your kids are picky eaters. It's possible that there are several challenges at the same time. But try to figure out what is the primary issue for you on a given day, and then look for recipes in this book that will satisfy your needs. Keep checking back here to figure out where to start, and then just keep the categories in mind when thinking about dinner or food shopping. Here are a number of situations you might recognize and some of my suggestions.

Other tools you might find useful in choosing recipes for weekend meals are the phrases listed below the recipe titles, highlighting dishes that offer certain benefits, such as Easy Preparation (for moments when you want something that requires only a little attention); Make-Ahead (letting you get the preparation out of the way in advance, so there is little to do at mealtime); No Cooking Needed (just do some simple prep work and plate it attractively); Take-Along (foods that will travel to a bring-your-own-dish dinner, or might be the hit of an impromptu picnic); and Something Special (a dish worth the effort it might take to produce that little something extra for your family and friends).

This isn't a cooking bible with thousands of recipes, but a source of ideas based on real-life needs. Some weekends you will want to cook special foods, either for family celebrations or perhaps for a much awaited dinner party; other weekends you might want something ready and waiting in the oven when you return from skiing, or that all-important ball game. Cooking at home naturally ebbs and flows with the yearlong schedule of activities and obligations. Even the most sophisticated cooks (professional or home-based) have secret cravings for junk foods—just like the rest of us. Even if you, on occasion, use prepared seasonings, bottled salad dressings, even boxed cake mixes when the need arises—you will still want to make good home-cooked dishes when energy and time permit.

I know people who might think it's not permissible to serve an omelet for dinner, or who wouldn't call salads real cooking, but good food is good food at any time. Do not feel hemmed in by convention; cook what you and your family like to eat. As long as you keep an eye on nutrition and aim for variety, you, as the cook, have the final say about what to prepare.

Is Your Kitchen Ready?

In order to enjoy cooking regularly, whether all through the week or just on weekends, it's simpler if you get yourself and your kitchen into gear—literally and figuratively. The more your workspace is arranged to eliminate extra effort, the more it will become a family haven, where extra weekend time can be spent enjoying the preparation of meals as well as the eating of them. Put your mind toward organizing your kitchen so that it is well-stocked and arranged in a way that makes it a comfortable, safe, and inspiring place to work. Clean out your pantry and refrigerator, make sure you have the right cooking equipment and pans, and plan food shopping that will provide a balance of fresh, seasonal foods.

A Well-Stocked Pantry

To keep shopping time to a minimum, you will need to maintain a properly stocked pantry. And properly stocked may mean different things to different cooks. There is a set list of items well worth everyone having on hand, but then your supplies will also be based on what you like to cook most and what your family eats most often. Before you take a look into your cupboards, try this exercise: Make a list of ingredients that you think should be on hand. Base it on what you like to cook or what is on your shelves. Then, go have a look at what you actually have on your shelves, decide what you need, and start getting your kitchen into shape.

A Trip Through Your Pantry

The weekend—when you are more relaxed, and you might be in cleaning and organizing mode anyway—is a perfect time to launch an attack on kitchen clutter, or if your cupboards are bare, to plan a focused shopping trip aimed at making your kitchen a convenient and functional place.

Setting the Scene

Put your work clothes on and plan to spend some time. Get a few trash bags out, and be ready to fill them. It's quite possible you have been shopping for food for years, but have never thought to clean out stuff that you might not even remember you have and is probably out of date anyway. Some things have just been taking up space and cluttering your cabinets since the day you bought them. There is no telling how long the job will take, especially if you are a serious saver, so let's begin with a few guidelines:

A Guide to Organizing Your Pantry

1. If you don't use it, lose it. Stop waiting for those "just in case" moments that never happen and get rid of it. Odds are you will re-buy that special ingredient anyway since you won't remember it is there somewhere.

2. Dried herbs last one year; dried spices last one and a half years. That is all! So if you still have the cans and bottles of spices and herbs you bought when you moved in years ago—throw them away. The natural oils dry up when they get much older. P.S. If you just can't bear to part with them, before using them heat them in a dry skillet over medium heat—just until you can smell their aroma. This activates whatever oils remain—but there won't be much left.

3. Beans and grains are best used within one and a half years. Once a box or package is opened, you can maintain the food's shelf life a little longer by storing it in a tightly sealed container.

4. Oils, such as vegetable, canola, and olive oil, last about one year (best stored in the fridge); vinegar, vanilla, and other extracts last two years. Some oils have a shorter shelf life, such as walnut oil or other nut oils. Flavored oils have a very short shelf life once opened because of the additional organic elements such as garlic or chiles—not usually more than a few days in the refrigerator.

5. If you have kitchen equipment that you use infrequently, like an ice cream machine, try and find an out-of-the-way spot for it.

6. Make a map of your kitchen. What are your cooking and food preparation patterns? If you have your pans stored more than five feet away from the stove, that is too far. Consider that you need to be able to reach the cabinets where you store the glasses and plates while standing close to the dishwasher. What about your spices? They should be near your food preparation area (but not near the heat or the quality will deteriorate).

7. Exposure to the elements can decrease food's usable life. In general, keep foods—fresh or dry—away from heat, light, air, and moisture and they will last longer. The exceptions are cereals and crackers, which will stay fresh longer if stored in the cabinet over the stove.

Here's my suggested list of what to keep on hand:

Dried Herbs and Spices

_____ Allspice

_____ Basil

_____ Bay leaves

_____ Cayenne pepper

_____ Celery seed

_____ Chili powder

_____ Cinnamon, ground and sticks

_____ Coriander, whole seeds and ground

_____ Cumin, ground

_____ Curry powder , whatever strengths you like

_____ Ginger, ground and crystallized

_____ Marjoram, dried

_____ Mustard, dried powder

_____ Nutmeg, seeds and ground

_____ Old Bay Seasoning (spicy seasoning with great pepper flavor)

_____ Oregano, dried

_____ Paprika, Sweet Hungarian

_____ Peppercorns, black and white (and a grinder)

_____ Poppy seeds

_____ Crushed red pepper

_____ Rosemary, dried

_____ Sage, dried

_____ Salt (if possible, sea salt—ground and coarse)

_____ Seasoned pepper (such as Mrs. Dash, for quick seasoning of everyday foods)

_____ Sesame seeds

_____ Tarragon, dried

_____ Thyme, dried

_____ Turmeric

Other Seasonings and Flavorings

_____ Anchovy fillets in olive oil

_____ Double-acting baking powder

_____ Baking soda

_____ Barbecue sauce (choose one or two really good commercial ones for quick grilling)

_____ Beans: white, great Northern, black, dried and in cans

_____ Bouillon cubes and powder (to use in a pinch if you have no broth or stock)

_____ Brandy

_____ Bread crumbs: unseasoned and panko

_____ Low-sodium chicken broth, canned or boxed

_____ Chocolate: unsweetened and semisweet morsels

_____ Cocoa, unsweetened baking

_____ Cornmeal, yellow

_____ Cornstarch

_____ Cream of tartar

_____ Flour, unbleached all-purpose

_____ Gelatin, powdered and unflavored

_____ Honey

_____ Horseradish, jarred

_____ Ketchup

_____ Mustard: Dijon and yellow

_____ Nuts: pecans, walnuts, almonds, peanuts, and pine nuts

_____ Oil: olive (regular and extra-virgin), vegetable, peanut, Asian sesame, and walnut

_____ Dry Sherry

_____ Sugar: white granulated and dark brown

_____ Soy Sauce: light and, possibly, low-sodium

_____ Tabasco sauce

_____ Tomatoes: whole plum, diced, tomato paste, and tomato puree in cans, and sun-dried

_____ Vanilla extract, pure

_____ Vinegar: white wine and red wine (if you like vinegars add balsamic, cider, and rice wine)

_____ Wine: Chardonnay, Sauvignon Blanc, Cabernet, sweet Muscat, Madeira, and Port (optional)

_____ Worcestershire sauce

_____ Yeast, dry active

Pasta and Grains

_____ Bulgur

_____ Couscous

_____ Lentils

_____ Thin pastas (i.e. linguine, spaghettini, or angel hair)

_____ Rice: white and basmati

_____ Risotto, or other round grain rice

_____ Small pasta shells and other shapes

Fresh Basics

____ Butter, unsalted (or salted if you prefer, except for baking)

____ Eggs, large grade A

____ Garlic: fresh cloves (or finely chopped in oil to use in a pinch)

____ Lemons

____ Margarine

____ Mayonnaise

____ Milk: whole and fat-free

____ Yogurt, plain nonfat

Kitchen Equipment

Do you have the kitchen equipment you need? From sharp knives to good pans, quality equipment makes your job easier and more enjoyable. Just as with new or high-quality running shoes or sports gear, good cooking equipment makes you want to get going.

How to Outfit a Working Kitchen

Knives

Knives are your most important kitchen tools. If you can, invest in high-quality knives. I prefer nonserrated knives. Although serrated don't need to be sharpened, their edges aren't suitable for all foods and can make your work more difficult. Keep all knives sharp (read directions and talk with a knife seller) and carefully stored in a butcher block, on a magnetic rack, or in a drawer (always cover the blades in a drawer, or they well become dull more quickly and can develop nicks and scratches when they touch each other). Remember that dull knives are dangerous—more so than very sharp ones.

Knives should be professionally sharpened every six months or at least once a year. Ask the meat cutter in your supermarket where you can get your knives sharpened. If you bought a knife set, sharpen the knife with the steel rod that came with it every two to three times you use it.

(You can buy the sharpening steel on its own too, but the steel can only hone a generally sharp blade. Once it is truly dull, it must be resharpened with a honing rod or wet stone, or by a professional. Review the instructions or ask for a demonstration to understand the technique.) And never put knives in the sink. Wash them separately, dry them, and put them away as you use them. Here's the set I recommend:

____ 3-inch paring knife: for all those small cutting jobs; very useful for people with small hands

____ 8- or 9-inch chef's knife: the workhorse knife; for slicing, dicing, and most other cutting jobs

____ Bread knife

____ Tomato knife (long knife with a scalloped edge): not essential but very useful tool for slicing tomatoes, cheese, and foods that tend to stick to flat knives

____ 10-inch slicing/carving knife: this is very useful for slicing roast meats, ham, etc., or for carving poultry

____ Sharpening steel/rod, diamond edge: an everyday tool used for bringing back a fine edge; cannot sharpen a very dull knife

Equipment and Utensils

____ One set of 11 glass nesting mixing bowls

____ One set of measuring spoons consisting of ¼ teaspoon, ½ teaspoon, 1 teaspoon, and 1 tablespoon measures.

____ Two sets of measuring cups, one for dry foods, one for liquid. Liquid measures are glass or plastic and are available in 1-, 2-, and 4-cup sizes. Dry measures come in four sizes, ¼ cup, ⅓ cup, ½ cup, and 1 cup.

____ An instant-read meat thermometer and a frying thermometer

____ One oven thermometer: oven temperature controls are not always accurate; it is easy to be certain if you use a separate oven thermometer

____ Several wooden spoons for stirring foods or serving

_____ One stainless steel slotted spoon: a long-handled spoon useful for removing foods from liquids

_____ One stainless steel cook's spoon: the same as the slotted spoon without holes, used for basting, mixing liquids, and removing foods from pots and pans

_____ One large strainer/colander

_____ One fine-mesh strainer

_____ Two whisks, a large balloon wisk and a small sauce whisk, or, if you can only have one, a medium whisk

_____ Two rubber spatulas

_____ One flat metal spatula: for transferring and serving food

_____ One ladle

_____ One cook's fork: a three-tined or two-tined fork used for moving foods around while cooking, and for holding meats and poultry steady while carving

_____ One set of tongs: spring action are extremely useful for moving meat and poultry in and out of pans, off and on the grill, or for turning without piercing the exterior and releasing essential juices

_____ One grater, box or flat, stainless steel is best

_____ One bulb baster

_____ One heavy can opener with bottle opener

_____ One vegetable peeler

_____ One citrus zester (my favorite is the Microplane zester)

_____ One wine opener: several recipes call for wine and although many quality wines these days are bottled with screw-caps, most still have corks

Pots and Pans

_____ 1-quart and 2½-quart saucepans, both with lids

_____ 8-quart stockpot with lid

_____ 4-quart soup kettle

_____ 8-inch skillet, nonstick preferred, with ovenproof handle

_____ 10- or 12-inch slope-sided skillet with ovenproof handle

_____ Heavy Dutch oven, or 4-quart heavy ovenproof casserole dish with a lid (Le Creuset is good)

_____ 12-inch straight-sided skillet with ovenproof handle (sauté pan)

_____ Roasting pan with rack

Baking Equipment

_____ One rolling pin

_____ One 10-inch springform pan

_____ One 8- or 9-inch loose-bottom tart tin

_____ Two large cookie sheets, heavy stainless steel

_____ Two baking sheets (also called half-sheets) with raised edges

_____ Two 8-inch round cake pans

_____ Two 9- × 5- × 3-inch loaf pans

_____ One 9-inch glass pie plate

_____ One 12-cup muffin tin plus one 24-cup muffin pan

_____ One 9- × 13- × 2-inch ovenproof glass dish

_____ One flour sifter

_____ One wire cooling rack

_____ One pastry brush

Machines

These items can be expensive but are worth every penny. With proper care they will last a lifetime. Because these are big purchases, I offer my favorite brands, which have stood the tests of use and time.

_____ Food processor: preferably one with a large capacity. My preference is for the 11-cup Kitchen Aid for versatility and power. It has a mini chopper built in, which is so convenient.

_____ Stand Mixer: Preferably the 5-quart Kitchen Aid, though a 4½-quart mixer should be fine for most uses. My grandmother's big Kitchen Aid has been working since 1943. Now that's a great investment.

_____ Heavy-duty blender: 40-ounce capacity. My preference is Waring though Oster is another good brand—I have Gram's Waring from 1942 and it works better than most new ones.

_____ Digital kitchen scale: a spring-action scale with a digital readout is useful for weighing ingredients and for portion control.

_____ Immersion blender: a very useful appliance for mixing and pureeing in the container in which the food is being prepared. Wonderful for pureeing soups, for quickly beating eggs, for making homemade mayonnaise, and for whipped drinks such as milk shakes. Saves cleanup and the mess of transferring food from one container to another.

_____ Electric ice-cream maker: optional, but great to have

_____ Fondue pot and forks: pottery for cheese, stainless steel for meat, fish, and vegetables; optional, but the source of much fun.

Grilling Equipment

You don't need to have multiple grills for great grilling. Below is a brief review of different grills to help you choose and of other tools to help you grill successfully and more often.

_____ Small hibachi grill: small tabletop charcoal grill, adequate for two or three servings. It uses a small amount of charcoal and is convenient to store.

_____ Kettle grill: covered charcoal grill, available in several sizes that are good in windy situations and can be used in light rain or snow. It also acts as a high heat oven. It uses charcoal and/or wood chips, which burn hotter and give more flavor to foods than gas grills.

_____ Large, rectangular or drop-in charcoal grill: a covered grill with a very large grilling surface for families with a great love for barbecue. It functions just the same as a kettle grill but managing indirect and direct cooking is easier because of the larger cooking area.

_____ Gas grill: a covered grill that uses propane gas instead of charcoal. It requires no fire starter, no long preheating time, and grilling temperature (and indirect and direct grilling) is easy to control.

_____ Vegetable grate or basket: a grid with small holes that allows grilling vegetables without losing them to the coals below.

_____ Fish basket or fine grill: a fine meshed cooking grill for grilling fish.

_____ Electric rotisserie: useful for roasting chicken or other whole poultry, roasts, or even racks of ribs. Sometimes one is included with a gas grill, but if not it is an easy-to-add accessory.

_____ Large turner or spatula: essential for turning fish or other fragile foods.

_____ Flashlight or battery lamp: very useful for grilling in the dark.

_____ Food-quality wooden plank: usually available in packs of four, in cedar, alder, apple, etc. (as used in the cedar-planked salmon recipe, on page 153).

Once your kitchen is in order, learning to shop well is the next step.

Making the Most of the Market

In addition to organizing your pantry and kitchen, it is important to make the most of every trip to the food market. The core principle of good cooking is: use the best available ingredients. I don't mean excessively expensive or exotic vegetables and condiments. I mean searching local markets for the most vibrantly fresh, brightly colored fruits and vegetables, quality condiments, freshly butchered meats and poultry, and just-out-of-the-water fish and shellfish.

Today, the range of foods accessible to us across the country is truly incredible. While cities and sophisticated urban areas may offer a wider selection than smaller communities, all Americans have a greater variety of fruits, vegetables, and other fine edibles within reach than ever before. After all, supply is a question of demand. As restaurant chefs and experienced home cooks are demanding more choice and better quality in fresh foods, supply has begun to catch up with demand.

At farmers' markets, green markets, and well-stocked supermarkets everywhere, you may likely see a new fruit or vegetable nearly each week. Old, familiar vegetables are reappearing in new guises. Tiny yellow pear-shaped tomatoes are offered as well as several varieties of the customary cherry tomatoes. More familiar red and green bell peppers are seen in company with varieties of orange, purple, black, and white ones.

Even sizes are changing. Petite culinary gems are pushing out the old bigger-is-better prizewinners. Small and toothsome seem to be watchwords in today's world of vegetables. Tiny, crisp carrots, pencil-slim leeks, and miniature ears of corn are just a few of the varieties available.

It shouldn't be long before eating well does not mean eating expensively. For now, knowing how to buy fresh foods at the peak of their quality, how to store them, how to prepare them, and, ultimately, how to cook them appropriately so that they retain the best of their flavor is key in making the most of the market. And that is where I come in.

Fine food does not have to be exotic, complex, or complicated. A perfectly fresh piece of Atlantic salmon, roasted or grilled with olive oil and garlic alongside freshly steamed or perhaps grilled vegetables is both nutritionally and gastronomically superior to a heavily sauced portion of fettuccine Alfredo.

Convenience has become the working family's mantra. Readily available in stores now are cleaned and pared vegetables, washed and dried greens, even boned meats and fishes, portioned and often already marinated or stuffed. Everything seems ready to pop into the pot or oven, or toss onto the grill. When time or energy is short, you can take advantage of the fact that some of the kitchen work has already been done, enabling you to put more interesting food on the table in a short period of time. The convenience comes at a cost, though the price still remains

low enough that very little home effort can produce an excellent meal less expensively than even a low-end restaurant.

Here are a few tips for a successful trip to the market:

_____ Choose ingredients that are in full season—when they are at the peak of quality, full of flavor, and capable of being prepared with minimum effort. An easy way to know what is in season is by watching your local newspaper circulars to see what is in great supply, at the best prices, at area markets, such as sweet peas late in May, asparagus in June, cherries in June and July, corn on the cob in August, apples in September, pumpkins in October, and all the wonderful citrus fruits in January and February.

_____ Leafy vegetables should be bright or richly green—without yellow patches. Leaves must be crisp and sound, not limp, slimy, brown, or full of holes.

_____ Root vegetables must be plump and firm, not floppy or limp, with no shiny, soft, or damp patches, or other surface damage such as nicks and cuts. Look for potatoes with few if any eyes, and no greenish tint.

_____ Tomatoes and peppers should have taut, shiny skins, full of bright color—no bruises or soft spots.

_____ Herbs must be vibrantly colored, with strong scent and flavor. Avoid any that are wilted, yellowed, or showing signs of rot. Trim the stems and store them stem down in a jar of water in the refrigerator. If you like, cover with a plastic bag to protect other foods from their strong scents.

_____ Plan to use items from the farmers' market within two days of purchase at the very most. Almost all vegetables are more nutritious if they are at their freshest when you use them—ideally the same day picked or purchased. In fact, most fresh produce, with a few notable exceptions, is best within hours of being harvested. This follows a smart tradition long followed on farms, where they say one should have the kettle boiling before one picks the corn for dinner. Now that's last-minute freshness!

____ Ask local growers or purveyors about the foods they are selling. Usually they take great pride in what they produce, and often they will provide a wealth of information on how to prepare what they sell. Ask to sample things you haven't tried before. Often you will enjoy the new flavor or food, and you may decide to introduce it to your family.

____ While bringing a list helps you to shop efficiently, don't consider it written in stone when you are in fresh food markets or aisles of the supermarket selling produce, meats, and fish. Decide what appeals to you and looks freshest, then form your menus around what you have bought, just as many great chefs do. This may take a little more time and effort, but can be more rewarding than following your list or a recipe that calls for food not at the peak of quality, or even in season.

Kitchen Safety

Safety in the kitchen is mostly common sense, though there are definitely things to remember. Here are just a few:

Utensils

Knives

____ Keep out of reach of children. If possible, always store them with the blades covered. If using one of the magnetic racks, store with the sharp edge away from you.

____ Never put a knife in the sink, whether it is full of water or not.

____ Never cut with the sharp edge pointed at you, always cut away from yourself.

Pots and Pans

____ Always turn handles away from the front edge of the stove so children cannot pull pots down on them, and so you don't accidentally hit a handle and spill hot liquids.

____ Always use dry cloths or potholders to take hot pans from the oven—a wet or damp cloth will transfer the heat quickly to your hand and burn you.

____ Always drain liquids away from you so the steam will not burn your face.

____ Be very careful of noninsulated pot and skillet handles. While they are wonderful for going directly into the oven, they become quite hot. One chef I knew sprinkled the handle with flour the minute he took a pan out of the oven to remind him the handle was extremely hot.

____ Do not wear dangling jewelry or extremely long or loose sleeves when cooking as they may catch on pot handles and lead to spills or burns from the hot stove or pots.

Appliances

____ Check all cords to be sure they are not frayed and are plugged in correctly, without too many appliances on one circuit.

____ Be sure appliance cords are not tangled, which could make them fall or spill when you move them.

____ Hold the covers on blenders and food processors with your hand to keep them from splashing liquid—especially hot liquid. Use a potholder or folded towel to prevent burns if a hot liquid should leak.

____ Always have a small kitchen fire extinguisher readily available—not in the broom closet or under the sink—just in case there is a flare-up in a pan or in the oven. Learn how to use it.

____ Anchor any mats or rugs to the floor so you do not slip while holding a knife or a pot full of hot food. Wipe all spills as soon as they happen, taking particular care if you spill oil or fat.

Grilling Safety

Using a grill is not only a wonderful way to cook foods of all kinds, it can be the center of a very social situation. Just remember that while an open fire is inherently dangerous, following these easy rules makes safe grilling just a step away.

_____ Whether grilling with wood, charcoal, or gas, rule number one is to check your grill components often and keep them in good working order.

_____ Be sure the grill is on a level surface, and on a fireproof mat if you are grilling on a wooden deck or balcony.

_____ Keep your grill at least ten feet from any wood structure, wall, fence, or tree limbs.

_____ Never grill in an enclosed area such as the garage, or on a three-sided covered balcony. Burning fuel creates carbon monoxide, a toxic, odorless gas that can harm you unless there is plenty of ventilation.

_____ Grill carefully when the wind is blowing. If you cannot tame the flames, don't grill at all until the wind dies down.

_____ Don't wear loose sleeves, fluttery ribbons, or billowing shirts or dresses when grilling. These can inadvertently catch fire if they come too close to the hot coals.

_____ Keep safety mitts close at hand.

_____ Have a spray bottle of plain water on hand nearby. In case of flare-ups, spray the coals, not the food. A small dry-spray fire extinguisher can be useful, too, provided you know how to use it.

_____ When using a gas grill, know where the gas cut-off is so you can shut it off quickly if there is an accidental fire.

_____ Check the hoses and canister connections each time you use the grill.

_____ Use the minimum amount of liquid fire starter, or none at all, on charcoal or wood, and never spray it on a warm or hot grill (it will flash sometimes, even if the grill isn't lit). The grill flames can travel back up the stream of fluid and cause the whole can to explode in your hands. Better to use a pyramid starter, or compressed sawdust starter cubes, which burn safely, long enough to ignite the charcoal. In addition to the safety factor, petroleum starter product leaves a strong aroma and frequently makes foods taste unpleasant.

_____ Check your fuel supply often so you will always have plenty on hand and won't run out in the middle of grilling. It can be very frustrating having to find another tank of propane at 8:30P.M. with a hungry hoard of guests cooling their heels at home.

Basic Food Safety

Shopping

_____ Buy the freshest foods possible. Check expiration dates and buy the freshest of the lot. Don't buy anything you don't think you can use before the expiration date—it is a waste of money.

_____ Do not buy dented cans or cans that have a bulge in the top or bottom, often indicating the seals are compromised and the contents contaminated with dirt or bacteria.

_____ Do not buy meat if the wrapping has been cut or torn, as the contents may be contaminated.

_____ Do not buy food in plastic bottles or packages if they are dented or cracked, as the contents may be contaminated.

_____ Arrange your trip around the supermarket to buy the most perishable things last. Dairy products, juice, eggs, and frozen food products should go in the cart last and come out first at home.

_____ Do not refreeze ice cream or frozen products that have melted on your way home.

_____ In warm weather, keep a cooler in the back of your car or truck and transfer the refrigerated and frozen foods to it for the trip home.

_____ Go through the refrigerator regularly and discard anything that is over its expiration date, or has been cooked and then left for more than two or three days. It's best to throw it away in a tightly closed container so pets and animals cannot get to it.

Preparation

_____ Wash your hands frequently before, during, and after food preparation and cooking—especially after handling anything raw, such as meat, poultry, and fish.

_____ Use plastic cutting boards for meat, poultry, and fish and wash thoroughly between uses. Do not cut meat on a board that has been used for poultry or fish without thoroughly washing it with hot soapy water first, or, if possible, putting it through the dishwasher.

_____ A good rule of thumb, if you can follow it, is to cut fruit first, then vegetables, then the meat, poultry, or fish you will be using. That isn't always practical, so:

_____ Wash cutting boards that have been used for meat, poultry, or fish with hot soapy water before using to cut up fruits and vegetables, most especially if the produce will be eaten raw.

_____ A good idea is to buy several cutting boards in order to be sure you will always have a clean one at hand. Reserve one for meats, poultry, and fish, and one for other foods. Colored plastic boards are ideal: use red for meat, green for produce, blue for fish, etc.

_____ Don't leave raw eggs, meat, poultry, or fish out of the refrigerator for more than about 20 minutes—or the length of time to warm to room temperature—before cooking or re-refrigerating.

_____ Throw away marinades that have been used on raw meat, poultry, or fish. If you want to use some for basting, reserve a quantity in a separate container before you add the rest to the meat, etc. Don't put cooked food on the same plate that has held raw food without washing it in hot soapy water first.

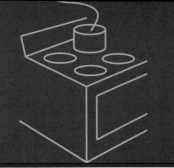

Brunch with
Friends & Family

Brunch conjures up the vision of a great gathering of family and friends. The foods are often simple, and definitely have lots of flavor. (Many people think brunch is an American invention, but that's not really true. The British "began" brunch around 1900. At first, they called it "Sunday lunch," and used the time between breakfast and tea to leisurely dine with friends, drink Champagne, and relax in preparation for the stresses of the week ahead.) Americans have taken brunch to another level, serving an array of breakfast and lunch dishes, and topping them off with Champagne, Bloody Marys, or mimosas. Brunch has become a Saturday or Sunday morning ritual to many of us, and creating a satisfying brunch at home is a perfect way to connect with your family and friends while enjoying some great fare.

When I cook breakfast during the week, the family is usually in a hurry to get to the table, eat, and rush out the door to work or school. The weekend provides them with a leisurely morning, a time when I can linger in the kitchen and treat them to a special first meal.

I always relish the idea of having the kitchen all to myself while everyone is still sleeping. This provides me with some much-needed time to myself, to replenish my energy. I like that it gives me time to reflect. I think about things like my grandmother, and the way she cooked—a few cherished and frequently made dishes that provided both sustenance and comfort for her family. I think about my mother and the things she has taught me in the kitchen. This is time to slow down, to enjoy the sounds and smells of the kitchen. I love the fact that, for a change, I can thoroughly read the recipe I'm making. I enjoy the process of laying out the ingredients, of measuring and then leveling flour off carefully with a spatula, of stirring, of cooking fragrant foods that will draw the family back into the hub of the kitchen—the heart of my home.

As I hear the family begin to stir, I remember the times I have spent cooking with and for them. I really do enjoy having the opportunity to give them such a great gift.

Fresh Fruit Smoothies

✓ *EASY PREPARATION*   ✓ *NO COOKING NEEDED*

Smoothies work for snacks or as a great starter to a weekend brunch. The fruit used in them can be fresh or frozen, depending on the season. I change the juice I add, depending upon the type of fruit I use, so consider what I've listed as suggestions; change it to your taste, if you like. You can easily freeze any leftover fruit, such as peaches or strawberries, as they ripen, for a great addition to your smoothies in the wintertime.

2 cups fresh strawberries

2 large ripe bananas

1½ cups cranberry juice

5 ice cubes

2 teaspoons honey

1. Clean the strawberries and remove the stems. Peel the bananas and break them into chunks. Place the strawberries and the bananas in a blender. Add the juice, ice cubes, and honey.

2. Place the lid on the blender. Fold a kitchen towel over the blender so that it drapes over the top, then if the mixture bubbles out from under the lid, it will not splatter. Turn the blender on high and blend the mixture until smooth. Pour into tall, frosted glasses and serve at once.

VARIATIONS

Try creating your own special smoothie. Using the same proportions of fruit to juice, combine fresh peaches with apple juice, vanilla yogurt, and a dash of cinnamon, or freshly cut up pineapple, pineapple juice, and ⅓ cup sweetened coconut milk. ✱

✱ TIP: One cup of **vanilla yogurt** or **sorbet** gives a smoothie even greater impact. Whichever you choose will add a tremendous amount of flavor and an even creamier texture to the drink.

Cinnamon Sour Cream Coffee Cake

✓ *SOMETHING SPECIAL*   ✓ *MAKE-AHEAD*   ✓ *TAKE-ALONG*

I love coffee cakes! They are extremely versatile—equally great for brunch, as an afternoon snack, or even for dessert. The best thing about them is that they freeze well, so make two or three extra to freeze and have on hand for another occasion.

BATTER

2 cups all-purpose flour

1 teaspoon ground cinnamon

1 teaspoon baking powder

1/2 teaspoon baking soda

1/4 teaspoon salt

1/2 cup butter (1 stick), at room temperature, plus 1 tablespoon more for buttering the pan

1 cup sugar

2 large eggs, at room temperature

1 cup sour cream (from 1/2 pint)

1 teaspoon vanilla

TOPPING

1 cup chopped toasted walnuts (about 4 ounces)

1/4 cup sugar

2 teaspoons ground cinnamon

2 tablespoons butter, melted

1. Preheat the oven to 375°F. Butter an 8- × 8-inch baking pan.

2. Sift together the dry ingredients in a medium bowl. Set aside.

3. Cream the butter and sugar in a mixer on medium speed until light and fluffy. While the mixer is running, add the eggs one at a time. When incorporated, add the sour cream and the vanilla. Remove the bowl from the mixer and fold in the dry ingredients. The batter will be fairly stiff.

4. Pour the batter into the prepared pan and smooth the top with a spatula. Combine the topping ingredients in a small bowl. Spread the topping over the batter, gently pressing it down into the batter. Bake for approximately 45 minutes, or until a toothpick inserted in the center comes out clean. Cool on a wire cooling rack. ✶

✶ TIP: When freezing these coffee cakes, tightly wrap the completely cooled cakes in plastic wrap and then either wrap in foil or place the plastic-wrapped cake in a freezer bag. They will freeze nicely for up to three months.

Papa's Pancakes

✓ SOMETHING SPECIAL

My grandfather used to make the best buttermilk pancakes every Saturday morning, and I love to continue the tradition. My son also likes to eat them for breakfast during the week. I just freeze the extras and pop them in the toaster to warm them through whenever he wants them.

2 cups all-purpose flour

1½ tablespoons sugar

1 teaspoon salt

1 teaspoon baking powder

1 teaspoon baking soda

1½ cups buttermilk

½ cup whole milk

2 large eggs, separated, at room temperature

4 tablespoons butter, melted

Vegetable oil, to brush the griddle

1. Sift the dry ingredients into a medium bowl. In a small bowl, combine the buttermilk, milk, egg yolks, and melted butter. Add the wet mixture to the dry mixture and stir together briefly with a wooden spoon. Do not overmix; the batter should still be fairly lumpy. *

2. With an electric mixer, beat the egg whites at medium speed just until frothy. Increase the speed to high and beat until stiff peaks form. *

3. Stir one-third of the egg whites into the batter to lighten it. Carefully fold half of the remaining egg whites into the batter, inserting a wooden spoon or spatula into the center, then drawing it toward you and up and out. Turn the bowl slightly and continue until the egg whites are incorporated. Finally, fold in the rest of the egg whites in the same manner. At this point, the batter will be nice and light. Lumps may still exist, but do not mix them out.

4. Heat a griddle or large skillet to medium heat. This may take 5 or more minutes. Brush the griddle with oil. When a few drops of water splashed over it sizzle and skitter about, the surface is hot enough. Pour ¼ cup of the batter at a time onto the hot griddle, creating several pancakes. Do not overcrowd the griddle.

5. When the pancakes are light brown, the top surface has begun to bubble, and some of the bubbles break, flip the pancakes. Cook the second side until it has browned. *

6. Serve very hot with your favorite toppings.

*TIP: As a time-saver, measure out an **extra recipe's worth of dry ingredients** and seal in a plastic bag for the next time you want to make these. Then just sift the dry ingredients, add the liquid ingredients, and you have almost instant pancakes!

*TIP: **Egg whites** have reached a stiff peak when you can remove the beater from them, hold it up and the sharp tip that forms when you pull out the beater does not flop over, but remains stalwartly upright. Be careful not to overbeat egg whites. They become grainy and will no longer be smooth and shiny.

*TIP: **To keep the pancakes warm,** heat the oven to 200°F, wrap the pancakes in a clean cotton kitchen towel, and place the bundle on a cookie sheet in the oven. Layer the pancakes, separating each layer with a clean towel to keep them from sticking. They should hold well for about 30 minutes.

Country Frittata

✓ *SOMETHING SPECIAL*

Frittatas are thick Italian omelets. Instead of being filled and rolled, the filling ingredients are stirred into the egg mixture and then cooked on both sides until puffy and golden brown. Making frittatas is fun and easy to put together—they don't require a time-consuming crust the way their quiche cousins do. I make two frittatas with this recipe. They can be cooked up to an hour in advance and served at room temperature. If you are serving a buffet, try dividing the filling into muffin tins and baking the mini omelets at 350°F for ten minutes.

4 tablespoons butter

1/2 cup finely chopped white onion (from about 1/2 medium onion)

1 cup seeded and deveined, sliced red bell pepper (from about 1 small pepper)

Pinch of salt

1 cup seeded and diced tomato (from about 1 medium tomato)

1 teaspoon finely chopped garlic (from 1 medium clove)

12 large eggs, at room temperature

1 cup half and half (from 1/2 pint)

1 cup grated Parmigiano-Reggiano cheese (from 4 ounces)

1/4 cup freshly chopped basil ✱

1 teaspoon Tabasco sauce

1 teaspoon salt

1/2 teaspoon freshly ground pepper

1 cup grated Swiss or Gruyère cheese (from 4 ounces)

Lightly seasoned sour cream and fresh basil, for garnish

1. Preheat the oven to 325°F.

2. Melt 2 tablespoons of the butter in a frying pan over medium heat. Add the onion and red bell pepper, season with a pinch of salt, and cook until soft and tender, without browning, about 10 minutes. Add the tomato and garlic and cook until the garlic is tender and fragrant, another 3 minutes. Divide the vegetable mixture between two 10-inch ovenproof skillets.

3. While the vegetables are cooking, in a large bowl, whisk together the eggs, half and half, Parmigiano-Reggiano cheese, basil, Tabasco sauce, salt, and pepper.

4. Add 1 tablespoon of the remaining butter to each skillet with the vegetables. Over low heat, as the butter is melting, swirl the pans to coat the bottom of each. Pour half of the egg mixture into each skillet and stir the eggs with a fork from the outer edges to the center of the pan, just until the eggs begin to set, about 5 minutes. ✱

5. Place the pan in the preheated oven and bake for 5 minutes.

6. Sprinkle the top of the frittata with the grated cheese and continue to bake about another 2 minutes, until the center is just set.

7. Remove from the oven, cool slightly, slice, and serve with some lightly seasoned sour cream and fresh basil.

✱ **TIP:** Always **chop basil at the last minute** to keep it from becoming an unappetizing black color.

✱ **TIP:** The key to a great, creamy **frittata** is to keep slowly stirring the eggs with a fork into the center of the pan just until they begin to set.

Franny's Granola

✓ *SOMETHING SPECIAL*   ✓ *MAKE-AHEAD*   ✓ *TAKE-ALONG*

Granola has a long history as a healthy breakfast, and with good reason since it is packed with whole grains and fruit. It also makes a nutritious out-of-hand snack or take-along school bus breakfast. This mixture will keep well for four to six weeks in a tightly sealed container.

3 cups rolled oats—old fashioned or quick cooking, not instant

²/₃ cup wheat germ

½ cup shredded sweetened coconut

½ cup toasted almond or pecan pieces (from 2 ounces)

3 tablespoons brown sugar

1 teaspoon ground cinnamon

½ cup canola oil

½ cup honey, golden syrup, or dark corn syrup

¼ cup hot water

1 teaspoon Madagascar vanilla, or other pure vanilla extract

½ cup raisins

½ cup dried date pieces

¹/₂ cup chopped dried apricots

1. Preheat the oven to 300°F.

2. In a large bowl, combine the oats, wheat germ, coconut, nuts, brown sugar, and cinnamon.

3. In a small saucepan, combine the oil, honey (or other syrup), hot water, and vanilla. Heat just until the honey dissolves. Pour over the oat mixture and combine well. ✱

4. Spread the mixture in a thin layer on a large, flat baking sheet with a rim and bake 30 to 40 minutes, stirring well every 10 minutes. ✱

5. Remove the pan from the oven and stir in the dried fruit until thoroughly mixed. Cool completely and store in airtight jars or tins.

SERVING SUGGESTION

Plain yogurt or milk go wonderfully with this granola for breakfast; or heat it briefly and top with a scoop of vanilla ice cream and some fresh berries for a quick weeknight dessert.

✱ **TIP:** The secret to really good **granola** is making sure the dry ingredients are well coated with the oil and honey mixture.

✱ **TIP: Divide the mixture** between two sheets if it is too thick on one baking sheet. Granola needs to be toasted evenly in a thin layer.

Italian Sausage and Cheese Brunch Bake

✓ *MAKE-AHEAD*   ✓ *SOMETHING SPECIAL*

While this recipe suggests refrigerating the mixture before baking, in a pinch it can go straight into the oven. A light green salad or a mix of freshly cut fruit makes this a full lunch or dinner meal. Add some good crusty Italian bread if you like.

½ pound bulk Italian sausage—
as hot as you like

2 tablespoons butter

6 ounces fresh mushrooms,
brushed and sliced

2 tablespoons chopped green or red
bell pepper (from ¼ pepper)

2 teaspoons finely chopped garlic
(from 2 medium cloves) (optional)

1 bunch green onions (about 5 thin),
white and light green parts thinly
sliced

6 large eggs

⅓ cup milk

2 tablespoons all-purpose flour

Salt and freshly ground pepper,
to taste

¼ teaspoon crushed red pepper

2 tablespoons chopped fresh parsley

1½ cups grated fontina cheese
(from 6 ounces)

1. In a large skillet over medium-high heat, cook the sausage, breaking up the large pieces with a fork, until well browned, about 8 to 10 minutes. Drain and reserve the sausage.

2. In the same skillet, melt the butter. Add the mushrooms and bell pepper and cook, tossing, over medium-high heat until the mushrooms are golden, about 6 to 8 minutes. Add the garlic and sliced onions and cook for 1 minute more. Combine with the sausage and spread in the bottom of a 9-inch square glass or ceramic baking dish.

3. In a small bowl, beat together the eggs, milk, flour, salt, pepper, crushed red pepper, and parsley. Stir in 1 cup cheese. Pour over the sausage. Stir lightly to combine. Refrigerate, covered, 2 hours or up to 8 hours.

4. Preheat the oven to 350°F.

5. Top the mixture with the remaining cheese and bake 20 to 30 minutes or until puffed, golden, and just set in the middle. The eggs will continue to cook a bit after removing them from the oven, so do not overbake them.

6. Remove from the oven and cool for 5 minutes before cutting into 3-inch squares.

VARIATION

For a more robust dish, add 2 cups shredded potatoes—refrigerated (packaged) are fine—to the mushrooms and bell pepper while they are cooking, and then combine with the sausage before spreading in the bottom of the baking dish.

Scones

✓ MAKE-AHEAD

These easy pastries can be served any time of the day—sweet for breakfast or tea, savory for accompanying lunch or dinner. Lots of fresh butter goes very well with any of these varieties, or do as they do in England and serve the sweet varieties with strawberry jam and thick Devonshire cream or whipped cream. *

Basic Scones

TIP: English Devonshire cream, or the American version, is available in small jars or pots, usually in the cheese section of many supermarkets.

MAKES 8 SCONES

1½ cups unbleached all-purpose flour

⅓ cup sugar

2 teaspoons baking powder

Pinch salt

5 tablespoons cold butter, cut in pieces

1 egg, beaten

¼ to ⅓ cup half and half

1. Preheat the oven to 400°F.

2. In a medium bowl, combine the flour, sugar, baking powder, and salt. Use two knives or a pastry cutter to cut in the butter until it is reduced to pieces the size of peas.

3. Combine the beaten egg and half and half in a measuring cup. Stir the liquid into the dry mix just until combined and the dough begins to hold together. Don't overmix.

4. Turn the dough out on a lightly floured board and knead two or three times, adding a little flour if the dough sticks to your fingers. *

5. Shape the dough into a flat circle about 8 inches in diameter and 2 inches thick. Prick the surface with the tines of a fork. Transfer to an ungreased baking sheet. Cut across the round to make 8 wedges. Do not separate the pieces. *

6. Bake 15 to 20 minutes until golden brown.

TIP: It is essential to **work the dough as little as possible** or the scones will be tough rather than crumbly. Combine the ingredients only enough to form a smooth dough. You will still be able to see small pieces of butter.

TIP: **Try not to cut the dough all the way through** when forming the wedges. This will let the scones bake with soft sides, making them slightly less crusty and easier to split and slather with butter or whipped cream.

Brown Sugar Raisin Scones

2 cups unbleached all-purpose flour

1/3 cup packed light brown sugar

2 teaspoons baking powder

Pinch salt

1/2 teaspoon ground cinnamon

5 tablespoons cold butter, cut into pieces

1/2 cup raisins, plumped for 15 minutes in boiling water and well drained

1 large egg, beaten lightly with a fork

1/4 to 1/3 cup half and half

1. Preheat the oven to 400°F.

2. Follow the preparation directions for basic scones (above), stirring the cinnamon into the dry ingredients. Add the raisins once the butter is cut into the flour and before stirring in the egg and half and half.

3. Bake 20 to 25 minutes until golden brown.

Ginger Pecan Scones

1 1/2 cups unbleached all-purpose flour

1/3 cup sugar

2 teaspoons baking powder

Pinch salt

1/2 teaspoon ground ginger

5 tablespoons cold butter, cut in pieces

2 tablespoons finely chopped candied ginger

1/2 cup lightly toasted pecan pieces (from 2 ounces)

1 large egg, beaten lightly with a fork

1/4 to 1/3 cup half and half

1. Preheat the oven to 400°F.

2. Follow the preparation directions for basic scones (above), stirring the ground ginger into the dry ingredients. Add the candied ginger and pecan pieces to the flour mixture once the butter has been cut in and before stirring in the egg and half and half.

3. Bake as for basic scones.

Cheddar Cheese and Green Onion Scones

In this recipe the cornmeal takes the place of the sugar in the basic scone.

1¼ cups unbleached all-purpose flour

⅓ cup yellow cornmeal

2 teaspoons baking powder

Pinch salt

5 tablespoons cold butter, cut into pieces

½ cup grated sharp cheddar cheese (from 2 ounces)

3 tablespoons finely chopped green onion (from about 3 onions)

1 large egg, beaten lightly with a fork

⅓ cup whole or 2% milk

1 teaspoon Dijon mustard

1. Preheat the oven to 400°F.

2. Follow the preparation instructions for basic scones, adding the cheddar cheese and green onions to the flour mixture once the butter has been cut in. Beat together the egg, milk, and mustard before stirring into the flour mixture.

3. Bake 20 minutes until golden brown.

SERVING SUGGESTION

These savory scones are perfect to serve with our vegetable-filled frittata, or alongside a steaming bowl of soup or chili.

Dried Fruit Compote

✓ *EASY PREPARATION*   ✓ *MAKE-AHEAD*

Serve this delicious winter breakfast or dessert dish with a topping of yogurt, sour cream, or whipped cream. A slice of coffee cake goes very well with it for breakfast, or serve your favorite cookies alongside the fruit for a delicious dessert. This compote keeps for several days in the refrigerator.

TIP: Cut the fruit into **bite-sized pieces** if you like.

½ cup pitted prunes

½ cup dried apricots

½ cup dried apples

½ cup dried pears

½ cup raisins

½ cup dried cranberries

4 cups dry white wine, such as Chardonnay, or apple juice, or white grape juice

1 cup sugar (decrease sugar by half if using juice instead of wine)

1 tablespoon chopped candied ginger

Peel of 1 lemon, julienned

1. Combine all the fruit in a 3-quart stainless steel saucepan. Add the wine or juice, sugar, ginger, and lemon peel. If there isn't enough liquid to cover the fruit completely, add water until it does. ✱

2. Simmer, uncovered, over medium-low heat until the fruit is very tender and the liquid is thick and syrupy, about 10 minutes.

3. Cool the fruit completely in the syrup, and refrigerate for several hours before serving. Serve the compote chilled, at room temperature, or warm, with a drizzle of cream if you like.

SERVING SUGGESTION

Just before serving, stir in ½ cup each toasted pecan pieces and shredded coconut.

Finger Foods

With a little preparation, and the help of these recipes, you can throw a cocktail party that you will enjoy as much as your guests will. Finger foods are also fun dishes to bring to gatherings at someone else's home. So, before special occasions approach, the holidays arrive, or you get invited to a potluck, learn a few simple recipes and some efficiency tips. Making party food will be easier and more enjoyable, and you'll make it more often.

Ever since I was in college, I have always been the one who brought something special that I made myself, rather than store-bought snacks. I prefer something simple and homemade to dry vegetables with ranch dip from a plastic tub, or chips from a bag, and so do others at the parties. Homemade dips or grilled foods are fun to make and are crowd-pleasers, so that's what I made then and still do.

For entertaining in your own home, a cocktail party is ideal; you can make it happen with a limited investment of time. It doesn't require toiling over multiple courses, dusting off the old china, or borrowing tables to seat everyone.

Tips for a successful cocktail party:

- Preparation is key. Plan your list of invitees—and be sure to mix it up a bit so everyone has someone interesting to talk to (how great your snacks are can be an easy topic of conversation to break the ice).

- Make a list of dishes and the ingredients needed so you can coordinate your shopping trips.

- Mix store-bought items with homemade. (No one will criticize if you didn't make the breadsticks yourself.) Decide on one or two easy-to-prepare snacks like a very good wedge of cheese with some juicy grapes and flavorful flat bread, or a plate of your favorite deviled eggs.

- Choose some recipes that can be made well in advance. For example, in this chapter, Marinated Shrimp on a Stick (page 32), and Crispy Phyllo Stuffed with Prosciutto and Figs (page 33) will make delicious, varied options for the party menu. Both can be substantially prepared well before party time, with a bit of just-before-the-guests-arrive attention.

The notion that you cannot enjoy your own party will be a thing of the past.

Parmigiano-Reggiano Frico with Baby Greens

✓ SOMETHING SPECIAL   ✓ EASY PREPARATION

Frico are the lacy thin cheese crisps made in Italy. You can replace the Parmigiano-Reggiano with Asiago, cheddar, or Gruyère cheese, though the result will not be the same. The fresh herbs used in it can vary; try basil or oregano.

2 cups freshly grated Parmigiano-Reggiano cheese (from 8 ounces)

1 tablespoon all-purpose flour

1½ teaspoons chopped fresh thyme leaves

4 cups baby greens (about 6 ounces)

2 tablespoons extra-virgin olive oil

2 teaspoons fresh lemon juice (from 1 medium lemon)

Salt and freshly ground pepper, to taste

1. In a medium bowl, toss together the cheese, flour, and thyme.

2. Heat a nonstick frying pan over low heat. When hot, sprinkle 2 tablespoons of the cheese mixture to form a 4-inch circle in the pan. Cook it until the cheese is melted into a circle and slightly firm, about 1 minute. The cheese should be just lightly brown.

3. Using a spatula, turn the frico and cook on the other side for 30 seconds more.

4. Remove the frico from the pan and place it over a rolling pin, pressing it down lightly to form the shape of an upside-down taco. Let the frico rest there until cool. Gently remove from rolling pin and place on a cookie sheet. *

5. Repeat with the rest of the cheese.

6. Place the clean baby greens in a small bowl. Toss with the olive oil, lemon juice, salt, and pepper.

7. Place a small amount of the greens in each of the frico and serve.

＊TIP: To shape these frico you will need to work quickly. Lift each frico from the pan with a spatula directly onto the rolling pin and mold it while it is still warm. Gently mold the hot cheese around the rolling pin so that it curves slightly.

Eggplant Caviar with Pita Crisps

✓ *SOMETHING SPECIAL*   ✓ *MAKE-AHEAD*

This pureed eggplant recipe was one of my favorites as a child. My mom would make it for dinner parties and I would take the leftovers with crackers to school for lunch. Now you can serve it with crisp pitas. No one will know there is eggplant in it!

2 medium eggplants

1/4 cup olive oil

1 cup finely chopped white onion (from 1 medium onion)

1/2 cup seeded and finely chopped green bell pepper (from 1/2 medium pepper)

1 teaspoon minced fresh garlic (from 1 medium clove)

1/2 teaspoon sugar

One 6-ounce can tomato paste

1/4 teaspoon Tabasco sauce

2 teaspoons salt

Freshly ground pepper, to taste

2 tablespoons fresh lemon juice (from about 1 lemon)

Grilled Pita Crisps (below)

1. Preheat the oven to 425°F. Place the 2 whole eggplants on a cookie sheet. Bake them in the preheated oven, turning once, about 1 hour, until the inside is soft and the skin is charred. Remove the eggplants from the oven and cool. Cut off the stems and cut the eggplants in half. Scoop out the inside and spoon the flesh into a food processor or blender. Puree until smooth and set aside.

2. Heat the olive oil in a large skillet over medium-high heat. Add the onion and cook for 3 minutes.

Add bell pepper and garlic to the pan and cook until soft, but not browned, about 5 minutes.

3. Pour the eggplant puree into the skillet with the onion mixture and stir in the sugar, tomato paste, Tabasco, salt, and pepper. Stir to combine.

4. Bring this mixture to a boil, lower the heat, cover, and then simmer gently for 20 minutes. Remove cover and add lemon juice. Chill and serve with grilled pita crisps. ✱

✱TIP: This **eggplant caviar** makes a great spread for sandwiches. Try it spread on toasted white bread, with crisp lettuce and fresh tomato slices for a low-fat lunch.

Grilled Pita Crisps

✓ *MAKE-AHEAD*   ✓ *EASY PREPARATION*

To make quick work of cutting the pita, use a sharp pair of kitchen scissors to cut the pita into halves, then quarters, then pull the two pita pieces apart. Each pita round should give you eight pieces.

4 pita rounds

Olive oil

Salt

1. Heat a grill or grill pan to high heat. Brush the pita with olive oil and season with salt. ✱

2. Grill the pita until brown, turning once. Then cut the pita into quarters. Serve with the eggplant caviar. (They will get crisp as they cool.)

✱TIP: For **spicy pita crisps**, sprinkle with ground cumin, finely chopped garlic and parsley, or a commercial pepper combination such as Old Bay.

Oven-Dried Tomatoes on Polenta Rounds

✓ SOMETHING SPECIAL   ✓ EASY PREPARATION

Polenta is a wonderful side dish, but it can also be the foundation of a great appetizer. In this recipe, you make soft polenta. Once it is cold and set, you cut it into two-inch rounds that can be topped with anything from fresh tomatoes to fresh cheeses.

Polenta Rounds

4 cups water

2 cups whole milk (from 1 pint)

1 teaspoon salt

4 tablespoons butter

1½ cups polenta

1 cup Parmigiano-Reggiano cheese, finely grated (from 4 ounces)

¼ teaspoon cayenne pepper

1 teaspoon unsalted butter, softened, for buttering wrap

2 tablespoons olive oil

1. In a medium saucepan, combine the water, milk, salt, and butter and bring to a simmer. Pour the polenta into the simmering liquid in a slow, steady stream, whisking continuously so lumps do not form. Reduce the heat to low, cover, and continue to cook, stirring frequently, until the mix is very thick and begins to pull away from the side of the pot, about 15 minutes.

2. Remove from the heat and stir in the grated Parmigiano-Reggiano cheese and cayenne pepper. Check the seasoning and add more salt, to taste.

3. Line a cookie sheet with buttered plastic wrap, letting it extend over the edges. Spread the polenta evenly over the plastic wrap, about ¼ to ⅓ inch thick, and chill until firm, at least 1 hour, or as long as overnight.

4. Cut chilled polenta into 2-inch diameter rounds with a biscuit cutter or a glass.

5. Heat the olive oil in a medium frying pan over medium-high heat. If you like, you can use a greased griddle. Cook the polenta rounds until golden brown, turning once, about 5 to 6 minutes all together. Place the rounds on a cookie sheet, and keep at room temperature until ready to serve. They can also be kept warm in a 250°F oven. ✳

6. Top each of the polenta rounds with a dried tomato. Garnish with Parmigiano-Reggiano cheese and fresh basil.

✳ **TIP:** Grilling polenta is a great way to add flavor to a simple side dish. Try cutting the polenta into squares, triangles, or 4-inch rounds. Brush with olive oil and grill over high heat until lightly browned on both sides, about 2 minutes on each side.

Oven-Dried Tomatoes

✓ *MAKE-AHEAD*　　✓ *EASY PREPARATION*

I like to use these tomatoes in pastas, salads, or as an appetizer with the polenta. They can be drizzled with olive oil and stored, in an airtight container, in the refrigerator for up to two weeks.

4 medium vine-ripened tomatoes

2 tablespoons balsamic vinegar

¼ cup olive oil

1. Preheat the oven to 250°F.

2. Slice the bottoms and the tops off of the tomatoes and then slice the tomatoes into ¼-inch-thick slices.

3. Place sliced tomatoes on a cookie sheet lined with parchment paper. Drizzle the balsamic vinegar and then the olive oil over tomatoes. Bake for 3 hours or until dried but still soft and pliable. Cool and reserve.

＊TIP: Make these tomatoes a day in advance if you like. Store them in the refrigerator in a tightly sealed plastic container. Separate each layer with a piece of waxed paper or plastic wrap. Return to room temperature before using.

Marinated Shrimp on a Stick

✓ *MAKE-AHEAD*　✓ *SOMETHING SPECIAL*

Serve these delicious skewered shrimp arranged on a bed of cracked ice on a serving tray as part of a cocktail buffet. The vegetables that accompany the shrimp in the marinade make these shrimp extremely flavorful.

2 pounds medium (31–35 per pound) shrimp, peeled except for the tail, deveined

²⁄₃ cup olive oil

¹⁄₃ cup fresh lime juice (from about 3 limes)

1 teaspoon dry mustard

1 teaspoon sugar

3 tablespoons chopped fresh curly parsley (curly is better for marinades)

3 sprigs fresh rosemary

½ small onion, thinly sliced

½ bulb fennel, very thinly sliced

¼ red bell pepper, very thinly sliced

2 bird tongue hot peppers, or ½ teaspoon crushed red pepper

3 cloves garlic, very thinly sliced

Salt and freshly ground pepper, to taste

Twenty 6-inch wooden skewers or dried rosemary stems *

1. Bring 2 quarts salted water to a boil. Add the shrimp and cook for 2 to 3 minutes, just until they turn pink. Drain well and cool in cold, running water.

2. Combine all the marinade ingredients (everything except the shrimp and the skewers) in a large glass or china bowl.

3. Place the cooled shrimp in a large, sealable plastic bag. Pour in the marinade and seal well. Marinate, refrigerated, for 3 to 4 hours, turning the bag several times.

4. To serve, drain the marinade and skewer the shrimp, 2 or 3 to a skewer. The drained vegetables can be served alongside as a crunchy condiment, or can be used later in a colorful salad.

VARIATION

Drain the marinade, but reserve the vegetables. Serve the shrimp and vegetables as a salad on a bed of crisp lettuce. Season to taste with more salt and pepper.

✻TIP: As these **skewers** are not cooked, they do not need to be soaked in water before skewering the shrimp. Large round toothpicks or colorful plastic cocktail picks can also be used.

Crispy Phyllo Stuffed with Prosciutto and Figs

✓ SOMETHING SPECIAL   ✓ MAKE-AHEAD

These surprisingly simple to make snacks will wow your friends. Just a little care will produce delicious, crispy sweet-savory bites. If fresh figs are not in the market, use well-drained canned Kadota figs, which are available in most supermarkets. The flavor and texture will be a little milder, but still delicious.

12 thin slices prosciutto

¾ cup crumbled blue cheese (from 3 ounces)

9 large ripe figs, quartered

Freshly ground pepper, to taste

6 sheets phyllo pastry

4 tablespoons butter, melted

1. Preheat the oven to 450°F. Line a heavy-duty baking sheet with parchment paper or a silicon baking pad.

2. Spread out 2 slices of prosciutto on a work surface. Sprinkle with blue cheese. Arrange 6 to 8 fig quarters (depending on their size) along the long side of 1 of the prosciutto slices. Season with freshly ground pepper. Roll up the prosciutto into a long tight cigar, and then roll in the second slice in the same way. Repeat with the remaining prosciutto, blue cheese, and figs, ending with 6 cigar-shaped rolls.

3. Spread out 1 sheet of phyllo on a work board. Immediately cover the remaining sheets with a damp towel. Lightly brush the entire sheet of phyllo with melted butter. Place 1 prosciutto roll along the short end of the sheet of phyllo. Roll up tightly, disregard the ragged ends as you will cut them off later. Brush the roll with melted butter and place on the lined baking sheet. Repeat with remaining phyllo, always recovering the unused sheets of pastry with the damp towel. *

4. Bake 8 or 9 minutes until the pastry rolls are well browned and crisp.

5. Remove from the oven. Cool for 1 minute. Cut off ragged ends of the rolls on an angle. Slice the rolls on an angle into bite-sized pieces, about 6 per roll. Cool 5 minutes and serve on a napkin-lined plate. *

* TIP: Filled phyllo rolls can be tightly wrapped with plastic wrap on the baking sheet and refrigerated for an hour or two at this point. Uncover and bake when you are ready to serve.

* TIP: A serrated bread knife is the ideal tool for slicing these delicate fig rolls without crushing them.

Maryland Crab Cakes with Chipotle Aioli Sauce

✓ *SOMETHING SPECIAL*

These succulent cakes are so quick and easy you will serve them for any festive occasion. The spicy aioli sauce is a perfect zesty accompaniment.

Chipotle Aioli Sauce (next page)

1 pound jumbo lump crabmeat

1/2 cup panko bread crumbs, or cracker crumbs *

1 tablespoon Dijon mustard

1/4 cup finely chopped green bell pepper (from about 1/4 medium pepper)

1/4 cup finely chopped celery (from about 1 medium rib)

1/4 cup finely chopped green onion (from about 4 to 5 thin onions, or 1 bunch)

1 tablespoon Worcestershire sauce

1/4 cup mayonnaise

1 large egg

Pinch cayenne

3 tablespoons chopped fresh curly parsley

Salt and freshly ground pepper, to taste

Flour for dredging

1 tablespoon olive oil or butter, for frying

1. Prepare the chipotle aioli sauce.

2. In a large bowl, very gently pick over the crabmeat with your fingers to remove any remaining shell. *

3. Add the panko, mustard, bell pepper, celery, green onions, Worcestershire, mayonnaise, egg, cayenne, and parsley. Season well with salt and pepper. Mix well, but gently. Form the crab mixture into 8 flat cakes or patties. Dust each lightly with flour.

4. Heat the oil in a large heavy skillet. Fry the cakes until golden brown, 3 to 4 minutes per side, turning very carefully so they do not fall apart.

5. Serve very hot with chipotle aioli sauce on the side.

✳ TIP: Cracker crumbs—in this case saltine crumbs—are available in many supermarkets, or you can quickly crush your own. Where panko remains crisp even in the presence of liquid, the cracker crumbs tend to melt into the crab mixture without making them taste bready. I prefer panko, but, choose whichever you like, or use plain dry bread crumbs instead.

✳ TIP: When picking over crabmeat, unless the recipe calls for the end result to be shredded, be careful not to break up the lumps. You pay a premium to have the large lumps and they give the finished cake substance and elegance.

Chipotle Aioli Sauce

✓ *SOMETHING SPECIAL*　　✓ *MAKE-AHEAD*

This variation on the garlic rich aioli sauce that is so popular in southern France is delicious with many kinds of poached or steamed fish, too. Classic aioli has a bread base, which makes it thick like mayonnaise; this version is thinner, more like a sauce—just right for drizzling over the hot cakes.

5 cloves garlic

2 hard cooked egg yolks

2 tablespoons drained, canned chipotle peppers in adobo sauce (from about 1 whole pepper)

3 tablespoons fresh lemon juice (from about 1 large lemon)

½ cup olive oil

Salt to taste

1. Just before serving, in the jar of a blender or food processor, process the garlic, egg yolks, peppers, and lemon juice until smooth. With the machine running, add the olive oil in a very thin stream until the sauce thickens slightly and is creamy-smooth.

2. Season with salt and more lemon juice if you like.

Curried Crab Bites

✓ *MAKE-AHEAD* ✓ *SOMETHING SPECIAL*

This is probably the most popular appetizer recipe I have ever written. My cooking students from all over the country have served this at parties with great results. You can slice the bread and make the crab mixture up to three days ahead.

¾ cup mayonnaise

¼ cup finely chopped white onion (from ¼ medium onion)

1 cup finely grated cheddar cheese (from 4 ounces)

¼ teaspoon Tabasco sauce

1 tablespoon curry powder

One 6½ ounce can crabmeat, drained

2 French bread baguettes, cut in ½-inch-thick slices

1. Preheat the oven to 400°F.

2. In a medium bowl, combine the mayonnaise, white onion, cheddar cheese, Tabasco, curry powder, and crabmeat.

3. To serve, spread tablespoons of the mixture on bread rounds and bake about 6 to 8 minutes, until golden brown and puffy. Serve immediately.

VARIATION

This is also wonderful served on baked puff pastry rounds. Cut store-bought puff pastry into 2-inch rounds. Place the rounds on a parchment-lined cookie sheet and top with another piece of parchment. Place another cookie sheet on top of the rounds (yes, we are going to bake the puff pastry between 2 cookie sheets) and bake in a 350°F oven for 10 to 12 minutes. Remove the upper cookie sheet, top the half-baked rounds with the crab mixture and continue baking about 3 or 4 minutes more, until heated through.

Great Salads
with Any Meal

A weekend meal wouldn't be complete without a salad, and you can make great ones quickly and simply without a lot of fuss. On the weekends, you can introduce your family to something more adventurous than greens and dressing. Try using just about anything that you can think of as a base for your salads. Think about what is in season: fresh peas, sweet corn, the first tiny tender beets, marble-sized new potatoes, those lusciously sweet home-grown tomatoes from the local farm stand.

Plan ahead for weekend salads. Take a trip to that market or supermarket that features the freshest greens and vegetables. When you bring them home, lay out your ingredients, and to save on prep time, slice everything at once, and have it ready on the counter. Slice extra vegetables for the salad the next day to save time on a hectic Monday night.

Many foods can be kept on hand for side salads. In winter, ingredients such as frozen vegetables, canned beans, artichoke hearts, canned fruit, rice, grains, or even pasta, can all be ready to use when you come home and toss them into a salad. In summer, take advantage of all the finest local produce you can find. If you see something new, ask how it should be prepared, or how you can incorporate it into your selection of favorite salads.

Prewashed greens are available everywhere now and can save time, but sometimes they come out of the bag wilted. To refresh wilted greens, place them in ice water with lemon juice for twenty minutes. Drain them well and spin them dry or wrap them in a towel. If you do this as soon as you get the greens home from the store, they can be kept in a resealable bag for one week or in the refrigerator in a bowl for up to four hours.

The ingredients for creative dressings are there in your pantry in the form of oils, vinegars, and mustards, as well as cheeses, herbs, and spices. You just need to dive in and start experimenting.

Green Salad with Sun-Dried Tomatoes and Tuscan Olive Oil Vinaigrette

✓ SOMETHING SPECIAL   ✓ NO COOKING NEEDED

Sun-dried tomatoes, packed in olive oil, are the backbone of this salad. Balsamic vinegar is the aged, sweet-flavored vinegar that brings all of the seasoning together. Buy the best quality you can afford so the flavor will be smooth and full-bodied rather than too acidic.

VINAIGRETTE

1 tablespoon finely chopped shallots (from about 2 medium cloves)

2 teaspoons Dijon mustard

2 tablespoons whole grain mustard

3 tablespoons balsamic vinegar

1/2 teaspoon salt

1 teaspoon sugar

1/3 cup Tuscan extra-virgin olive oil *

SALAD

8 cups mixed greens, well washed and dried (about 12 ounces) *

Salt and freshly ground pepper, to taste

1/4 cup oil-packed sun dried tomatoes, sliced into strips

1. In a small bowl, whisk together the shallots, mustards, vinegar, salt, and sugar. Add the olive oil in a slow stream, whisking constantly, until the dressing thickens. Taste and adjust the seasonings. Allow the dressing to stand for 30 minutes at room temperature.

2. When ready to serve, season the greens with salt and pepper in a large salad bowl. Add the sun-dried tomatoes. Drizzle with the vinaigrette, toss, and serve.

✳TIP: Tuscan olive oil is one of the finest in the world. It is deep green in color with exceptional fresh, fruity flavor—perfect for dressing and for garnishing. Use another extra virgin olive oil, if you prefer, though.

✳TIP: For the **perfect crisp greens,** soak the salad greens in cold water for about 20 minutes. Dry well and toss with the dressing. If you want to do this 6 to 8 hours early, just place the well-dried greens in a bowl, top with a damp paper towel, and refrigerate until ready to serve. Toss with the dressing at the last minute.

Chicory Salad with Avocado Slices and Red Wine Vinaigrette

✓ NO COOKING NEEDED   ✓ SOMETHING SPECIAL

As an appetizer salad, this is a great opener for a special weekend dinner. It is just hearty enough to cut the worst of your hunger, but still whets the appetite for what follows.

VINAIGRETTE

2 tablespoons red wine vinegar

1 tablespoon Dijon mustard

Salt and freshly ground pepper, to taste

½ cup extra-virgin olive oil

SALAD

4 slices thick-cut bacon, cut across into ½-inch pieces

1 head chicory or curly endive

4 hard cooked eggs, quartered

1 ripe Haas avocado, halved, pitted, and sliced *

1. In a small bowl, beat together the vinegar, mustard, salt, and pepper. Add the oil in a slow stream, whisking constantly, until the dressing thickens. Set aside.

2. Fry the bacon in a heavy skillet until crisp. Drain well on paper towels and set aside.

3. Trim the root end of the head of chicory, wash well, dry, and tear into bite-sized pieces.

4. In a large bowl, combine the chicory, eggs, and bacon pieces. Just before serving, toss in the avocado and ¼ cup of the dressing.

5. Serve the remaining dressing on the side.

VARIATION

This would also be delicious using leaves of fresh romaine, coarsely torn into bite-sized pieces.

★TIP: Two main types of **avocado** are widely available in supermarkets today. The Haas variety with wonderful buttery flesh and a dark green or black nubbly skin; and the larger Fuerte or Ettinger varieties with smooth green skins and pale green, slightly watery flavored flesh. If the Haas are ripe, they will be far more flavorful.

Grilled Corn and Butter Leaf Salad with Spiced Pecans

An appealing salad is the perfect beginning to almost any lunch or dinner. The inspiration for this recipe was wanting to make a great beginning to a full-flavored main dish, such as the Grilled Porto-bello Mushroom Burgers with Gruyére Cheese and Thyme Onions (page 102), or the Grilled Cajun Shrimp and Grilled Corn with Cumin Butter (page 110). It might even make a light luncheon salad to serve along with Cheddar Cheese and Green Onion Scones (page 125).

SPICED PECANS

1/4 cup vegetable oil

1 tablespoon sugar

1 teaspoon salt

1 teaspoon ground cumin

1/4 teaspoon cayenne

1/2 cup pecans (about 2 ounces)

GRILLED CORN

3 ears of corn, husk removed, cleaned

1 tablespoon olive oil

CUMIN VINAIGRETTE

3 tablespoons white wine vinegar

1 teaspoon ground cumin

1 tablespoon sugar

3 tablespoons finely chopped shallot (from about 5 or 6 medium cloves)

1/2 teaspoon salt

1/4 teaspoon freshly ground pepper

1/4 cup olive oil

SALAD

2 heads butter leaf lettuce, washed, dried, and torn into pieces

1/2 cup finely sliced red onion, soaked in ice water (from about 1/4 medium onion) *

1/2 cup finely chopped red bell pepper (from about 1/2 medium pepper)

1. Preheat the oven to 250°F. Preheat the grill to medium heat. Clean and season grill.

2. In a small bowl, combine the oil, sugar, salt, cumin, and cayenne pepper. Toss the pecans with the mixture and pour them out onto a cookie sheet. Place them in the oven and bake them about 30 minutes, until slightly dry.

3. Brush the ears of corn lightly with oil and place them on the preheated grill. Grill until the corn is lightly browned, turning the ears as they cook so the entire ear gets color—this will take 6 to 8 minutes. Remove the corn from the grill and cool. Once the corn is cooled, carefully cut the kernels off of the cob. *

4. In a small bowl, combine the vinegar, cumin, sugar, shallot, salt, and pepper. Add the olive oil in a slow stream, whisking constantly, until the dressing thickens. Taste and adjust the seasonings. Reserve.

5. In a large bowl, arrange the lettuce, red onion, and bell pepper. Add the prepared corn and toss with 1/4 cup of the vinaigrette. Adjust seasoning with salt, freshly ground pepper, and additional vinaigrette, as desired. Toss in the spiced pecans and serve.

★TIP: Soaking the **onion** slices in ice water for about 30 minutes will make them crisper and milder in flavor.

★TIP: To cut the **corn** off the cob, break the cooked cob in half. Place the flat end down on the cutting board or in a shallow bowl, holding it at the top with your free hand so that the cob doesn't slip, and cut down in a sawing motion between the kernels and the ear.

Grilled Asparagus Salad with Sherry Shallot Vinaigrette

✓ *EASY PREPARATION*

My favorite way to prepare asparagus is to grill it. In the wintertime, when I don't feel like firing up the grill, I simply use my grill pan on the stovetop. If you don't have a grill pan, try the broiler—the flavor won't be quite the same, but the small difference will not be enough to make you want to stand out in the cold.

ASPARAGUS

1 pound fresh asparagus

2 tablespoons olive oil

Salt and freshly ground pepper, to taste

VINAIGRETTE

1 tablespoon finely chopped shallots (from about 2 medium cloves)

3 tablespoons sherry vinegar

2 tablespoons red wine vinegar

Salt and freshly ground pepper, to taste

2 tablespoons walnut oil

½ cup extra-virgin olive oil

1. Using a sharp paring knife or simply by snapping the ends of the asparagus, remove the tough ends. Preheat the grill, or grill pan, for 5 minutes to medium heat, or preheat the broiler and move the top shelf to the second level from the top. Toss the asparagus in the 2 tablespoons of olive oil, season with salt and pepper, and grill or broil, turning often—this will take 5 or 6 minutes. Do not allow the asparagus tips to blacken. Remove from the heat and place on a serving platter. *

2. In a small bowl, combine the shallots, vinegars, and salt and pepper. Add the walnut oil and the extra-virgin olive oil in a slow stream, whisking constantly, until the dressing thickens. Taste and adjust the seasonings. Spoon the dressing over the warm asparagus and serve.

VARIATION

A creamy blue cheese–based dressing would be a wonderful alternative to Sherry Shallot Vinaigrette. Spoon a bit over the tip of room temperature–asparagus and pass more for anyone who wants it.

★TIP: For the perfect serving texture, cook the **asparagus** just long enough for it to begin to get tender, about 5 or 6 minutes. It will still have a crisp texture. In the time it takes you to drizzle on the dressing and serve it, the asparagus will continue to cook a bit and soften slightly.

Green Bean and Herb Salad

✓ SOMETHING SPECIAL   ✓ EASY PREPARATION

If your garden contains nasturtium flowers or purslane, add a few to this late summer side dish for a delicious peppery flavor and lots of attractive color.

SALAD

1 pound thinnest green beans (haricots verts), tipped and tailed

1 small Vidalia onion, halved from root to tip, very thinly sliced (1½ cups)

½ small red bell pepper, seeded and very thinly sliced (about ¾ cup)

1 teaspoon very finely chopped garlic (from 1 medium clove)

1 cup arugula, washed and dried (about 1½ ounces)

¼ cup fresh basil leaves

3 tablespoons fresh oregano leaves

½ cup fresh Italian flat-leaf parsley leaves

2 tablespoons minced chives

DRESSING

2 teaspoons fresh lemon juice (from 1 medium lemon)

Salt and freshly ground pepper, to taste

⅓ to ½ cup extra-virgin olive oil

1. Bring 4 quarts salted water to boil. Boil green beans until they are crisply tender, 3 to 5 minutes. Drain well and refresh with cold water. ✱

2. In a large bowl, combine the cold beans, onion, bell pepper, and garlic. Toss with the arugula, basil, oregano, parsley, and chives—and with the nasturtiums or purslane if you have them.

3. In a separate bowl, beat together the lemon juice, salt, and pepper. Add the olive oil in a slow stream, whisking constantly, until the dressing thickens slightly. Taste and adjust the seasonings. Pour the dressing over the beans. Toss and serve.

VARIATION

For a heartier salad, toss in a little feta cheese and some halved cherry tomatoes.

✱ TIP: To keep **green beans** and other green vegetables bright green and crisply fresh, drain and douse them with ice or cold running water to stop any further cooking.

Endive with Blue Cheese, Dried Cranberries, and Pecans with Sherry Vinaigrette

✓ *SOMETHING SPECIAL*   ✓ *NO COOKING NEEDED*

Even a side salad can be more satisfying than just a forkful of greens. The slightly bitter flavor of the crisp endive and sharpness of the cranberries mellow with the addition of blue cheese and pecans.

SALAD

3 large heads Belgian endive, ends trimmed and cut across into 1/2-inch slices—leaves separated

3 cups mesclun or European baby greens, well washed and dried (about 41/2 ounces)

1/3 cup dried cranberries

1/2 cup toasted pecan halves (about 2 ounces) or almonds or walnuts *

1/2 cup crumbled blue cheese (about 2 ounces)

VINAIGRETTE

1 tablespoon sherry vinegar

1 tablespoon dry sherry

1 teaspoon Dijon mustard

Salt and freshly ground pepper, to taste

1/3 to 1/2 cup vegetable oil, such as canola

1. Toss together the endive and mesclun in a large salad bowl. Toss in cranberries and pecan halves. Top with crumbled blue cheese.

2. In a small bowl, beat together the vinegar, sherry, and mustard. Season with salt and pepper. Add the oil in a slow stream, whisking constantly, until the dressing thickens slightly. Taste and adjust the seasonings.

3. Pour a little dressing over the salad and toss just before serving. Pass the remaining dressing separately.

* TIP: To toast the nuts, spread the nuts on a baking sheet or the pan of a toaster oven, and cook at 450°F for 3 to 4 minutes, watching very carefully. Nuts have a tendency to burn very quickly and can go from toasted to charred in a matter of seconds.

Strawberry Salad with Sugared Almonds and Champagne Vinaigrette

MAKES 8 SERVINGS

✓ *EASY PREPARATION*   ✓ *SOMETHING SPECIAL*

This salad combines the succulence of fresh summer greens and the sweetness and color of ripe strawberries. The dressing and sugared almonds add a sweet surprise. This is a wonderful side salad with grilled or roasted pork ribs, and it also goes very well with grilled tuna.

SALAD

¼ cup sugar

½ cup slivered almonds
(about 2 ounces)

8 cups baby greens, cleaned and
well dried (about 12 ounces)

2 tablespoons finely chopped green
onions (from about 2 to 3 whole thin
onions)

1 pint strawberries, cleaned, hulled,
and sliced

DRESSING

2 tablespoons sugar

1 tablespoon chopped Italian
flat-leaf parsley

2 tablespoons champagne vinegar

½ teaspoon salt

Freshly ground pepper to taste

¼ cup olive oil

1. Heat the sugar in a small skillet over medium-high heat until it begins to melt. Add the almonds to the pan and toss rapidly until all of the almonds are coated with sugar and lightly browned. Pour the almonds into a glass baking dish and separate them with a fork. Cool until hardened, and break into pieces. *

2. In a small bowl, combine all of the dressing ingredients except for the olive oil. Add the oil in a slow stream, whisking constantly, until the dressing thickens. Taste and adjust the seasonings.

3. In a large salad bowl, combine the greens, green onions, and strawberries. Toss them with the dressing. Add the almonds, toss lightly, and serve.

＊TIP: Watch the **almonds** carefully in the skillet because they will brown very quickly once the sugar melts. Toss them with two forks and pour the mixture out quickly into a glass (Pyrex) dish or onto a cookie sheet. Take the forks and spread the sticky nuts into a single layer so they will cool quickly. Then you can break the mixture into pieces.

First Courses

When served to start the meal, appetizers should set the tone for everything that follows. They can be simply prepared or as complex as you like, and should represent the tone, or seasonal emphasis, of the meal. For example, Chilled Dijon-Marinated Shrimp (page 48) might be the perfect opener for a cold summer dinner that includes a hearty salad, a selection of cheeses, and chunks of crusty whole-grain bread. Or, Potato Pancakes with Apple-Pear Compote (page 51) would be terrific to begin a dinner of roast pork, or grilled steak. Appetizers are really meant to tempt the palate. As the Italians say, "the appetite comes with the eating." Just remember to keep servings small.

If you're being more adventurous on the weekend, you can also try what's all the rage these days: make appetizers the entire meal. You can satisfy different cravings—for something spicy, for something comforting, or for something rich—or a little of each, all at one meal. With today's emphasis on less is more, two or three smaller—but equally delicious—dishes will satisfy hunger and appetite for being creative.

Vegetable-Stuffed Artichokes

These satisfying artichokes are hearty enough to serve as a main course for lunch or a late evening supper. Add some whole-grain artisanal bread on the side. Hold the glass of wine, though, as artichokes tend to make everything taste sweet and will make all but the most crisply acidic wines taste off. Do as the Italians do and wait until the next course to pour the wine.

Lemon-Curry Mayonnaise
(next page)

ARTICHOKES

6 large artichokes

2 lemons

1/2 teaspoon whole black peppercorns

2 whole garlic cloves

2 tablespoons olive oil

STUFFING

2 tablespoons olive oil

1/2 cup finely chopped yellow onion
(from about 1/2 large onion)

2 teaspoons finely chopped fresh
garlic (from about 2 medium cloves)

3/4 cup thinly sliced zucchini
(from about 1 small zucchini)

1/2 cup seeded, chopped green bell
pepper (from about 1/2 medium pepper)

1/2 cup seeded, chopped red bell
pepper (from about 1/2 medium
pepper)

1/2 teaspoon salt

1/2 teaspoon freshly ground pepper

1/2 cup julienned baby carrots,
steamed 2 or 3 minutes

3/4 cup seeded and diced tomatoes
(from about 1 small)

1 cup cubed day-old sourdough bread
(the cubes should be small, no larger
than 1/2 inch)

3 tablespoon chopped fresh Italian
flat-leaf parsley

2 tablespoons balsamic vinegar

2 tablespoons extra-virgin olive oil

1. Make the lemon-curry mayonnaise.

2. Clean the artichokes. ∗

3. Fill a pot large enough to hold the artichokes in one layer, side by side, with 3 inches of water. Add the peppercorns, garlic cloves, and olive oil to the water. Bring this to a simmer. Add the artichokes, stem end up, and cover the pot. Steam about 45 minutes, until the heart is tender. Drain them well, upside down, and cool them to room temperature. Working from the top, spread the leaves as far open as possible. Using the tip of a spoon, carefully remove the fuzzy choke. ∗

∗**TIP:** To **clean an artichoke**, follow these steps:

1. Snap off the bottom outer leaves. 2. Cut off the top third of the artichoke, then with scissors trim the rest of the leaf tips. Trim the stem off the bottom. 3. Rub the whole artichoke with a lemon wedge to prevent discoloration. 4. Spread the leaves open so that they will look uniform.

∗**TIP:** The choke is made up of the hairlike fibers that fill the **artichoke heart**. While you can probably eat them, they have a tendency to stick in your throat and choke you. Scoop the fibers out, taking care not to remove much of the heart, and discard them. I like to use the sharp tip of a grapefruit spoon to do this.

(continues)

4. Heat the 2 tablespoons of olive oil in a skillet. Add the onion and the garlic. Cook and stir the onions until tender, then add the zucchini, bell pepper, salt, and pepper and cook 4 to 5 minutes more. Transfer the mixture to a medium bowl. Cover and chill the mixture for several hours.

Add the carrots, tomatoes, bread cubes, parsley, balsamic vinegar, and extra-virgin olive oil, and season again with salt and pepper.

5. Spoon the mixture into the artichokes, chill, and serve on chilled salad plates with the lemon-curry mayonnaise on the side.

SERVING SUGGESTION

For a simpler dish, serve the warm artichokes (after the choke has been removed) with a small bowl of the Lemon-Curry Mayonnaise alongside. Or, try melted butter, simple vinaigrette, or our Sherry Shallot Vinaigrette (page 41) for dipping.

Lemon-Curry Mayonnaise

MAKES ABOUT 1 ⅓ CUPS

✓ NO COOKING NEEDED   ✓ EASY PREPARATION

You can make this dressing ahead and serve it on the side with the stuffed artichokes. Any extra can be refrigerated, covered, to serve with cold meats or fish, or as a sandwich spread with grilled or roast chicken.

1 cup prepared mayonnaise

3 tablespoons grainy-style Dijon mustard

3 tablespoons lemon juice, plus zest for garnish (from about 1 large lemon)

½ tablespoon curry powder, or more, to taste

Salt and freshly ground pepper, to taste

Combine all the ingredients in a small bowl and stir with a wooden spoon or heavy fork until well mixed. Chill until ready to serve.

Chilled Dijon-Marinated Shrimp

✓ *SOMETHING SPECIAL*   ✓ *MAKE-AHEAD*

Make this recipe at least eight hours in advance so the shrimp has a chance to pick up the flavors of the marinade. Somewhat like a seviche, this preparation emphasizes the fresh flavor of the shrimp. Be careful not to overcook the shrimp before putting them into the marinade or they will become tough while marinating.

3 pounds extra-large (16–20 per pound) shrimp, peeled and deveined *

1/2 cup finely chopped Italian flat-leaf parsley

1/4 cup finely chopped shallots (from about 6 to 8 medium cloves)

1/2 cup white wine vinegar

1 cup olive oil

2 tablespoons fresh lemon juice (from 1 medium lemon)

1/2 cup Dijon mustard

2 teaspoons crushed dried red pepper flakes

1 teaspoon salt

Freshly ground pepper, to taste

1. In a large kettle of simmering salted water, cook the shrimp until just pink, no longer than 3 minutes. Drain in a colander and transfer to a large bowl.

2. Combine the remaining ingredients in a small bowl and pour over the still-warm shrimp. Toss well so that every shrimp is coated. Cover and refrigerate for at least 8 to 10 hours (overnight is best). *

3. Thoroughly drain excess marinade from the shrimp before serving. Serve chilled, in a large bowl lined with lettuce.

＊TIP: Use your fingers to **remove the shell** from each shrimp. Once the shell is removed, use the tip of a small, sharp knife to make a small cut along the upper side of the shrimp and to pull out the dark vein as it is exposed. Rinse lightly. This vein is edible, but isn't very pretty in an otherwise very pretty preparation.

＊TIP: Tossing the warm shrimp in the dressing just after they are cooked and are still warm helps them absorb more dressing and creates very tender shrimp.

Potato-Rice Cakes with Baby Greens and Balsamic Cream

The dressing on this salad is a flavorful balsamic vinaigrette that will be a crowd pleaser every time. You can look in the market to decide what type of potato or other vegetable to use in these yummy little cakes. Hard winter squash, such as butternut, or even yams would also be delicious. The potato cakes are the star of this appetizer. It could also be a light main course for lunch or a late supper, but is essentially a first course.

POTATO-RICE CAKES

1 tablespoon olive oil

1/3 cup finely chopped white onion (from 1/2 small onion)

1/4 cup finely chopped shallot (from about 6 to 8 medium cloves)

Pinch salt

1 cup grated russet potato, lightly packed (from about 1 medium, peeled potato) *

3/4 cup grated sweet potato, lightly packed (from about 1 medium, peeled sweet potato) *

2 cups cooked wild rice *

2 teaspoons chopped fresh thyme

1 1/2 teaspoons salt

1/2 teaspoon freshly ground pepper

3 large eggs, beaten lightly with a fork

1/2 cup all-purpose flour

1/4 cup olive oil, for frying

SALAD AND DRESSING

Balsamic Vinaigrette (next page)

1/4 cup sour cream

1 teaspoon chopped fresh thyme

8 cups baby greens (12 ounces)

1. Heat 1 tablespoon olive oil in a small skillet over medium heat. Add the onion, shallot, and a pinch of salt and cook just until soft, about 4 minutes. Reserve.

2. Place the dried potatoes in a medium bowl and add the wild rice, cooked onion mixture, thyme, salt, and pepper.

3. Stir in the beaten eggs and then lightly fold in the flour.

4. Heat the oil in a large skillet at medium-high heat. Using a 1/4-cup measuring cup, scoop and drop the batter into the skillet. Flatten the pancake gently with a spatula and fry until each side is golden brown, about 4 minutes per side. Remove the pancake from the skillet and drain on paper towels. Repeat until the batter is gone. *

5. Make the balsamic cream by combining 2 tablespoons of the balsamic vinaigrette with the sour cream and thyme.

6. Toss the greens with 4 tablespoons of the remaining balsamic vinaigrette. Adjust seasoning as desired.

* TIP: A food processor fitted with the large grating blade can easily **grate the potatoes**, or use a box grater to grate them by hand. Place the grated potatoes in a colander and rinse with cold water until the water runs clear, to remove the starch in the potato. Pat the grated potatoes dry with a paper towel.

* TIP: Cooking wild rice requires more care than other rice—it isn't actually rice at all, but a type of wild water grass. If you have plenty of time, you can soak the wild rice overnight, drain, and then simmer in salted water to cover until all the water is absorbed, about 30 minutes. For quicker cooking, measure the dry rice and combine it with 3 times as much salted water in a heavy saucepan along with 1 teaspoon butter. Cover tightly and simmer over medium-low heat for about an hour until the rice is tender and most or all of the water is absorbed. Drain well in a strainer and serve hot.

(continues)

7. Reheat the pancakes if necessary. Arrange the dressed greens on individual plates and top with 2 pancakes. Garnish each serving of the pancakes with a dollop of the balsamic cream mixture and serve immediately, while warm.

★ TIP: These cakes can be kept warm on a cookie sheet for 30 minutes in a 200°F oven. Or, they can be made 6 hours ahead and reheated in a 350°F oven for 15 minutes.

Balsamic Vinaigrette

MAKES APPROXIMATELY ¾ CUP

✓ EASY PREPARATION   ✓ NO COOKING NEEDED

This is especially good on mixed greens with the wild rice cakes.

2 teaspoons finely chopped shallot (from about 1 medium clove)

1 tablespoon Dijon mustard

¼ cup balsamic vinegar

½ teaspoon salt

1 teaspoon sugar

¼ teaspoon freshly ground pepper

⅓ cup extra-virgin olive oil

1. In a medium bowl, combine the shallot, mustard, vinegar, salt, sugar, and pepper and whisk until well mixed.

2. Add the olive oil in a slow stream, whisking constantly, until the dressing thickens. This dressing can be made up to a day before serving. Bring to room temperature before serving.

Potato Pancakes with Apple-Pear Compote

The rule of thumb for potato pancakes is one egg for every potato. Using a buttermilk baking mix was my Gram's secret. She knew it adds flavor and creates a light pancake. (These are light and crispy. If you're in the mood for richer, more complexly flavored cakes, see the Potato-Rice Cakes, page 49.)

Apple-Pear Compote (next page)

4 large russet potatoes, peeled

4 large eggs, at room temperature, lightly beaten with a fork

¼ cup buttermilk baking mix, such as Bisquick®

1 teaspoon salt

Up to ½ cup vegetable oil, for frying

1. Make the apple-pear compote.

2. Grate the potatoes by hand with a box grater, or in the food processor fitted with the large grating blade. Next, place the grated potatoes back in the food processor fitted with the chopping blade and lightly chop them pulsing once or twice. ✴

3. Place the chopped potatoes in a colander and rinse them with cold water until the water runs clear to remove the extra starch. Drain them well by pressing them against the side of the colander. You can also press them with a paper towel to remove the excess water. Transfer them to a large bowl.

4. Add the beaten eggs, baking mix, and salt. Mix well. ✴

5. Heat ⅛ inch of oil in a large skillet over medium-high heat. With a spoon add 2 tablespoons of the batter to the oil and flatten it with the back of the spoon. Cook until golden brown, 3 to 5 minutes, turning only once. The best way to turn it is with two spatulas. Just turn the pancake over with one spatula, gently catching it with the other spatula. Then gently place it in the oil. This way it won't spatter oil when you turn. Drain on paper towels. Repeat until the batter is gone. Serve the pancakes with the apple-pear compote.

SERVING SUGGESTION

For a great-looking appetizer, cut the pancakes into 2-inch rounds with a small sharp cookie cutter. Place a spoonful of the compote on the top and garnish with a leaf of Italian parsley. Serve 2 or 3 on a plate of well-dried, undressed mixed baby greens.

✴**TIP:** You can **chop the potatoes** by hand with a knife. Using finely chopped potatoes in about ⅛-inch dice rather than in long grated shreds of potato results in a potato pancake with a finer texture.

✴**TIP:** For a lighter **potato pancake,** pour off the extra water that the potatoes will lose as the batter sits; do not stir it back into the potato mixture. Add more baking mix to absorb any excess moisture if you need to.

Apple-Pear Compote

✓ *EASY PREPARATION*   ✓ *MAKE-AHEAD*

The trick with this recipe is to cut the apple and pear very finely. They will cook evenly and you will get a little of the apple and pear in every bite of this chunky mixture. This compote is delicious with roast pork, or when spooned warm over a dish of vanilla ice cream for a quick dessert.

1 small Granny Smith apple, peeled, cored, and finely diced

1 small Bosc pear, peeled, cored, and finely diced

½ tablespoon fresh lemon juice (from ½ medium lemon)

1 tablespoon butter

1 cup thinly sliced yellow onion (from about ½ large onion)

1 tablespoon sugar

Salt and freshly ground pepper, to taste

1. Place the apple and pear in a bowl and toss with the lemon juice.

2. Heat the butter in a large skillet over medium-high heat. Add the onion and cook until softened, about 5 to 6 minutes. Add the sugar, lower the heat, and cook, stirring, until golden. Increase the heat to medium-high and add the apple and pear. ✱

3. Cook until golden, 10 to 12 minutes. Season with the salt and pepper. Serve warm with the pancakes.

SERVING SUGGESTION

You can make this up to 3 days ahead. Just make sure to warm the compote slightly in a heavy skillet with 1 tablespoon melted butter before topping the pancakes.

✱ TIP: To create a golden apple and pear mixture, make sure the pieces of apple and pear are in a single layer and do not toss it until the bottom is golden. Stirring it constantly will cause the mixture to steam instead of brown.

Herb-Cured Salmon with Rye Bread and Sour Cream Dressing

✓ *NO COOKING NEEDED*   ✓ *SOMETHING SPECIAL*

Cured salmon is commonly referred to as "graved lox" or gravlax. This dish is of Swedish origin, and is essentially raw salmon that is allowed to marinate in a dry cure of salt, sugar, and herbs. It's wonderful on rye bread with a dollop of the tart cream.

★TIP: This type of **salmon** should be sliced as thinly as possible. Using a sharp long, flexible serrated or carving knife, begin at a sharp angle and cut the salmon on the bias or slant, making the slices as large and thin as you can.

SALMON

1 pound fresh center-cut salmon fillet, boned, skin on

1/2 cup kosher salt

1/2 cup sugar

2 tablespoons freshly ground pepper

1/3 cup chopped fresh curly parsley

1/3 cup chopped fresh chive

1/3 cup freshly chopped basil

SOUR CREAM DRESSING

1/2 cup sour cream

1 tablespoon vodka

1/8 teaspoon salt

2 teaspoons fresh lemon juice (from 1/2 medium lemon)

1/2 teaspoon grated lemon zest (from 1 medium lemon)

One loaf of rye bread, thinly sliced, lightly toasted

1. Rinse the salmon and dry with paper towels.

2. In a small bowl, combine the salt, sugar, pepper, and herbs.

3. Sprinkle 1/4 cup of the salt mixture on the bottom of an ovenproof, glass baking dish large enough to lay the salmon flat. Set the salmon fillet, skin side down, in the baking dish. Pour the remaining salt mixture over the fillet.

4. Cover the salmon fillet with plastic wrap and place a gentle weight on the fish (a smaller baking dish works well). Refrigerate the salmon for 24 hours.

5. To make the dressing, in a small bowl whisk together the sour cream, vodka, salt, lemon juice, and zest. Reserve.

6. Remove the salmon from the refrigerator and rinse well to remove the salt cure. Dry thoroughly.

7. Thinly slice the salmon on a steep slant and arrange on a platter. Garnish the platter with toasted bread slices and serve with the sour cream dressing. ★

Elegant Soups

Soups are the cornerstones of a good meal. You may consider making an extra soup course just added work at dinner time, but there are probably ten ingredients in your pantry right now from which you can choose and then combine to make a great soup. And with leisurely weekend meals, either impromptu or long-planned, adding a soup course is a good way to relax and slow down the pace of normally hectic family dining.

Soup is one of the most versatile of foods. They range from the ultimate crystal clear, full-of-flavor broth, a simple vegetable soup, a creamy puree, or a hearty stew that makes the entire meal. Here are some things to remember when you make your own:

- To make a really flavorful soup, start out with a rich base. You can buy or make good stocks, but most often a recipe will call for a low-salt canned broth.

- While canned broths are now quite good, for better flavor, add vegetables such as carrots, celery, and onion to the broth from the can. Allow them to simmer for about an hour. Once the vegetables are soft, strain the broth and use it as the base for your soup. This was my family's "trick" for homemade soup.

- Once you have the base, almost anything can be added to make it a distinct soup. Try using any combination of meat, fish, or vegetables.

- Soups freeze beautifully, so take advantage of your extra time in the kitchen on the weekend to freeze extra servings that can be reheated for a little special touch to a busy worknight dinner. To freeze vegetable-based soups, pour the cooled soup into well-labeled resealable freezer bags. Make sure to remove any air as you are sealing the bag. Place the bags of soup in a single layer in the freezer on a cookie sheet. Once frozen, the bags can easily be stacked in minimum space. When you are ready to eat the soup, place the bag in boiling water and simmer until the soup is hot. If the soup has any type of dairy product in it, freeze it without the dairy, and then add it before serving, when the base has been thawed and reheated—otherwise the soup will separate when you thaw it.

While you're enjoying the extra course, know that you're treating your body well. Health experts say that dieters who begin their meals with a small bowl of soup are more quickly satisfied, eat less, stick to their diets longer, and therefore lose weight more successfully. This is especially true of clear soups, or soups that call for pureeing the vegetables before serving—giving the illusion of creamy richness without the addition of heavy cream.

In this chapter are soups to make a weekend meal a little more special. In the next chapter are soups that are more substantial for more casual nights.

Creamy Tuscan Artichoke Soup

✓ SOMETHING SPECIAL

Every time I serve this soup, my family and friends think I have added cream to it. In fact, it is the starches in the artichokes and potato that make the soup seem very rich. Make this the first course the next time you have guests, and your culinary reputation will be set.

¼ cup olive oil

1 cup finely diced white onion (from about 1 medium onion)

Pinch salt

1 cup peeled and diced russet potato (from about 1 medium potato)

Two 14-ounce cans artichoke hearts, drained, rinsed, and chopped

Salt and freshly ground pepper, to taste

6 cups low-salt vegetable broth or chicken broth (1½ quarts)

¼ cup freshly shredded Parmigiano-Reggiano cheese (from 1 ounce)

1. Heat the olive oil in a large pot over medium-low heat. Add the onion, season with a pinch of salt, and cook until soft, about 5 to 6 minutes. Add the potato and cook until slightly tender, about 5 minutes. Add the chopped artichokes and season with salt and pepper to taste. Cook for 10 minutes and then stir in the broth.

2. Increase heat to medium-high and bring to a simmer. Lower the heat slightly and simmer, skimming off any foam that appears on the surface of the soup, until the artichokes are tender, about 20 minutes.

3. Remove the soup from the heat and allow it to cool slightly. Puree the soup in batches in a blender until smooth, or use an immersion blender. Return the soup to the pot, reheat, adjust seasonings, and serve garnished with the shredded cheese. ✱

✱ **TIP:** Pureeing the soup gives it a slightly thicker texture. You can strain the soup through a fine mesh strainer if you want it to be even smoother.

Squash, Apple, and Curry Bisque

✓ *SOMETHING SPECIAL*

I love a soup that uses all of the great flavors of the season, just like this one, which is great for autumn. You can create this soup with fall squash, apples, pears, or even canned pumpkin.

2 tablespoons olive oil

1½ cups finely chopped white onion (from about 1 large onion)

1 cup finely chopped carrots (from about 2 medium carrots)

½ cup finely chopped celery (from about 1 large rib)

1 teaspoon salt

4 cups diced butternut squash (from about 2 pounds squash)

1 cup peeled, cored, and chopped Granny Smith apple (from about 1 large apple)

1 teaspoon curry powder

¼ teaspoon freshly ground nutmeg

¼ teaspoon ground cinnamon

2 teaspoons brown sugar

1 cup apple juice

¼ cup cider vinegar

5 cups low-salt chicken broth (from 2 quarts)

1 cup heavy cream, heated just until bubbles appear around the edges of the pan

Salt and freshly ground pepper, to taste

1. Heat the olive oil in a stockpot over medium heat. Add the onion, carrots, and celery. Season with salt and cook until the vegetables are soft and tender, about 8 minutes.

2. Add the butternut squash and Granny Smith apple and stir to combine with the vegetables. Add the curry powder, nutmeg, cinnamon, and brown sugar. Cook just until fragrant, about 1 minute. Add the apple juice, vinegar, and broth. Increase heat to medium-high and bring to a simmer, skimming off any foam that collects on the top of the soup.

3. Reduce the heat slightly and simmer until the squash is tender, about 20 minutes.

4. Puree in a blender in batches, then push through a mesh strainer for a smooth, velvety texture. Stir in the warmed cream and season with salt and pepper. Serve hot.

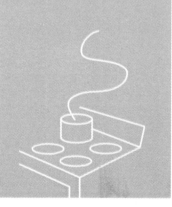

Nutmeg Carrot Soup

✓ SOMETHING SPECIAL ✓ MAKE-AHEAD

This chilled soup is both rich and creamy. It fits well with any summer or fall meal, and can be served with fresh chives and butter-crisped carrots for a garnish.

*TIP: This soup **can be made up to 2 days ahead**, and stored tightly covered in the refrigerator.

1/4 cup olive oil

4 cups peeled and thinly sliced carrots (from about 8 medium carrots)

3 large leeks, white part only, cut lengthwise, thoroughly rinsed and sliced (2½ cups)

1/2 teaspoon salt

1½ teaspoons fresh thyme leaves

2 teaspoons brown sugar

3/4 teaspoon freshly ground nutmeg

6 cups low-salt chicken broth, heated (1½ quarts)

1 cup fresh orange juice (from 2 to 3 large oranges)

Salt and freshly ground pepper, to taste

2 tablespoons chopped fresh chives, for garnish

1/2 cup sour cream, for garnish

1. Heat the olive oil in a large skillet over low heat. Add the carrots and leeks, season with salt, and cook until soft, stirring from time to time, 30 to 45 minutes, being careful not to caramelize or brown the vegetables.

2. Add the thyme, brown sugar, and nutmeg and cook until the sugar dissolves and the thyme is fragrant, about 3 minutes.

3. Stir in the broth, cover the pot, and simmer until the carrots are very soft, about 10 minutes more. In a blender, puree the vegetables with the cooking liquid in batches, until smooth. Strain the soup through a bowl strainer into a clean pot.

4. Stir in the orange juice and season to taste with salt and pepper.

5. Chill until cold. Garnish with chives and sour cream.

Cumin-Mushroom Soup

✓ SOMETHING SPECIAL

I love to make a mushroom soup for dinner. The richness of the dried mushrooms gives this soup great depth of flavor even when you cannot find a wide variety of mushrooms at the grocery store.

1 cup boiling water

1 ounce assorted dried mushrooms, such as morel, oyster, and porcini

3 tablespoons olive oil

1½ cups finely chopped yellow onion (from about 1 large onion)

1 teaspoon salt

2 cups diced portobello mushrooms, stems and dark brown gills removed (from about 5 ounces)

2 cups sliced shiitake mushrooms, stems removed (from about 6 large or 10 small mushrooms, 3 ounces)

2 teaspoons all-purpose flour

2 teaspoons ground cumin

½ cup dry red wine

4 cups low-salt chicken broth (1 quart)

2 tablespoons dry sherry

Salt and freshly ground pepper, to taste

1 tablespoon chopped fresh chives, for garnish

1. Pour the boiling water over the dried mushrooms and set aside to soak for 15 minutes. When rehydrated and soft, drain the mushrooms, and reserve the water, now known as mushroom liquor. Roughly chop the mushrooms and set aside.

2. Preheat a heavy stockpot over medium-low heat and add the olive oil. Add the onion and salt and cook until soft, stirring often, about 8 minutes.

3. Add the diced portobello and sliced shiitake mushrooms and stir to combine. Cook until the mushrooms soften and start to caramelize or begin to turn golden brown, about 6 minutes. Add the chopped, rehydrated mushrooms and stir to combine.

4. Sprinkle on the flour and cumin, stirring to combine evenly, until just fragrant. Add the red wine and reserved mushroom liquor, stirring, and reduce by half, about 5 minutes. Add the broth and bring to a simmer over medium heat.

5. Continue to simmer for 15 minutes more, skimming off any foam from the top of the soup.

6. Stir in the sherry and season as desired with salt and pepper. Garnish with chives and serve hot.

✱ TIP: Dried mushrooms often have a lot of grit in them. Be sure to swish them around in the soaking water to release it all before using the rehydrated mushrooms. Strain the liquor carefully before adding to any soup, stew, or sauce.

Grilled Corn and Roasted Red Pepper Soup

MAKES ABOUT 10 LARGE SERVINGS

✓ *SOMETHING SPECIAL*   ✓ *MAKE-AHEAD*

This is hands-down my very favorite soup for the late summer and early fall. I even freeze ears of corn when it is in season so I will have it to make this soup in the middle of the winter. Not only does it combine two of the sunniest summer flavors, but it is colorful enough for any occasion.

6 ears corn, husked, rinsed well to remove the silk, dried, brushed with olive oil*

6 cups low-salt chicken broth (1½ quarts)

8 bacon slices, diced

2 tablespoons butter—more or less

2 cups finely chopped white onions (from about 2 medium onions)

½ teaspoon salt

¼ cup all-purpose flour

3 cups peeled, diced russet potatoes (from about 3 medium potatoes)

½ cup jarred roasted red bell peppers, chopped

2 cups whole milk (1 pint)

1 teaspoon fresh lemon juice (from ½ medium lemon)

Salt and freshly ground pepper, to taste

2 tablespoons chopped fresh chives, for garnish

1. Preheat the grill for 5 to 10 minutes to medium-high. Clean and season grill.

2. Place the prepared ears of corn on the preheated grill. Grill until the corn is lightly browned, turning frequently so that the corn cooks evenly, about 10 minutes. Remove the corn from the grill and cool. Once the corn is cooled, carefully cut the kernels off the cob.*

3. Place the broth in a 3-quart saucepan. Add the cobs and heat over medium heat. Simmer the cobs in the broth to infuse corn flavor, about 15 minutes. Discard the cobs and reserve the stock.

4. Fry the bacon in a heavy stockpot over medium-low heat until just crisp, about 4 to 6 minutes. Remove the bacon and drain on absorbent towels. Add enough butter to the rendered bacon fat to equal about 3 tablespoons. Add the onions, season with salt, and cook, stirring from time to time, until pale golden in color, about 12 minutes.

5. Sprinkle with the flour and cook, stirring constantly, about 2 minutes.

6. Add the infused broth to the stockpot, whisking continuously to incorporate. Increase the heat to medium-high, stir in the potatoes, and simmer about 10 minutes, covered, until tender. Skim any foam from the surface of the soup with a ladle or spoon.

7. Stir in the corn, roasted red pepper, and milk. Simmer until slightly thickened, for 10 to 12 minutes.*

8. Stir in the lemon juice and season with salt and pepper. Serve very hot, garnished with bacon and chopped chives.

*TIP: Taste the raw corn before you grill it. If it is not very sweet, soak the corn in the husk with the silk removed in a mixture of sugar and water for an hour. This will help sweeten the flavor of the corn.

*TIP: To cut the corn off the cob, break the cooked cob in half. Place the flat end down on the cutting board, or in a shallow bowl, and cut down in a sawing motion between the kernels and the ear, holding it at the top with your free hand so that the cob doesn't slip.

*TIP: At this point, the soup can be tightly covered and refrigerated up to 2 days. **This soup can also be frozen** before the milk is added. Simply thaw, reheat, and add the milk when the mixture is hot, season with salt and pepper and serve.

Hearty Soups

As the chill of fall and winter sets in, our appetite for soup seems to grow. We look foward to wonderfully hearty foods that satisfy not only the stomach, but also the soul. A bowl of hot, steaming soup is the ultimate comfort food.

Soups are not tricky to put together; you just need to plan in advance to make sure you have basic flavoring ingredients like onion, garlic, leeks, and tomatoes (canned, most likely). Then, what kind of flavors does your family like to eat? Do they love melted cheese? Then onion soup might really hit the spot. Do your children love noodles? Then make sure to have many different kinds in your cupboard so that, even when you are trying a new recipe, if you put noodles in it, they are more likely to try and possibly even love it.

Weekends are the perfect time to make soup. All the chopping and preparation can be done without rushing, and long-cooking soups such as Ribbolita (page 61) can be simmering while you are folding laundry or raking autumn leaves. Remember, though, that many soups don't need to be cooked for hours and hours to taste great. Frequently 30 minutes to an hour of cooking results in a hearty, fresh-tasting finished dish.

Add a salad, a simple omelet, and lots of good bread to dip in the bowl and you have a meal for even the biggest appetite. All this means that on certain days, soup is one of the most perfect foods. Have you had your soup today?

Ribbolita

✓ *MAKE-AHEAD*

Like many old-fashioned dishes, easy-to-make ribbolita is really much better when served the day after it is first made. Even its name means reboiled—which you do when you reheat it. I like making it one day and serving it for a virtually no-work dinner the next night. The hearty vegetable flavor is wonderful and the added bread makes this chunky soup a very satisfying dish—perfect after a day of skiing, snow shoveling, or even a day full of errands and children's activities.

✱TIP: Although it isn't classic, for an even heartier dish, add 2 cups diced cooked meat (chicken or beef) to the kettle now.

✱TIP: At this point **the soup may either be served, or cooled and refrigerated overnight.** Just before serving, reheat to boiling.

2 tablespoons olive oil, plus more for serving

1 cup chopped yellow onion (from about 1 medium onion)

1/2 cup chopped celery (from about 1 large rib)

1 cup scraped and sliced carrots (from about 2 medium carrots)

1 tablespoon finely chopped garlic (from about 3 cloves)

Two 15 1/2-ounce cans cannellini beans, drained and rinsed until the foam subsides

2 medium white potatoes, peeled and cut up

1 large 28-ounce can plum tomatoes with their juice

5 cups well-flavored low-sodium chicken broth (from 2 quarts)

1/2 small head savoy or napa cabbage, shredded

1/2 cup chopped fresh Italian flat-leaf parsley

Salt and freshly ground pepper, to taste

8 thick slices densely textured Italian bread—at least 1 day old, or lightly toasted

Extra-virgin olive oil for garnishing

1. Heat the oil in a heavy soup kettle. Add the onion, celery, and carrots. Cook over medium-high heat until softened and the onions are transparent, 6 to 8 minutes. Add the garlic and cook 1 minute more. Stir in the drained beans and cook 1 minute. ✱

2. Add the potatoes and cook 2 minutes more, stirring once or twice. Add the tomatoes, their juice, and about 1 cup broth, breaking up the large pieces. Add the cabbage and parsley. Season with salt and pepper. Add the remaining broth and simmer until the vegetables are very tender, 30 to 40 minutes. ✱

3. To serve, place 1 thick slice of Italian bread or toast in each flat serving bowl. Ladle the soup over the bread and drizzle each serving with a little extra-virgin olive oil.

Corn-Crab Chowder

✓ *SOMETHING SPECIAL*

For this thick and chunky cream soup, it is best to buy fresh crabmeat from the fish market or grocery store. Make sure to drain any excess moisture from the crabmeat and then add it at the very last minute, so it does not become overcooked and chewy. (It is already cooked when you buy it.)

6 tablespoons butter

1 cup chopped white onion (from about 1 medium onion)

1 cup sliced celery (from about 2 large ribs)

Salt to taste

1½ cups peeled, diced russet potato (from about 1 extra large potato)

½ cup clam juice or fish stock

1 cup chicken broth

1 bay leaf

3 ears of corn, husked, rinsed, dried, and brushed with olive oil

⅓ cup all-purpose flour

1½ cups whole milk

2 cups half and half (1 pint)

2 tablespoons dry sherry

¼ teaspoon freshly ground pepper

8 ounces special grade crabmeat, cleaned and picked through for shells, flaked *

2 tablespoons chopped fresh chives, for garnish

1. Preheat an outdoor grill to medium-high. Clean and season grill.

2. Melt 2 tablespoons of the butter in a large saucepan over medium-low heat. Add the onion and celery, season with salt to taste and cook until just tender, stirring often, about 15 minutes.

3. Add the potato and cook 5 minutes more. Add the clam juice, chicken broth, and bay leaf and simmer, covered, for 30 minutes. Remove the bay leaf and reserve.

4. Place the prepared ears of corn on the preheated grill. Grill until the corn is lightly browned, turning frequently so that the corn cooks evenly, about 10 minutes. Remove the corn from the grill and cool. Once the corn is cooled, carefully cut the corn off the cob. *

5. In a 3-quart saucepan, melt the remaining butter over medium heat. Stir in the flour and cook for 5 minutes, stirring constantly. Whisk in the milk and half and half, all at once, and continue to stir until the mixture comes to a simmer and thickens.

6. Add the simmering vegetables and corn to the thickened milk and season with sherry, salt, and pepper. Skim any foam from the surface of the soup with a ladle or spoon.

7. Add the fresh crabmeat just before serving and heat through to just a simmer. Serve immediately, garnished with the chives.

SERVING SUGGESTION

Pass a bowl of oyster crackers, or serve with a plate of Common Crackers to crumble into the chowder for an even more substantial meal.

✱ TIP: Buy **"special" grade crabmeat** for this chowder. It is already in bits and flakes and costs much less than lump crabmeat. No need to use premium-priced lump crabmeat, which should be reserved for crab cakes or fresh salads.

✱ TIP: To cut **the corn off the cob**, break the cooked cob in half. Place the flat end down on the cutting board and cut in a sawing motion between the kernels and the ear, holding it at the top with your free hand so that the cob doesn't slip.

Rich and Hearty Onion Soup

✓ *SOMETHING SPECIAL*   ✓ *MAKE-AHEAD*

Instead of using only one kind of onion, I like to use four different varieties in this delicious soup. While the style may be familiar, very like French Onion Soup, the flavor of the combined onions is decidedly heartier. The slicing and browning of the onions, while simple tasks, take time—so pop in your favorite music to sooth you or inspire you to sing along and enjoy the moment.

* TIP: Using red wine makes this a deliciously hearty soup, though the color is a bit murky—if you want a more golden soup, use dry white wine instead.

3 tablespoons butter

4 large shallots, very thinly sliced (about 3 tablespoons)

2 large leeks, well washed, white and light green parts very thinly sliced (about 1½ cups)

4 large yellow onions, halved and sliced (about 8 cups)

2 bunches green onions, white and light green very thinly sliced (about ⅔ cup)

2 tablespoons all-purpose flour

1 cup red wine *****

5 cups beef broth (from 2 quarts)

Salt and freshly ground pepper, to taste

½ teaspoon ground cumin

½ cup freshly shredded Parmigiano-Reggiano cheese (from 2 ounces)

1. Melt the butter in a heavy 3-quart covered saucepan. Add the shallots, leeks, onions, and green onions. Cook over low heat until soft and well browned— a slow process that may take 30 minutes or more. Be careful to stir from time to time and watch carefully to keep the onions from burning.

2. Sprinkle the onions with flour and cook, stirring, for 3 to 4 minutes more.

3. Stir in the red wine and cook over high heat for 5 minutes to reduce slightly. Stir in the broth, season well with salt, pepper, and ground cumin, and simmer gently for 25 to 30 minutes.

4. Serve ladled into bowls and topped with shredded Parmigiano-Reggiano cheese.

SERVING SUGGESTION

If you would like an even heartier flavor, fry 8 strips bacon until crisp, drain on paper towels, and then crumble to sprinkle over each bowl of soup along with the cheese. This soup makes a great lunch or supper, along with a simple salad and some crusty bread.

Potato, Leek, and Bacon Soup

✓ *MAKE-AHEAD*

I love to use the sweet flavor of leeks in this soup for the perfect accompaniment to the smoky flavor of the bacon. Leeks and potatoes, along with milk or buttermilk, combine to make an almost perfectly nutritious dish—a wonderful way to end an exhausting day.

½ pound bacon, cut into small pieces *

3 tablespoons olive oil

6 small leeks, white part only, sliced lengthwise, rinsed, and then chopped (about 3 cups) *

6 cups peeled and diced russet potatoes (from about 6 medium potatoes)

6 cups low-sodium chicken broth (1½ quarts)

4 cups half and half (1 quart)

Salt and freshly ground pepper, to taste

1. Fry the bacon in a small skillet over medium-high heat, stirring frequently, until the pieces are crisp. Make sure to pour off the excess fat as it is rendered in order to crisp the bacon faster. Drain the bacon thoroughly on a paper towel.

2. Add the olive oil to a large 6-quart stockpot over medium heat. Add the leeks and cook, stirring often, until they are soft, about 8 minutes. Do not allow them to brown.

3. Stir in the potatoes, add the broth and half and half, and bring to a boil. Lower the heat and simmer until the potatoes are tender, about 30 minutes.

4. Adjust the seasonings with salt and pepper. Stir in the bacon, and serve.

✻ TIP: It's simple to **cut bacon with scissors**. Cut the entire slab across the layers rather than cutting the individual slices, creating small 1-inch "stairs" of bacon. As the bacon cooks, the pieces will break apart and cook into perfect ½-inch diced pieces.

✻ TIP: Make sure you **choose small leeks**, and remember they must be cleaned thoroughly. Cut them lengthwise, rinse in between the layers to remove all of the dirt, then chop and add to the pot.

Minestrone

✓ *EASY PREPARATION*   ✓ *SOMETHING SPECIAL*

This wonderfully simple vegetable soup, perfect for a vegetarian meal, tastes deceptively rich, though it is easy, natural, and uncomplicated. Once you have sampled it, you will be amazed it was made with just water, not chicken stock.

¼ cup olive oil

1½ cups very thinly sliced onion (from about 1 small onion)

2 small zucchini, trimmed and diced

2 medium white- or red-skinned potatoes, washed and diced

1 cup diced celery (from about 2 large ribs)

1 cup finely diced carrots (from about 2 medium carrots)

1 cup small cauliflower florets (from about ⅓ medium head cauliflower)

3 cups stemmed, halved, seeded, and diced tomatoes (from 3 large tomatoes)

2 large portobello caps, diced

20 large fresh green beans, cut into ½-inch pieces

6 cups water

Salt and freshly ground pepper, to taste

½ cup uncooked elbow macaroni

¼ cup chopped fresh Italian flat-leaf parsley

½ cup freshly shredded Parmigiano-Reggiano cheese (from 2 ounces)

1. Heat the oil in a heavy kettle. Stir in the onion and cook, stirring, for 2 to 3 minutes. Stir in the remaining vegetables and toss to coat with oil. Stir in 6 cups of water. Season well with salt and pepper. Simmer, partially covered, over low heat for about 30 minutes or just until the vegetables are very tender.

2. While the soup is cooking, bring 3 quarts salted water to a boil and boil the pasta for 6 to 7 minutes, until just al dente or slightly firm in the middle when you bite it. Drain well.

3. Stir the cooked pasta into the soup and cook 2 minutes more.

4. Just before the soup is finished, stir in ¼ cup minced fresh parsley and cook 1 or 2 minutes. Serve while the parsley still gives its fresh flavor to the soup.

5. Serve in heated bowls topped with a tablespoon of freshly shredded Parmigiano-Reggiano cheese.

Adventures in Pizza

Pizza is a great dish for the weekend because to do it right, it's best to work with homemade dough, which is not always feasible on a weeknight. (Kneading dough is actually wonderfully relaxing and a great way to work out any stress you may have accumulated during the week.) When it comes to the crust, you have many choices. On the weekend, a traditional crust can be made from yeast, flour, water, salt, and sugar. It slowly rises an hour or more to become the perfect base for the toppings. But, this is not the only way. Pizza dough will also rise nicely in the refrigerator, which improves the texture of the dough. It can rise for up to 24 hours in the refrigerator, tightly covered with plastic wrap. The crust can also be leftover bread, tortillas, pitas, or even store-bought dough.

Toppings can be your old favorites, or think about adding an extra hamburger to the grill, or a chicken breast on Friday night. The shredded chicken or the crumbled hamburger will make a great pizza topping the next day.

The cheese is the final element. Conventional wisdom tells us to use mozzarella cheese. I think this cheese is very mild and needs to have a stronger tasting cheese added to it, such as Parmigiano-Reggiano or even Pecorino. Specialty cheeses such as goat cheese, blue cheese, or even gorgonzola can turn an ordinary pizza into a spectacular pizza.

A busy-weekend dinner can be made easier with some make-ahead pizza tips.

- You can cook your sauce ahead. Sauces also freeze well, so add an extra batch and freeze some for the next time you make pizza.

- Prepare all of your topping ingredients before the dough is ready. By slicing, chopping, and grating in advance you will save time when topping your pizzas.

- Pizza making may also be inspired by the extras left over from last night's dinner. Leftover grilled meats, roasted vegetables, or bread dough from another weekend meal can turn into beautiful pizzas for a Saturday night dinner or an early Sunday treat. Some of my favorite pizzas are topped with grilled chicken or leftover breakfast sausages.

- Pizza is the perfect family food because everyone can get involved with the rolling, topping, and baking of a pizza.

- Small pizzas can be made for each family member so that everyone gets exactly what they like. Survey your family and friends and gather up all of your own creative pizza ideas, and enjoy!

- Remember, each 12-inch pizza round can be cut into 4 to 6 slices. Two to three of these slices makes a reasonable serving.

Grilled Pizza Bread with Garlic-Herb Oil

MAKES TEN 6-INCH ROUNDS OR 5 TO 6 SERVINGS

This recipe can easily be prepared with premade pizza dough from the supermarket. Just make the infused oil and grill the dough as directed. Pass this bread, cut into small wedges or pieces, along with drinks before dinner, or serve it instead of regular bread with soups, stews, and pasta dishes. Make plenty; it seems to please nearly everyone.

GARLIC-HERB OIL

1 cup extra-virgin olive oil

2 teaspoons curry powder

1 teaspoon garlic powder

1 teaspoon onion powder

1/2 teaspoon dried oregano

1 teaspoon crushed dried red pepper

1/2 teaspoon salt

1/4 teaspoon freshly ground pepper

DOUGH

1 envelope (2 teaspoons) dry yeast

1 tablespoon sugar

1 1/4 cups hot water (120°–130°F)

2 tablespoons extra-virgin olive oil

2 teaspoons salt

3 1/2 cups bread flour (this measure is approximate)

1 tablespoon coarse-grained sea salt, for sprinkling on top

1. In a small saucepan, combine the olive oil, curry powder, garlic powder, onion powder, oregano, red pepper, salt, and pepper.

2. Heat the mixture over low heat just until the oil is warm. Remove the saucepan from the heat, and let herbs steep for 2 hours.

3. Strain through a coffee filter into a clean jar and reserve.

4. Combine the yeast, sugar, and water in the bowl of a mixer. Let stand until the yeast begins to work, making the mixture frothy. Add olive oil, salt, and 3 cups of the flour. Stir until mixed, adding up to 1/2 cup more flour if the dough seems too wet, and then knead vigorously for 15 minutes by hand. ✳✳

5. Place the kneaded dough in an oiled bowl, cover it with plastic wrap, and let rise in a warm place for 1 hour or until doubled in size. ✳

6. Preheat the grill on medium-high heat for 10 minutes.

7. Punch down the dough with your knuckles and then divide it into 10 pieces. Allow the pieces to rest under a towel for 10 minutes and then roll them out into 6-inch circles. Brush one side of each piece of dough with the infused oil.

8. Place the dough on the preheated grill rack or griddle, oil side down. Brush the top with the infused oil. Turn them only once, until cooked through and golden brown on each side, about 3 minutes per side. ✳

9. Serve the rounds on a warmed plate and garnish with coarse salt and infused oil.

✳**TIP:** Kneading pizza **dough**, like the dough for many types of bread, is a wonderful way to work off frustration, anger, or just nervous energy. The more vigorously it is kneaded, the more developed the gluten, the better the crust.

✳**TIP:** If using an **electric mixer**, combine the ingredients with the paddle attachment and then knead for 15 minutes with the dough hook. Add more flour if necessary to yield a soft, tender dough that is not sticky to the touch.

✳**TIP:** The dough will have **doubled** in bulk when the marks of two fingers pressed into the surface remain there and do not fill in immediately.

✳**TIP:** To **avoid wrinkling the dough**, place it gently on the grill grate. Handle it as though you are laying a wet washcloth on the counter, so you will end up with a flat bread. If you throw it on the grill, you will end up with large folds in the final bread.

Mexican-Inspired Pizza

✓ *SOMETHING SPECIAL*

This is a family pleaser—kids love pizza and everyone usually enjoys the layering of flavors and the variety of Mexican food, so here you get them in one dish. This pizza has all of the makings to provide you with the pizza you crave, combined with the tastiness of a Mexican meal.

Cornmeal Pizza Dough (next page)

2 tablespoons olive oil

1 cup thinly sliced white onion (from about ½ large onion)

3 fresh poblano chiles, seeded, deveined, and sliced (about 1 cup)

Pinch salt

1 pound chorizo sausage, casings discarded

1 cup commercial green chili sauce

½ teaspoon salt

2 cups grated Monterey Jack cheese (from 8 ounces)

2 cups grated cheddar cheese (from 8 ounces)

2 vine-ripened tomatoes, thinly sliced

1 cup sliced black olives

1 cup canned black beans, rinsed until the foam subsides

1. Preheat two pizza stones in the oven for 15 minutes or more at 500°F. *

2. Make the cornmeal pizza dough, forming two 12-inch rounds.

3. Heat the oil in a large skillet over medium heat. Add the onion, sliced poblano chilies, and a pinch of salt and cook until soft, 3 to 4 minutes. Add the sausage and cook, stirring occasionally, until fully cooked, about 6 minutes. Remove the mixture from the skillet with a slotted spoon, leaving all fat behind.

4. Lightly brush the entire surface of each pizza with ¼ cup of the green chili sauce. Sprinkle each pizza with ¼ teaspoon salt and ½ cup of each cheese. Sprinkle the sausage mixture over the cheese. Arrange the sliced tomatoes over the sausage and sprinkle with the black olives and black beans. Finish with a layer of green chili sauce and the remaining cheese. *

5. Transfer the pizzas to the preheated pizza stone and bake for 12 minutes or until the crust is golden and the cheese is melted. Remove the pizzas from the oven and allow them to rest for 5 minutes. Cut into wedges to serve.

✱ TIP: A **pizza stone** gives the crust a wonderful chewy and yet crispy texture. If you don't have one, you can also use a heavy cookie sheet, though the result will be slightly different.

✱ TIP: Build the pizzas on a **wooden or metal peel** dusted with fine cornmeal. The cornmeal acts like little roller bearings and lets the completed pizzas slide off easily onto the preheated stone.

Cornmeal Pizza Dough

✓ SOMETHING SPECIAL

Use extra-fine ground cornmeal so the texture of the dough will be as light as possible. As with whole-wheat dough, this crust is heavier, so use it with toppings that are hearty and full of flavor and texture; this full-bodied dough can overpower a delicate combination of toppings.

2¼ teaspoons active dry yeast (one envelope)

1 teaspoon sugar

1 cup warm water (110°–120°F)

2½ cups bread flour

½ cup very fine cornmeal

¼ cup extra-virgin olive oil

1 teaspoon sea salt

1. In a small bowl or a mixer fitted with the paddle attachment, combine the yeast, sugar, and water. Add 1½ cups bread flour and the cornmeal. Combine on low speed or with a wooden spoon until a rugged mass of dough forms.

2. Add the oil and the salt. Add enough of the remaining flour to form soft but kneadable dough. Place the dough on a floured surface and knead for 6 minutes or knead the dough in the electric mixer with the dough hook attachment.

3. Transfer the dough to a lightly oiled bowl and cover with plastic wrap. Allow the dough to rise in a warm spot until it has doubled in bulk, about 1 hour.

4. Once the dough has risen, punch it down with your hands and turn it out onto a lightly floured surface. Divide the dough into 2 equal pieces and allow it to rest for 15 minutes.

5. Roll the dough out into two 12-inch rounds. Build a 1-inch rim around each circle of dough. *

✱ TIP: If you only wish to **make one pizza**, wrap the second half of the dough tightly in plastic wrap, place in a resealable plastic bag, and squeeze out all the air. Refrigerate for a day or two, or freeze up to 3 months. Thaw completely, unwrap, and bring to room temperature before rolling out.

Stuffed Bread Pizza

✓ *SOMETHING SPECIAL*   ✓ *MAKE-AHEAD*   ✓ *TAKE-ALONG*

This pizza provides a unique crust and great fillings. Make this ahead, and then heat it up just before serving. It is a very hearty dish and one wedge makes a complete meal when accompanied by a salad of your choice.

One 1-pound sourdough bread loaf, unsliced

8 ounces lean ground beef

2 tablespoons olive oil

1 pound spinach, cleaned and trimmed (about 12 cups)

½ cup refrigerated commercial basil pesto

2 cups shredded mozzarella cheese (from 8 ounces)

Eggplant Caviar (page 29)

¾ cup canned or homemade plain tomato sauce

1. Preheat the oven to 375°F.

2. Cut off the top third of the bread. Use a sharp spoon or knife to scoop out the interior of the loaf, leaving a ½-inch shell. Place the bread shell on a large baking sheet. Keep the top layer and the interior of the loaf to use for bread crumbs, poultry stuffing, or for making bread pudding.

3. Cook the ground beef in a skillet over medium-high heat. Drain the ground beef on paper towels and wipe the skillet clean. Heat the olive oil in the same skillet over medium-high heat. Add the spinach and cook until just wilted, about 3 minutes. Add the basil pesto to the spinach.

4. Sprinkle half the cheese over the bottom of the bread shell. In even layers, spread the spinach mixture over the cheese, followed by the ground beef and the eggplant caviar.

5. Bake the pizza about 20 minutes, until the filling is heated. Combine the tomato sauce with the remaining cheese and spread it over the top of the pizza. Dot the top with any remaining basil pesto. Continue baking about 12 minutes, until the cheese melts. Cut into wedges and serve warm. ∗

∗ TIP: Before **cutting the pizza** into wedges, allow it to rest for at least 10 minutes. It will hold together better after it has a chance to cool slightly.

70 KITCHEN COACH: WEEKEND COOKING

Tomato Basil Pizza with a Phyllo Crust

✓ SOMETHING SPECIAL

Using phyllo dough is a quick and easy way to make a pizza crust. While not a common practice, here the delicate layers of the phyllo dough provide you with a crisp-crusted, innovative pizza choice. Children like the crispiness of these squares, and adults love them with before-dinner drinks. Working with phyllo dough takes a little extra effort, which makes it perfect for a weekend evening when you have more time to work in the kitchen.

4 tablespoons butter, melted and cooled slightly

10 sheets phyllo dough *

½ cup finely grated Parmigiano-Reggiano cheese (from 2 ounces)

½ cup basil pesto—homemade or good quality commercial

4 ounces goat cheese

1 cup thinly sliced white onion (from about ½ large onion)

3 vine-ripened tomatoes, seeded and sliced into rounds

¼ cup fresh basil, torn into pieces

1. Preheat the oven to 375°F. Brush a rectangular baking sheet with butter. Brush one sheet of phyllo dough with melted butter and place it on the prepared baking sheet. Brush another sheet of phyllo dough with butter, place on top of the first sheet and sprinkle it with Parmigiano-Reggiano. Repeat this layering, 2 sheets of buttered phyllo between each sprinkling of cheese, until you have used all 10 sheets of the phyllo dough, ending with phyllo.

2. Top the last layer of phyllo with the pesto, pieces of the goat cheese, the onion, and finally the tomatoes.

3. Bake about 30 minutes, until the crust is crisp and brown and the cheese softens. Let stand 5 minutes, sprinkle with the freshly torn basil, and cut into squares with a breadknife to serve.

***TIP:** When working with **phyllo**, keep the sheets you aren't working with under a damp towel until you are ready for them. This will keep them from drying out. If phyllo pastry dries out it becomes brittle and shatters, making it impossible to work with.

Endive, Pancetta, and Fontina Pizza

✓ *SOMETHING SPECIAL*

This pizza matches the sweetness of the pancetta with the bitterness of the Belgian endive to create an unusual and intriguing taste. The creamy texture of melted fontina and its mildly nutty flavor are perfect for this combination.

1 teaspoon olive oil

¼ pound pancetta, diced

4 cups thinly sliced Belgian endive (from about 4 to 5 large heads endive)

¼ cup freshly grated Parmigiano-Reggiano cheese (from 1 ounce)

1 teaspoon fresh lemon juice (from ½ medium lemon)

Salt and freshly ground pepper, to taste

One 12-inch cheese Boboli or other premade cheese pizza crust

1½ cups freshly grated fontina cheese (from 6 ounces)

1. Heat the olive oil in a large skillet. Add the pancetta and cook, stirring, until crisp. Add the endive and cook with the pancetta until softened, about 10 minutes. Stir in the Parmigiano-Reggiano and the lemon juice. Season with salt and pepper.

2. Preheat a pizza stone 15 minutes or longer in the oven at 500°F, or as specified by the manufacturer. Spoon the toppings over the crust and then sprinkle with the fontina cheese. Place the pizza on the stone and bake about 8 minutes, until the cheese melts and the crust is golden.

3. Cut the pizza into wedges and serve.

VARIATION

Use the homemade dough from the Grilled Pizza Bread (page 67) for this pizza if you want a thinner crust, building the pizza rim before adding the filling.

✱ TIP: A number of **different cheeses** make a delicious topping on this pie. Fontina is a mild melting cheese, but I have made it with goat cheese and even white cheddar.

Mom's Fruit Pizza

✓ *SOMETHING SPECIAL*   ✓ *MAKE-AHEAD*

You can make this dessert pizza with your own butter cookie recipe or premade sugar cookie dough. This quick tart dough will be the perfect base for the fresh fruit that is in season.

1 package refrigerated sugar cookie dough

One 8-ounce package cream cheese, at room temperature

1/3 cup sugar

1/2 teaspoon pure vanilla extract

3 cups assorted sliced fruit such as peaches, kiwi, strawberries, raspberries, blueberries, orange sections, etc., or more if needed

1 tablespoon water

1/2 cup seedless red raspberry jam

1. Preheat the oven to 375° F. Cut the roll of sugar cookie dough into ⅛-inch slices. Line a 14-inch round pizza pan with the slices of cookie, overlapping them slightly and pressing gently. Bake them for about 12 minutes or until lightly browned.

2. In a large bowl, blend the cream cheese, sugar, and vanilla until smooth. Spread over the cookie crust. Arrange the fruit in circles on the cream cheese.

3. Warm the water and the jam together in a small saucepan, stirring gently, to form a glaze for the fruit. Brush the glaze on the fruit with a pastry brush. Refrigerate for up to 3 hours.

4. Cut into wedges to serve.

＊TIP: When you see a shiny piece of fruit on a tart or pie, it is because the **fruit is glazed**. You can glaze the fruit with strained orange marmalade, seedless berry jam, or even currant jelly. Just warm your choice of glaze over low heat mixed with a little water and brush it on the fruit.

Perfect Pasta

There is something about a hot, fragrant bowl of cooked pasta that is both comforting and too good to resist.

Whether it originated in China or not, pasta has become a mainstay in Italian kitchens, and is now one of the most popular dishes in America because it's easy to prepare, serve, and enjoy.

Pasta is more than spaghetti or macaroni; it comes in a myriad of shapes, from bow ties to lasagna noodles and beyond. Even couscous, which many people think is a grain, is really a form of pasta.

In Italy, cooks are very conscious of pairing sauces and pasta shapes. They feel a dish is not quite right if the sauce is served with the wrong shape of pasta. The idea is to serve chunky sauces with shapes like rigatoni, orecchiette, or some other shape with enough nooks and crannies to hold on to the sauce so you taste everything at one time. Creamy, thick sauces are served with long strands of pasta such as linguine, fettuccine,

and angel hair. No matter what the combination, toss the pasta with the sauce in a bowl or cooking pot so that it is all moistened at the same time, rather than serving a bowl of pasta with a ladle of sauce spooned on top. That way the flavors of the sauce and pasta come together in every mouthful.

When you have time, and are thinking along the lines of fettucine with a rich cream sauce or homemade pesto, weekends provide the perfect opportunity to bring the kids into the kitchen to make your own fresh pasta. Let them crank the handle of the pasta machine, or catch the pasta as it comes out of the machine, laying it over a rack to dry for a time before cooking.

I love to make a big steaming bowl of pasta, and serve it to my family for a warm and satisfying Saturday night supper. It is a favorite at our house—and I bet it will be at yours, too.

Sausage, Red Bell Pepper, and Tomato Orecchiette

✓ MAKE-AHEAD

In this recipe, I like to use any interesting Italian or Mexican sausage I can find. My favorite is an Italian sausage made with fennel, or a traditional chorizo.

1 pound orecchiette pasta (these "little ears" pick up lots of sauce) *

Salt and freshly ground pepper, to taste

Splash of extra-virgin olive oil

1 tablespoon olive oil

1 pound Italian sausage, sliced— use the hot variety if you prefer

2 cups finely chopped yellow onions (from about 2 medium onions)

2 cups diced red bell peppers (from about 2 small peppers)

1 teaspoon salt

1 tablespoon finely chopped fresh garlic (from about 3 medium cloves)

¼ cup balsamic vinegar

One 28-ounce can crushed Italian tomatoes *

¼ cup freshly chopped basil, for garnish

1. Cook the orecchiette in a large stockpot with salted boiling water, until al dente. Drain the pasta, return it to the stockpot, season with salt and pepper, and drizzle with a touch of extra-virgin olive oil. Cover to keep it warm.

2. While the pasta is cooking, heat a large skillet over medium-high heat. Add the oil and the sausage slices in batches, and cook until lightly browned, about 1 minute per side. Remove the sausage to a plate and set aside. Reserve the skillet to make sauce.

3. In the skillet used to cook the sausage, over medium heat, add the onions and bell pepper, and season with salt. Cook, stirring from time to time, until the vegetables begin to soften, 8 minutes. Add the garlic and cook until fragrant, 30 seconds to 1 minute. Add the vinegar and simmer 5 minutes to reduce by half. Add the tomatoes and simmer until the sauce has reduced a little and thickened, 10 to 15 minutes. Adjust seasoning as necessary.

4. Add the sausage to the sauce and heat through. Pour the sauce over the warm, seasoned pasta and garnish with basil. Serve immediately.

＊TIP: Use pasta shells or even penne if you cannot find orecchiette.

＊TIP: Tomatoes that are grown and packed in Italy or are organic will have less acidity. I always keep canned whole tomatoes, crushed tomatoes, and tomato paste in my pantry for a quick and easy dinner.

Rigatoni with Lamb, Arugula, and Feta

✓ *SOMETHING SPECIAL*

Although not traditional, lamb and pasta are a delicious combination. You can find loin lamb chops in the supermarket. In this recipe, they are cooked on the bone, and then the tender, succulent meat is removed and added to the cooked pasta.

1 pound rigatoni

4 loin lamb chops, each about ¾ inch thick

Salt and freshly ground pepper, to taste

1 teaspoon paprika

1 tablespoon olive oil

1½ cups chopped white onion (from about 1 large onion)

1 teaspoon finely chopped fresh garlic (from 1 medium clove)

3 cups fresh arugula or baby spinach (4½ ounces)

1½ cups crumbled feta cheese (from 6 ounces), plus more for serving

2 tablespoons fresh oregano leaves, removed from the stem *

1. Cook the rigatoni in plenty of boiling salted water, until al dente. Drain the pasta and return it to the stockpot to keep it warm.

2. While the pasta is cooking, heat a large frying pan over medium heat. Season the lamb chops with salt, pepper, and the paprika. Add the olive oil to the pan and then the lamb chops. Cook the chops at medium heat until the meat is firm and still slightly pink in the middle, 4 minutes per side. Remove the lamb chops from the pan and drain on a plate lined with paper towels. Reserve frying pan to cook onion.

3. Once the lamb is cool enough to handle, cut the meat off the bone and slice into ½-inch-thick slices. Reserve. *

4. Add the onion to the frying pan, season with salt, cover and cook over medium heat 5 minutes, or until soft and beginning to turn golden. Add the minced garlic and cook until fragrant, about 30 seconds to 1 minute. Remove the cover, add the arugula or spinach, and cook until just wilted, 1 or 2 minutes. Add the lamb to the frying pan and toss just to warm.

5. Add the contents of the frying pan to the pasta and gently toss to combine. Stir in the feta cheese and oregano, and season with salt and freshly ground pepper. Heat 1 minute.

6. To serve, arrange a bed of the pasta on each dinner plate and top with a little more cheese. Serve very hot.

＊TIP: Substitute about 1½ teaspoons dried oregano for the fresh leaves if fresh oregano is not easily available. Normally the equivalent is 3 times fresh oregano for dried, but here the leaves are left whole, so they create a larger volume than chopped.

＊TIP: Once you have removed the meat from the **lamb bones**, place the bones in a resealable plastic bag and freeze them. At a later time, the bones can be roasted in the oven and then added to a soup broth you're making for richer flavor. You can keep them in the freezer for up to 2 months.

Spaghetti with Salmon, Zucchini, and Spiced Crumbs

✓ *SOMETHING SPECIAL*

You can make these spiced bread crumbs with store-bought dried bread crumbs. Or, if you have some leftover bread, from our Stuffed Bread Pizza (page 70) for example, you can grind it up and use it in this recipe.

1 pound spaghetti

2 tablespoons plus ¼ cup olive oil

2 teaspoons finely chopped garlic (from about 2 medium cloves)

1 teaspoon finely chopped, seeded serrano chile (from ½ pepper)

1 tablespoon grated lemon zest (from 1 medium lemon) *

1 teaspoon salt

1½ cups coarse bread crumbs

One 8-ounce center-cut salmon fillet, boned, skinned

Salt and freshly ground pepper, to taste

1 small zucchini, peeled into strips with vegetable peeler

½ cup halved, pitted Kalamata olives

1 cup baby spinach (1½ ounces)

¼ cup fresh lemon juice (from about 2 medium lemons)

1. Cook the pasta in a stockpot of salted boiling water until al dente. Drain and return to the pan to keep it warm.

2. Heat 1 tablespoon of the olive oil in a medium skillet over medium-low heat. Add the garlic, chile, lemon zest, and salt to the pan and cook until fragrant, about 1 minute. Add the bread crumbs and cook, stirring, until crisp and golden, 5 minutes. Spread the mixture onto a large plate to cool.

3. Wipe out the skillet and return it to the heat. Heat 1 tablespoon of the olive oil. Season the salmon with salt and pepper. Add the salmon to the hot skillet and cook until golden on the outside and just opaque in the middle, about 4 minutes per side. Remove the salmon from the pan, place it on a plate and gently flake the fish with a fork into bite-sized pieces. *

4. Add the zucchini to the same skillet and cook until just tender, 2 minutes. Add the olives and spinach and toss to heat and just wilt the spinach. Add to the pasta with the lemon juice and remaining olive oil. Toss and season with salt and pepper. Add the flaked salmon to the pasta. Toss well, divide among individual pasta bowls, sprinkle with the bread crumbs, and serve immediately.

★ TIP: Zesting citrus fruit is quick and easy with a Microplane grater. Now there is one with two grater sizes, coarse on one end, fine on the other.

★ TIP: Instead of cooking the **salmon fillets** in a pan, you can substitute grilled salmon or even leftover chicken. Add the pieces to the pan to warm them through, then add the vegetables.

Three-Cheese and Herb Lasagne

✓ SOMETHING SPECIAL ✓ MAKE-AHEAD

For family nights, party nights, potlucks, or just because you want something hearty, lasagne is a perfect dish. It's hard not to love the blend of flavors, the comfort of noodles and cheese. You may already know how to make the classic meat lasagne. This is a fun and healthier variation with spinach added and less meat—still irresistible.

Try to use fresh mozzarella cheese and fresh ricotta. I guarantee that you, your family, and your guests will notice how much better it tastes.

✱TIP: This lasagne can easily be **adapted to a vegetarian meal.** Eliminate the ground meat and add an equal amount of diced squash or carrots in its place.

✱TIP: The **lasagne can be made a day ahead** to this point and refrigerated, or frozen. Or, make smaller portions in disposable bread pans, cook them together, let the portions you're not eating for that meal cool, then freeze them for up to three months.

1½ pounds lean ground beef ✱

3 tablespoons olive oil

1½ cups finely chopped white onion (from about 1 large onion)

2 teaspoons finely chopped garlic (from about 2 medium cloves)

2 cups Italian-style crushed tomatoes (about one 14½ ounce can)

1 cup tomato sauce

½ cup tomato paste

2 teaspoons dried basil

1 teaspoon salt

½ teaspoon dried sage

¼ teaspoon freshly ground pepper

¼ teaspoon dried rosemary

¼ teaspoon Tabasco sauce

10 ounces lasagne noodles, fresh (next page) or dried

1 teaspoon butter

1 pound fresh mozzarella cheese, cubed

1 cup grated Parmigiano-Reggiano cheese (from 4 ounces)

1 pound fresh spinach, well washed, stemmed, chopped (about 10 cups)

1 pound low-fat ricotta cheese

1. In a large skillet, brown the beef, breaking up any large pieces, pour off the fat, and set the browned beef aside. Add the olive oil to the pan. Cook the onion, stirring, for about 1 minute, and then add the garlic. Cook the garlic, stirring, for about 2 minutes. Add the beef, the tomatoes, sauce, paste, basil, salt, sage, pepper, rosemary, and Tabasco. Simmer for at least 30 minutes.

2. Cook fresh lasagne noodles 3 to 4 minutes or dried noodles 9 to 10 minutes. They should be slightly underdone because they will absorb liquid from the sauce during the baking process. Separate the noodles as soon as they are drained and lay them out on a cookie sheet in a single layer.

3. Preheat the oven to 375°F. Spread a layer of sauce on the bottom of a buttered 9- × 13-inch baking pan. Top with half of the lasagne noodles, and one-third of the mozzarella. Sprinkle with one-third of the Parmigiano-Reggiano. Combine the spinach with the ricotta and spread half of this mixture over the cheeses. Top with another layer of sauce, noodles, cheese, and spinach. End with a layer of sauce and cheese. ✱

4. When ready, bake the lasagne in the preheated oven for 35 to 45 minutes until lightly browned and bubbling. Cool about 15 minutes before cutting. (If frozen, the lasagne should be thawed in the refrigerator and then baked.)

Homemade Lasagne Noodles

✓ *MAKE-AHEAD*

You won't believe the difference these simple homemade noodles make in your lasagne! Remember that fresh noodles cook quickly—4 to 5 minutes—so don't go far when they are cooking.

3 cups semolina flour

4 large eggs

1. Place the flour on a pastry board. Make a well in the center of the flour and crack the eggs into the well. Using a fork, slowly mix the eggs into the flour, drawing more of the flour in from the edges as you go.

2. When the dough begins to hold together as you work it, it is ready to be kneaded. Flour your hands and begin to work the dough into a ball. Knead the dough for 5 minutes by pulling the dough towards you, then folding it away from you, pressing with the heal of your hands. Rotate the dough a quarter turn between each fold. Add a little bit of flour if the dough becomes too sticky.

3. When fully kneaded, the dough should be smooth and very glossy. Wrap it in a clean, damp towel and let it rest 10 minutes. Divide the dough into 3 pieces. Flatten each piece into a rectangle about 5 inches wide. Insert one end into the pasta machine set on the thickest setting, according to the machine directions, and roll out into a long sheet. Change to next thinnest setting and repeat the rolling process. Continue rolling, making the setting one step thinner each time, until the dough is as thin as possible. Lay the sheets of dough out flat and let them dry for 5 minutes.

4. Cut the pasta sheets into 8- to 10-inch lengths, then into 2-inch-wide strips for lasagne noodles.

Irresistible
Breads

Baking delicious loaves of bread and other baked goods is not difficult once you understand the proper techniques. But, you may wonder, why bother to make your own bread when so many bakeries exist? It is because there are so many personal payoffs. You can start the bread, leave it as it rises and bakes, and then be rewarded with the wonderful aroma of bread baking (and the tasty result).

Bread baking is also one of the most therapeutic forms of cooking. There is something enormously soothing about working with the dough. The effort of kneading the dough for ten or more minutes to develop the gluten eases the stress of a long, busy week. In fact, the more effort you put into kneading the better the loaf, so push and punch it as hard as you like until it is shiny and elastic.

At its most basic, bread is made from flour, yeast, and water. Gluten in the flour becomes elastic when added to water. As the dough is kneaded, the yeast feeds on starches in the flour and releases gases. These gases are trapped in a weblike structure of gluten in the dough, which causes it to rise. In the following recipes I use the most common yeast, dry active yeast. This type of yeast requires no proofing, meaning you no longer have to add warm water and a little sugar to the yeast to start the growth process before adding the mixture to the dry ingredients. And as long as it is used while fresh, it will provide great structure in the bread.

Liquids added to the bread can range from water to beer, or from buttermilk to whole milk. Buttermilk adds tangy acidity, while beer adds full-bodied flavor. Milk makes a soft, delicate bread loaf. But any liquid must be cooled to 115°F temperature or less so that it doesn't make the dough too hot and ultimately kill the yeast.

Other added ingredients can contribute flavor to the dough, as well as change its chemistry. For example, salt can strengthen the gluten in the flour, control the yeast, and bring out the flavors in the bread. Bread without enough salt can taste flat and uninteresting. Olives, herbs, or spices can also be added to the dough, but never in such a large quantity that they overpower the bread's flavor.

So get out the mixing bowl, flex your muscles, and make bread.

Rustic Rosemary Round Loaf

✓ *SOMETHING SPECIAL*

This traditional artisanal bread can be made without any flavorings, or it can contain olives, sun-dried tomatoes, caraway seeds, or a combination of fresh or dried herbs. This fragrant rosemary loaf is especially good with egg dishes, such as our Country Frittata (page 20) or Italian Sausage and Cheese Brunch Bake (page 22).

2½ teaspoons dry active yeast (from 1 packet or measured from a jar of yeast)

1 teaspoon sugar

1¾ cups warm water (105°F)

5 cups bread flour

1 tablespoon plus 1 teaspoon salt

2 teaspoons chopped fresh rosemary

Olive oil, to grease bowl

1. In a large bowl or electric mixer bowl, dissolve the yeast and sugar in the warm water, until froth forms on the surface, an indication that the yeast is working.

2. Combine 3 cups of the flour with the salt and rosemary, and add it to the yeast mixture. Mix with a wooden spoon, or the paddle attachment of an electric mixer. Mix thoroughly, adding more flour, if necessary, to yield a soft pliable dough that is still slightly sticky.

3. Turn the dough out onto a lightly floured board and knead for 15 minutes, or replace the paddle attachment with a dough hook and knead for 10 minutes with the electric mixer. Sprinkle on more flour, a little at a time, if the dough is still a little sticky and clings to the beater or your hands, until the dough is soft, silky, elastic, and in one consolidated mass. Place the dough in a greased bowl, cover with plastic wrap, and let it rise in a warm, draft-free place until doubled in bulk, about 1 hour.

4. Punch the dough down with the knuckles of your hand, and remove it from the bowl. Knead 4 or 5 times, let the dough rest on the board for 5 minutes, and then form it into a ball. Sprinkle the bottom of a jellyroll pan with cornmeal and place the dough in

the center. Cover the dough loosely with a towel and allow it to rise for about 1 hour, until it is almost doubled in bulk again.

5. Thirty minutes before the dough finishes rising, preheat the oven to 450°F. When the dough has finished the second rising and is doubled in bulk again, carefully cut three long slashes in the top of the loaf, then place it in the hot oven, and bake for 15 minutes. Reduce the heat to 400°F and continue baking for another 30 to 40 minutes or until the bread is crusty, golden, and the loaf sounds hollow when rapped on the bottom with your knuckles or a spoon. Remove from the oven and cool completely on a wire rack.

✱ TIP: If you want a **crispier loaf**, place a heavy pan in the oven on a rack set below where the bread pan will be placed. Allow the pan to preheat in the oven. Before you add the bread, put 2 or 3 ice cubes in the hot pan and then immediately add the bread. This steam technique will give you a light crispy crust.

Basil Focaccia

✓ *SOMETHING SPECIAL*

This Italian flat bread is crusty, thick, chewy, and moist, almost like a pizza crust. In Italy, it may have lots of different toppings including sliced tomatoes, grated cheese, prosciutto or Parma ham, or a variety of fresh or dried herbs. In its simplest form, it is brushed with olive oil, and sprinkled with coarse salt. This version does not need a starter (like sourdough), so you can make it in few hours. It freezes beautifully.

2½ teaspoons active dry yeast (from 1 packet)

1¾ cups warm water (105°F)

3 tablespoons extra-virgin olive oil

1½ teaspoons salt, plus more for top

2 tablespoons dried basil

4 to 4½ cups unbleached all-purpose flour

Olive oil, to grease bowl and pan

1. In a large bowl or electric mixer bowl, dissolve the yeast in the warm water, letting it stand until bubbles begin to form on the surface, an indication that the yeast is working.

2. Add 1½ tablespoons of the olive oil, all of the salt, dried basil, and 3 cups of the flour.

3. Mix vigorously with a wooden spoon, or for 2 minutes with the paddle attachment of an electric mixer. Add additional flour in ½-cup increments, mixing thoroughly after each addition, to yield a soft, pliable dough. ✱

4. Turn the dough out onto a lightly floured board and knead for 15 minutes, or replace the paddle attachment with a dough hook and knead for 10 minutes with the electric mixer. Gather the dough into a ball, place in an oiled bowl, and turn it to coat the dough with oil on all sides. Cover the bowl with plastic wrap and let the dough rise in a warm, draft-free place until doubled in bulk, about 1 hour. ✱

5. When doubled, punch down the dough with your hand and turn out onto a lightly floured board. Knead briefly 4 or 5 times, gather into a ball, and allow the dough to rest, covered with a towel, for 3 minutes.

6. Using a lightly floured rolling pin, roll out the dough into a rectangle large enough to fit a 9- × 11-inch lightly oiled glass baking pan. Place the dough in the pan, loosely cover with plastic wrap, and let rise in a warm, draft-free place about 30 minutes.

7. Using your fingertips, make a few indentations about ½ inch deep in the dough. Sprinkle with the remaining olive oil, cover again lightly with plastic wrap and let rise in a warm place for another 2 hours or until doubled in bulk.

8. Thirty minutes before the dough has risen fully, preheat the oven to 400°F. Just before baking, sprinkle the surface of the loaf lightly with salt. Bake for 25 to 30 minutes or until golden brown.

9. When finished baking, immediately invert the bread onto a cooling rack. Drizzle with more extra-virgin olive oil, if desired.

✱ **TIP:** The **amount of flour** necessary can change according to the flour and weather. At times, I have used up to a total of 4½ cups.

✱ **TIP:** The **dough has doubled in bulk** when two fingers poked into the dough ball leave marks that do not instantly go away.

Irish Soda Bread

✓ *SOMETHING SPECIAL*   ✓ *EASY PREPARATION*

Soda bread takes only a few minutes to combine, and then just 30 to 40 minutes to bake. You can experiment with variations of herbs, olives, onions or sun-dried tomatoes, whatever flavors you'd like to add to this bread; for instance, just two tablespoons of any fresh herbs incorported into the dough makes a full-flavored herb bread. This loaf can be cut into scones as well.

3 cups unbleached bread flour

1 teaspoon salt

3/4 teaspoon baking soda

1 1/2 cups buttermilk

1. Preheat the oven to 450°F.

2. Sift the dry ingredients into a large bowl. Make a well in the center of the dry ingredients, and pour two-thirds of the buttermilk into it. With one hand, mix the flour into the buttermilk. Using only one hand leaves the other hand clean for adding more liquid or flour, and for holding the bowl. Add more buttermilk to create a soft dough that sticks lightly to your fingers. Gather the dough into a ball, turn it out onto a floured board, and knead lightly for a few seconds, adding a little more flour if the dough is so sticky it doesn't easily come off your fingers when they are rubbed together.

3. Pat the dough into a round about 1 inch thick and cut a cross into the top crust. Cut through the edges of the round, about halfway, but not completely through the loaf. Bake on a cookie sheet in the preheated oven for 20 minutes. Turn the temperature down to 375°F and bake for 10 to 20 minutes more. ✳

4. Cool on a wire cooling rack for 10 minutes and serve immediately.

✳ TIP: With your knuckles or the back of a spoon, **tap the bottom to see if the loaf is done.** If the tapping sounds hollow, the loaf is finished. If you don't hear the hollow sound, return the bread to the oven for 5 or 6 minutes longer.

Soft Buttermilk Biscuits

✓ *SOMETHING SPECIAL*

A wet dough creates these delicious biscuits. The steam created in a hot oven makes them fluffy and airy. This is a technique I learned from Shirley Corriher, a food science expert and author and a creative cook.

1½ **cups cake flour**

1½ **teaspoons baking powder**

¼ **teaspoon baking soda**

¼ **teaspoon salt**

1 **tablespoon sugar**

3 **tablespoons vegetable shortening**

¾ **cup buttermilk**

½ **cup heavy cream**

¾ **cup all-purpose flour, for shaping**

2 **tablespoons butter, melted**

1. Preheat the oven to 475°F. Spray an 8-inch cake pan with cooking spray. Sift together the cake flour, baking powder, baking soda, salt, and sugar into a mixing bowl. With a pastry cutter or two knives, cut the shortening into the flour mixture. When you are finished, the dough should have lumps only slightly larger than the size of a pea.

2. Gently stir in the buttermilk until it is barely combined with the flour mixture, being careful not to overwork the dough or the biscuits will be tough. Allow the mixture to sit for 3 minutes. Put the heavy cream in a small bowl and pour the all-purpose flour onto the work surface. Flour your hands, and spoon about 2 tablespoons of

the wet dough into the cream. Next transfer the biscuit to the flour, spooning a little over the entire surface of the wet dough. Pick up the soft round and shake off the excess flour. Repeat until all the dough is used and place the biscuits, one by one, into the cake pan until they are tightly packed. Let them rise but not spread out, about 5 minutes.

3. Brush the top of each biscuit with melted butter, place the pan in the oven, and bake in the center of the oven 15 to 20 minutes, until lightly browned. Cool in the pan on a wire rack for 3 minutes. Turn out, break apart, and serve warm with butter and jam or honey.

Homemade Raspberry Jam

✓ *SOMETHING SPECIAL* ✓ *EASY PREPARATION*

Making your own jams is quick and easy. You can substitute your favorite berry in place of the raspberries if you like. I sometimes make my jam with many different frozen berries to go with freshly baked bread.

1 pound fresh or frozen raspberries

1 pound sugar (about 2½ cups)

2 tablespoons powdered fruit pectin

2 teaspoons fresh lemon juice
(from 1 medium lemon)

1. Preheat the oven to 400°F.

2. Stir the fresh or frozen raspberries into a medium stockpot. Heat over medium-high heat until the fruit releases some of its liquid and bubbles slightly. Place the sugar on a cookie sheet and bake about 15 minutes until hot, without melting. Add the sugar to the berries, along with the pectin and lemon juice.

3. Boil the mixture until it thickens, about 7 minutes. ∗

4. Remove the kettle from the heat and allow it to stand for 5 minutes.

5. Ladle the jam into a container and store in the refrigerator for up to 2 weeks.

∗**TIP:** To determine if the jam is ready to set, chill a small plate in the refrigerator. After 7 minutes of cooking the jam, place a small amount on the plate and put the plate back in the refrigerator. Remove the jam from the heat. After a few minutes, take the plate out of the refrigerator. Push the jam with your fingernail. If it wrinkles, the jam is done. If it doesn't wrinkle, put the jam back on the heat, cook a few minutes more, and repeat the process.

Specials from the Sea

Fish and shellfish have become a prominent part of the American diet, due in part to the demands of a more health-conscious public. Improved preservation and transportation techniques have made good seafood widely available, just in time for the increase in demand. Flash freezing at sea brings the closest thing to fresh-caught fish to places that are far from major fishing ports.

Many types of fish and shellfish are expensive, and all are highly perishable. In many areas there is no choice but to buy fish at the supermarket. Develop a working friendship with its seafood department staff, and don't hesitate to ask how fresh the fish or shellfish are. Even if you have to alter your choice, buy the freshest fish available. And try to stay away from prepacked fresh fish as you cannot smell or touch it before you buy.

Tips for Great Fish Dishes

Some people don't like fish because it tastes and smells "fishy." The rule of thumb when buying fish is:

- If it smells unpleasant, it's not fresh, so don't buy it. Fish should smell of the sea, like salt water and ocean winds.

- Check for freshness by looking at the eyes if the fish is whole. They should be clear, with black centers. Avoid any fish with sunken, cloudy-looking eyes. They will not be at their freshest.

- Gills should be bright red, flesh should be resilient, not at all spongy when you touch it, and the surface should be smooth and slick. Don't buy fish if the skin feels sticky.

- Fish is an ideal weekend dish. Usually your store gets deliveries on Fridays so it will be fresh for the weekend. You can shop and prepare the fish on the same day, which means it will be at its peak. If you cannot use it within 24 hours, wrap it tightly and freeze it in the coldest part of the freezer.

- Frozen fish can be thawed in the refrigerator, or in a pan of cold, preferably running, water. Do not ever thaw at room temperature because the fish are very fragile and there is a great risk of spoilage.

- Because the flavors are more delicate and cooking times are shorter than other forms of protein, seafood preparation calls for special attention. Most fish and shellfish require very short cooking times. It's less than ten minutes per inch of thickness if cooking steaks, but only two to three minutes or less per side if cooking small fillets. Shellfish cook in minutes. Shrimp need only three to four minutes to be cooked through, so add them at the end of the cooking time.

- Because fish cooks quickly, be adventurous in how you flavor it. Or even be adventurous in choosing fish—weekends are great for trying new things—especially at the table.

Blackened Tuna with Softened Polenta and Garlic Beans

✓ *SOMETHING SPECIAL*

The simple marinade of honey and lemon juice is essential to the process of blackening this tuna. The sugar in the marinade along with the added pepper caramelizes quickly in the very hot pan, creating a blackened crust. Remember that for best flavor serve the tuna rare in the middle; you should only cook it about two minutes per side.

TUNA

¼ cup clove honey

¼ cup fresh lemon juice
(from 2 medium lemons)

2 tablespoons olive oil

¼ teaspoon salt

⅛ teaspoon freshly ground pepper

Six 6-ounce tuna fillets

POLENTA

4 cups (1 quart) whole milk

2 cups water

1 teaspoon salt

4 tablespoons butter

1½ cups quick-cooking polenta

Salt and freshly ground pepper,
to taste

Garlic Beans (next page)

1. In a glass dish, combine the honey, lemon juice, olive oil, salt, and pepper. Add the tuna fillets, turning to coat in the marinade. Refrigerate, covered, for about 30 minutes.

2. In a medium saucepan, combine the milk, water, salt, and butter and bring to a simmer. Pour the polenta in a slow, steady stream into the simmering liquid, whisking continuously so lumps do not form. Reduce the heat to low, cover, and continue to cook, stirring frequently, about 15 minutes, until the mixture is very thick and begins to pull away from the sides of the pan when you stir it. Season to taste with salt and pepper. Set aside. ✱

3. Heat a dry, nonstick skillet over medium-high heat until a drop or two of water flicked onto the surface skitters around before breaking to become steam. Add the tuna and cook until blackened on each side, turning once, 2 to 3 minutes per side. Tuna should be rare inside. Remove the tuna from the skillet and reserve, tented with foil to keep warm.

4. Make the garlic beans and reserve.

5. To serve, place a spoonful of polenta in the middle of each plate and top with a spoonful of beans. Place the tuna on the beans and serve hot.

✱TIP: To prevent a skin from forming over the **polenta,** cover the saucepan with plastic wrap, pressing it directly onto the polenta while you wait to serve it.

(continues)

Garlic Beans

This very easy side dish is also quite good with roast lamb or grilled chicken. Keep several cans of white beans on hand in the pantry for last minute additions to weekend and weeknight menus.

4 tablespoons butter

2 teaspoons finely chopped fresh garlic (from 2 medium cloves)

Two 14-ounce cans white beans (cannellini, great Northern, or navy), drained and rinsed

½ teaspoon salt

1 teaspoon lemon juice

Melt the butter in a medium skillet over medium heat. Add the garlic and cook until fragrant. Stir in the beans, toss until well coated and warmed through. Season with the salt and lemon juice. Serve warm.

Grilled Lemon Salmon with Vegetable Crisps

✓ *SOMETHING SPECIAL*

This light fish dish can be made with just about any type of fish you like. You can cook the fish outside on the grill, on a grill pan in the kitchen, or in the broiler.

¼ cup fresh lemon juice
(from 2 medium lemons)

¼ cup olive oil

2 teaspoons finely chopped fresh
garlic (from 2 medium cloves)

1 teaspoon fresh thyme

¼ teaspoon salt

Six 6-ounce center-cut salmon fillets

Vegetable Crisps (next page)

Lemon wedges from 1 fresh lemon

1. Combine the lemon juice, olive oil, garlic, thyme, and salt in a glass baking dish. Add the salmon, turning the fillets to coat with the marinade. Marinate in the refrigerator for 30 minutes. ✶

2. Make the vegetable crisps and drain well.

3. Preheat the grill to medium-high heat for at least 5 minutes. Clean and season grill.

4. Remove the fish from the marinade and pat dry with paper towels. Lightly oil the meaty side of the fish and place on the preheated grill, skin side up. Grill until just barely cooked through, 3 minutes per side, turning once. The salmon should still be very pink at the center.

5. Serve the grilled fish garnished with the vegetable crisps and lemon wedges.

✶TIP: Always **marinate fish** in the refrigerator for 4 hours or less. Leaving it in an acidic marinade too long can actually cook the fish and make it soft and flabby.

(continues)

Vegetable Crisps

Rice flour helps make a very light and crisp crust on the vegetables. It is available in the Asian section of many supermarkets. If it isn't available, cornstarch or potato starch can be substituted. I also like to serve these crisps as a nosh with drinks before dinner.

1 medium zucchini

1 small eggplant

1 fennel bulb, fronds and stems removed

3 cups vegetable oil (1½ pints)

4 egg whites, lightly beaten

2 cups rice flour

Salt and freshly ground pepper, to taste

1. Using a vegetable peeler, slice the zucchini and eggplant lengthwise into thin flat ribbons the length of the vegetable. With a very sharp knife, thinly slice the fennel bulb.

2. Heat the oil to 350°F in a deep, straight-sided, 3-quart pan, checking the temperature with a deep-fry thermometer or by adding one of the vegetable pieces to see if it sizzles.

3. Put the beaten egg white and rice flour into separate shallow bowls or cake tins.

4. Place the vegetable ribbons, one vegetable at a time, in a medium bowl, toss each vegetable with the egg whites, then coat them with the flour. Shake all excess flour off the vegetables and fry them in batches in the hot oil until crisp and golden brown. Place on paper towels and blot lightly to remove the excess oil. Season with salt and pepper. Repeat with the remaining vegetables.

Seared Halibut with Potatoes and Curry Broth

MAKES 8 SERVINGS

This is one of my favorite fish recipes. It combines the crunchiness of the seared fish with the soft texture of the potatoes and broth. Delicious!

Potatoes (next page)

BROTH

6 cups low-salt chicken broth
(from 2 quarts)

1 tablespoon curry powder,
hot or mild, to taste

2 tablespoons butter (optional)

FISH

1 cup whole milk

1 large egg, beaten

1 cup all-purpose flour

1 tablespoon curry powder,
hot or mild, to taste

Salt and pepper, to taste

2 cups panko bread crumbs,
or plain Italian bread crumbs

1½ pounds halibut fillets—
in 8 pieces

¼ cup peanut oil, for frying

1 cup pea sprouts or watercress
(about 1½ ounces), for garnish ∗

1. Make the potatoes.

2. For the broth: Add the chicken broth to a large saucepan. Heat over high heat and reduce to 3 cups to intensify the flavor. Whisk in the curry powder and warm gently. You can add 2 tablespoons of butter to the broth just before serving to make the broth richer, if you desire.

3. For the fish: In a small bowl, beat together the milk and egg, and set aside. On a plate, combine the flour and the curry powder. Season the mixture with salt and pepper. Spread the bread crumbs on a separate plate. Season the fish with salt and pepper. Dip each piece into the seasoned flour, then into the egg mixture, and finally into the bread crumbs. Repeat this with all of the fillets. Set aside on waxed paper to dry slightly.

4. Heat the peanut oil in a large skillet over medium-high heat. Cook the fish, in batches, until golden brown on each side and still slightly translucent in the middle, 3 to 4 minutes altogether. Set the fish on paper towels to blot off the excess oil.

5. To assemble the dish: Serve in shallow bowls with large rims. Place 1 cup of the potatoes in the center of the bowl. Top the potatoes with the sprouts and then with a fillet. Finish with a ladle full of the broth. Serve immediately.

∗TIP: Try using **radish sprouts, bean sprouts,** or even **arugula** as the greens in this dish. Each will give the fish a little extra crunch and color.

(continues)

Roasted Potatoes

Roasting the potatoes before peeling them and pushing them through a ricer gives them a richer, more concentrated flavor than boiling does.

3 pounds Yukon gold potatoes

2 tablespoons olive oil

1/2 cup whole milk

3 tablespoons butter

1 teaspoon salt

1 teaspoon freshly ground pepper

1. Preheat the oven to 400°F. Rub the potatoes with olive oil and place in a roasting pan.

2. Bake the potatoes for 1 hour or until they are soft. Cool slightly and peel.

3. Push the potatoes through the small screen of a potato ricer into a large bowl. Beat in the milk and the butter. Season with salt and pepper. Keep warm in a large saucepan until ready to serve. *

★TIP: Using a **potato ricer** is the quickest and easiest way to make lump-free mashed potatoes or other root vegetables. Press them when the vegetables are still hot and then just use a wooden spoon to beat in any additional liquid or seasonings you wish.

Braised Salmon with Caramelized Fennel and Wasabi Mashed Potatoes

MAKES 6 SERVINGS

✓ *SOMETHING SPECIAL*   ✓ *EASY PREPARATION*

The flavor pairing of the heat of wasabi with the richness of salmon is inspired by Japanese sushi and translated for the Western palate in this delicious dish. Braising is an excellent, almost foolproof, way to cook fish. The end result is tender and succulent with just a hint of the flavor of the braising liquid—and you can quickly monitor how cooked the fish is. The anise flavor of fennel goes so well with the salmon.

3 tablespoons butter

4 bulbs fennel, root and stem ends cut off, thinly sliced

1/2 cup chicken broth

Salt and freshly ground pepper, to taste

Wasabi Mashed Potatoes (next page)

1 tablespoon olive oil

5 shallots, very thinly sliced

3 sprigs fresh thyme

One 2-pound piece center-cut salmon fillet

1/2 cup dry white wine

*TIP: Fish should be braised, baked, or roasted for no more than 10 minutes for each inch of thickness. This "rule" isn't hard and fast, but it is a great place to start.

1. Preheat the oven to 400°F.

2. Melt the butter in a large heavy skillet. Add the thinly sliced fennel to the skillet along with the chicken broth. Cover and cook over low heat, 5 to 6 minutes, until the fennel is transparent and tender. Remove the cover and continue to cook, stirring from time to time until the fennel is golden brown and the broth is completely evaporated, about 6 minutes more. Season with salt and pepper.

3. Prepare the Wasabi mashed potatoes.

4. Heat the oil in a very small frying pan. Add the shallots and thyme, and cook over low heat until very soft. Spread in an oven-proof glass baking dish. Top with the salmon, skin side down. Season with salt and pepper. Pour the wine around the salmon. Cover tightly and braise in the oven for 8 to 10 minutes. *****

5. To serve: Divide the salmon into 6 servings. Arrange on individual serving plates with a serving of Wasabi and Potato Mash alongside—or set the salmon on a bed of potatoes. Top the salmon with caramelized fennel.

(continues)

Wasabi Mashed Potatoes

✓ *SOMETHING SPECIAL*   ✓ *EASY PREPARATION*

If you love potatoes and a little "heat," you'll enjoy this dish. The wasabi paste adds a kick to these potatoes, but won't overwhelm a sensitive palate.

Six large russet potatoes

6 tablespoons butter

Salt and freshly ground pepper, to taste

1½ cups half and half, heated just until tiny bubbles begin to appear around the edges of the pan

1 tablespoon plus 1 teaspoon Wasabi paste (or powder) ＊

1. Put the potatoes in a large pot, and cover with cold water by 2 inches. Bring to a simmer, cover, and cook them, 20 to 25 minutes, until they are knife tender.

2. Drain the potatoes and while they are hot, peel them and push them through a potato ricer into a large bowl.

3. Dot the riced potatoes with butter and season with salt and pepper.

4. Gently and quickly stir in the hot half and half to make a smooth puree. Beat in the Wasabi paste and finish with a final seasoning of salt and pepper. Serve warm.

＊TIP: Wasabi is a Japanese seasoning that is actually the root of an herb, though it has many of the same hot characteristics as horseradish. In Japan, is it often used fresh, but in the United States it is sold in the International section of many supermarkets, either in a paste or as a dried powder. Either will give you the heat and bite that makes wasabi so popular.

Come Over for Burgers

What could be more **American** than gathering family and friends in the backyard for a delightful hot-off-the-grill hamburger? Grilling and hamburgers just seem to go together. Grilling brings out the flavors of the ingredients and seasonings, and adds a smoky flavor of its own that can't be beat. Grilling isn't just a summertime activity in my house, so we enjoy grilled hamburgers the year 'round, and so can you. (Unless it's raining or snowing over your grill, consider the "summer-in-February" thrill of serving hot burgers on a cold day to perk up a meal.)

The Base

Hamburgers can be plain or fancy, grilled or fried, stuffed or not, but however you create them, hamburgers are perfect weekend family fare. You can adapt your favorite beef burgers in many ways, but burgers can also be made with a great range of ingredients such as ground turkey, chicken, even shrimp, or vegetables.

Try to avoid the leanest ground beef, too, because much of the flavor is in the fat. If you want to limit fat, eat beef burgers only occasionally, but when you do, enjoy them at their best. You can stick to poultry, shrimp, or vegetable burgers the rest of the time.

Seasonings

The beauty of burgers is that everything is mixed together into patties and all the flavors and seasonings are enjoyed in every satisfying bite. Think about your favorite flavors and mix them in: chopped onions, garlic, parsley, chili powder, barbecue spices—whatever you have on hand. When mixing ingredients into the ground beef or poultry, however, be gentle. Mix just enough to combine and ensure moist burgers.

Stuffings and Toppings

Once you have decided how to season the base of your burger, you can decide how to stuff it or top it. Stuff a burger with a cube of cheese, an onion slice, a spoonful of spicy salsa, nearly anything you can think of—make up your own specialty. Put out lots of toppings and watch what people do with them. Sliced cheeses like cheddar, blue cheese, Monterey Jack, and Pepper Jack all add distinctive tastes to burgers. Plain mayo, chipotle mayo, mayo with mustard added, ketchup, flavored mustards of all kinds, raw onion, sautéed onions, fried onions, pickle chips, jalapeño chips, relish—the list of add-ons is nearly endless. With a little imagination, you will never have to settle for a plain burger again, unless of course, that's the way you prefer them.

No matter how you fix them, it's always fun to have a crew come over for a burger off the grill.

Herbed Goat Cheese Stuffed Hamburger Patties

✓ *SOMETHING SPECIAL*

This recipe, with its additions of goat cheese and pesto, will transform a burger from typical to fantastic. Serve it with a warm potato salad and some sourdough rolls for a new family favorite.

1½ pounds ground beef chuck

¾ teaspoon salt

½ teaspoon freshly ground pepper

1 tablespoon Worcestershire sauce

3½ ounces soft goat cheese, such as Montrachet

2 tablespoons refrigerated commercial pesto

1. In a bowl, combine the ground beef, salt, pepper, and Worcestershire sauce. Combine the goat cheese and the pesto in a separate, smaller bowl. Refrigerate both the beef and the goat cheese mixtures for ½ hour.

2. Preheat the grill to medium-high heat for 10 minutes. *

3. To form the patties, portion the ground beef into 6 equal balls. Pick up 1 ball at a time, remove about one-third of the beef, and set aside. Make a dent in the larger piece of beef and fill it with approximately 1 tablespoon of the goat cheese mixture. Cover the goat cheese with the beef that has been set aside, pinching the edges to seal in the cheese. This step is crucial so that the cheese does not ooze out of the patty on the grill.

4. Grill the patties until cooked to desired doneness, about 4 minutes per side for medium.

SERVING SUGGESTION

Serve burgers in crusty sourdough rolls along with your favorite potato salad.

＊TIP: To tell if **the grill is hot enough** to cook the burgers, place your hand 2 to 3 inches over the grate and count: One thousand one, one thousand two, one thousand three, one thousand four. If the heat makes you pull your hand back between four and five, the grill has reached 450°–500°F, and is ready for the burgers. Too hot, cool the grill down because the burgers will burn. Too cold, the burgers will stick and fall apart.

Teriyaki Turkey Burgers

✓ *SOMETHING SPECIAL*

These teriyaki burgers bring fun new flavors to hamburgers on the grill. Pair them with a salad tossed with an Asian dressing made from the soy sauce, rice wine vinegar, and sesame oil.

2 tablespoons soy sauce

2 tablespoons dry sherry

1 tablespoon sesame oil

1 tablespoon minced ginger

½ teaspoon minced garlic

½ teaspoon brown sugar

½ teaspoon salt

½ teaspoon freshly ground pepper

2 pounds ground turkey

6 kaiser rolls

2 tablespoons butter, melted

Grilled yellow onion *, green leaf lettuce leaves, and sliced tomato for garnish

1. Preheat the grill to medium heat for 10 minutes.

2. In a small bowl, combine the soy sauce, dry sherry, sesame oil, ginger, garlic, brown sugar, salt, and pepper. Place the ground turkey in a large bowl. Add the soy sauce mixture to the turkey, mix well, and gently shape into 6 burgers of equal size and thickness (about ¾ inch thick). Season both sides of the burgers with salt and pepper.

3. Grill over direct medium heat until the internal temperature reaches 160°F for medium, about 5 minutes per side. Brush the rolls on the cut side with butter. About 2 minutes before the burgers are done, lay the rolls on the grill, cut side down, and grill until lightly browned, about 2 minutes. Remove the hamburgers and the rolls from the grill. Serve with the grilled onion, lettuce, and tomato.

★ TIP: To grill onion slices so they don't fall apart on the grill, cut the onion into thick slices and then skewer each slice together horizontally, so they will hold together and sit flat on the grill. Use two skewers at right angles for each slice. Brush the slices with olive oil and grill over direct medium heat until the onion begins to soften, turning once.

Meatloaf Burgers with Italian Tomato Jam

✓ *EASY PREPARATION*

Making a good meatloaf recipe can be time consuming, but these burgers take much less time and still have the satisfying meatloaf taste. Leftover burgers can be used in sandwiches. Serve with mashed potatoes or grilled whole potatoes (which develop a crisp, delicious skin), a green salad, and some steamed green beans.

2 tablespoons unsalted butter

2/3 cup finely diced onion (from about 1/2 large onion)

1/2 cup finely chopped green bell pepper (from about 1/2 medium pepper)

1 teaspoon salt

1/2 teaspoon cayenne pepper

1/2 teaspoon dried thyme, crumbled

1/2 teaspoon freshly ground pepper

1/4 teaspoon ground cumin

1 pound lean ground beef

1 egg, lightly beaten with a fork

1/2 cup fine dry bread crumbs

1/4 cup ketchup

1 teaspoon Worcestershire sauce

6 kaiser rolls

Butter for rolls

Sliced onion, lettuce, and tomato, for serving

Italian Tomato Jam (next page)

1. Preheat the grill to medium heat for 10 minutes.

2. Melt the butter in a heavy medium-sized skillet over medium-low heat. Add the onion, bell pepper, salt, cayenne, thyme, pepper, and cumin and cook until vegetables are tender, stirring frequently, about 10 minutes. Cool.

3. In a medium bowl, combine the meat, egg, bread crumbs, 1/4 cup ketchup, and Worcestershire sauce. Stir in the cooled vegetables, mixing until well combined. Form the mixture into 6 equal patties.

4. Grill the burgers over direct medium heat until the internal temperature reaches 160°F for medium, 4 to 5 minutes per side, depending on the thickness of the burger. Brush the rolls on the cut side with butter. About 2 minutes before the burgers are done, lay the rolls on the grill, cut side down, and grill until lightly browned, about 2 minutes. Remove the hamburgers and the rolls from the grill. Serve with onion, lettuce, and Italian Tomato Jam. *

∗ TIP: Use an instant-read thermometer to tell if a hamburger is done. Place the thermometer in the burger at an angle in the thickest part of the meat. The instant-read thermometers will register within 30 seconds or so. Make sure that the thermometer is not close to the bottom of the burger or it will read hotter than it is because of the heat of the grill underneath it.

Italian Tomato Jam

This jam makes a great savory spread for a burger or any sandwich—vegetarian, meat-filled, or otherwise, especially sandwiches with spicy or tart flavorings, which are balanced by the rich, mildly sweet jam. It comes together quickly and will keep in the refrigerator for up to two weeks.

1 tablespoon olive oil

½ cup finely chopped yellow onion (from about ½ small onion)

Salt, to taste

1 tablespoon finely chopped fresh garlic (from 3 medium cloves)

One 28-ounce can chopped Italian plum tomatoes

½ cup red wine vinegar

1 teaspoon honey

⅛ teaspoon freshly ground nutmeg

¼ teaspoon ground cinnamon

¼ cup firmly packed dark brown sugar

1. Heat the olive oil in a medium frying pan over medium-low heat. Add the onion and a pinch of salt. Cook until translucent, about 5 minutes. Add the garlic and cook just until fragrant, about 1 minute, being careful not to burn the garlic. Add the tomatoes and stir to combine.

2. Add the vinegar, honey, nutmeg, cinnamon, and brown sugar. Simmer over low heat, stirring occasionally, until the liquid has evaporated and the tomato mixture has thickened, about 1½ hours. Cool completely and serve.

Shrimp and Chicken Burgers with Creamy Chile Sauce

✓ *SOMETHING SPECIAL*

Grill or pan-broil these burgers for a lighter take on the classic hamburger. They're great as a no-red-meat choice for cholesterol watchers or for anyone who likes to try something a little different.

1 pound medium (31–35 per pound) shrimp, peeled and deveined

1 pound ground chicken

½ cup panko bread crumbs, or plain dried bread crumbs

¼ cup finely chopped green onion (from about 4 to 5 thin onions, or 1 bunch)

3 tablespoons chopped Italian flat-leaf parsley

Salt and freshly ground pepper, to taste

Creamy Chile Sauce (next page)

Hamburger or other rolls

1 head leaf lettuce, washed and dried, for garnish

1. Place the shrimp in the bowl of a food processor. Pulse in 10-second intervals, just until the shrimp are coarsely chopped. Do not overprocess or puree.

2. In a large bowl, combine the chopped shrimp, ground chicken, panko bread crumbs, green onion, and parsley and season well with salt and pepper.

3. Form the mixture into 6 patties. ✱

4. Make the creamy chile sauce.

5. Preheat the grill or grill pan over medium-high heat for 5 to 10 minutes. Grill the patties until no longer pink in the middle, turning once, 2 to 3 minutes per side.

6. To serve, set the patties on toasted buns garnished with fresh lettuce and topped with a dollop of creamy chile sauce. Tomato slices are also a nice addition.

VARIATION

Make bite-size burgers from tablespoons of the mixture and grill (on a vegetable or fish screen to prevent them from falling between the grates) or pan-fry for 3 to 4 minutes, turning once. Skewer with toothpicks and pass with the Creamy Chile Sauce for dunking as a wonderful snack with drinks.

✱ **TIP:** Lightly oil the palms of your hands to prevent the meat from sticking to them. Form patties that are slightly thinner in the middle and fatter around the edges as these burgers tend to draw in a little while cooking. This donutlike shape will permit the center to cook through without drying out the edges and make a uniform thickness when cooked.

Creamy Chile Sauce

✓ *SOMETHING SPECIAL*

Rouille is a peppery hot mayonnaise-like sauce that is traditionally spread on toast rounds and served with bouillabaisse—that delightful French fish stew. It is a shame to confine it to fish stew when it is wonderful as a garnish for cold meats, steamed or braised fish, and poultry, or anywhere a flavored mayonnaise might be appropriate. While this Creamy Chile Sauce isn't a classic rouille at all, it is incredibly simple to make and tastes as delicious as the original.

2 cloves garlic

½ cup mayonnaise

1 tablespoon harissa paste—or more, to taste (add as much as you like to make it as hot as you like) *

1. Peel, crush, and mash the garlic cloves into a creamy paste with the flat side of a heavy knife.

2. In a small bowl, beat together the mayonnaise, garlic paste, and harissa paste. Refrigerate 15 minutes or longer to give the flavors a chance to develop. Add more harissa if the sauce is too mild to suit your taste.

★ TIP: Harissa paste, made from hot red chiles and very popular in North African cooking, is available in tubes in the International section of many supermarkets and in specialty food stores. If you cannot find harissa, the new commercial chipotle mayonnaise mix can be used as an instant substitute for the mayonnaise and harissa combination.

Grilled Portobello Mushroom Burgers with Gruyère Cheese and Thyme Onions

✓ *SOMETHING SPECIAL*   ✓ *EASY PREPARATION*

It is hard to believe that these satisfying, meaty burgers are in reality grilled mushroom caps. They are so substantial that they often stand in well for meat in vegetarian dishes, and they are delicious and filling enough for the heartiest appetite.

6 tablespoons olive oil

6 cups thinly sliced Vidalia or other extra-sweet onions (from 3 large onions)

1/2 tablespoon fresh thyme leaves

Salt and freshly ground pepper, to taste

2 cloves garlic, peeled, crushed, and mashed into a paste with the flat side of a heavy knife

6 large portobello mushrooms, stemmed *

6 slices Gruyère cheese

6 hamburger rolls, toasted

Sliced fresh tomatoes, for garnish

Leaf lettuce, washed and dried, for garnish

1/2 cup mayonnaise, for garnish

1. Heat 3 tablespoons of the oil in a large, heavy skillet. Add the onions and fresh thyme. Season well with salt and pepper. Cook over low heat, stirring from time to time, until the onions are soft and very well browned. This will take 20 to 25 minutes. *

2. Preheat the grill to high heat for 10 minutes.

3. Combine the remaining 3 tablespoons of the oil and the garlic. Rub the mushroom caps all over with the oil and season well with salt and pepper. Grill over medium-high heat, cup side up, until well browned, 4 to 6 minutes. Turn the mushrooms over. Top each with a slice of cheese. Close the grill and cook 1 minute more, until the cheese is melted.

4. Serve the mushroom burgers on toasted rolls with onions on top. Serve with sliced ripe tomatoes, lettuce, and mayonnaise on the side. For added flavor, try the Creamy Chile Sauce (page 101) with these mushroom burgers instead of plain mayonnaise.

＊TIP: **Portobellos** should be cleaned by wiping with a moist cloth or brushing with a soft brush, just to remove any soil. Do not rinse or soak in water as they act like sponges, absorbing the water and then releasing it into the dish when they are cooked. If you wish, you may remove the "beard" or the gills of portobellos by scraping them out with the tip of a teaspoon. The gills will leach a dark color into finished dishes. The taste is delicious, but the color can be off-putting.

＊TIP: If your family or guests love **soft-cooked onions**, increase the number of onions you use because they diminish considerably in quantity as they cook. This part of the recipe is very easily doubled or even tripled. (Expect the cooking time to be longer.)

Veggie Burger Extraordinaire

✓ SOMETHING SPECIAL

These meatless burgers take a bit of time, but they will be good enough to please even confirmed carnivores. Just be sure to use a fine vegetable or fish grilling grid, and be careful that they do not fall apart when turning them on the grill.

½ cup cracked wheat or bulgur

1¼ cups salted water

2 tablespoons olive oil

2 teaspoons finely chopped garlic (from 2 medium cloves)

½ cup shredded carrot (from 1 medium carrot)

¼ cup seeded and finely chopped green bell pepper (from ½ small pepper)

½ cup finely chopped onion (from ½ small onion)

½ cup finely chopped celery (from about 1 large rib)

½ cup plain bread crumbs, or panko bread crumbs

½ cup chopped toasted pecans or walnuts (from 2 ounces)

¼ cup chopped parsley

1 teaspoon cumin

1 large egg, lightly beaten with a fork

Salt and freshly ground pepper, to taste

6 to 8 whole grain burger buns

Sliced fresh tomatoes, for garnish

Leaf lettuce, washed and dried, for garnish

½ cup mayonnaise (optional)

1. Combine the cracked wheat and salted water in a small saucepan. Bring to a boil, reduce the heat, and simmer until very tender, 10 to 15 minutes. Drain well.

2. Heat the oil to medium-high heat in an 8-inch skillet. Combine the garlic, carrot, bell pepper, onion, and celery. Cook, stirring, just until the vegetables are beginning to soften, 2 to 3 minutes. Cool slightly.

3. In a large bowl, combine the wheat, vegetables, bread crumbs, nuts, parsley, and cumin. Stir in the egg until well mixed. Season well with salt and pepper. Form the mixture into 6 to 8 patties. Refrigerate 30 minutes.

4. Preheat the fine grid on the grill or grill pan on medium-high heat for 5 to 10 minutes. Grill the burgers until well browned outside, turning very carefully once, 2 to 3 minutes per side.

5. Serve the burgers on toasted buns and garnish with fresh tomatoes and lettuce. Pass mayonnaise on the side.

Backyard Barbecue—
Beyond Burgers

Barbecuing means fresh air, family and friends gathered, flavorful food—good summer fun. Techniques and grills have come a long way since we learned to grill by watching our fathers in the backyard blowing on the Kingsford® coals. Many people prefer the flavors and adventure of charcoal grilling, but gas grills have made grilling easier and have broadened the realm of what can be cooked outdoors. Now, a grill can be used like an outdoor stovetop, with some considerations.

I like a barbecued hamburger just as much as the next person—just check out the recipes in the Come Over for Burgers chapter. But to stop there is like just learning how to play "chopsticks" on the piano. This chapter will help you refine your techniques and expand your outdoor cooking repertoire. So use the recipes in this chapter to try preparing some foods you've never grilled before.

Tips for Great Grilling:

- Light the grill well before you need to start cooking so the temperature will be high enough to sear or caramelize the outside of whatever you are grilling right away. Don't try to heat up the grill and cook at the same time or you will have overdone interiors before the outside turns grill golden.

- Use indirect and direct heat as needed; this helps you control the way your food cooks. To begin with direct cooking, set up the heat so the charcoal is banked to one side of the grill, or the burners are set to medium-high on one side and off or low on the other. You can begin by browning the food directly over the heat. Then switch to indirect cooking by moving it to the cool spot to cook it through more slowly. That way you will end up with the ideal combination of a crisp exterior with a succulent, evenly cooked center.

- To ensure even cooking on the grill, allow meats such as chicken, pork, lamb, or beef to come to room temperature before grilling. It will only take about 20 to 30 minutes out of the refrigerator. Fish and shellfish should be cooked cold.

- Always oil the food and not the grates. This will help you control flare-ups.

- Grill with the hood closed so the air circulates inside the grill and the heat is contained and constant, not lost in the surrounding air.

There are all kinds of benefits to grilling. It is a simple, fun way of cooking that helps us produce our own wholesome food—a comfort in a world that entices us with fast, frozen, preservative-laden, and high-fat food as modern conveniences. By grilling, we are able to produce high-quality and fresh-tasting dishes without adding extra fat. But the bottom line is that grilling can be a way for us to enjoy foods in backyards, on patios, terraces, and in parks, or at the dinner table.

Maryland Crab Cakes with Chipotle Aioli Sauce (page 34)
and Parmigiano-Reggiano Frico with Baby Greens (page 28)

**Grilled Portobello Mushroom Burgers
with Gruyère Cheese and Thyme Onions (page 102)**

Grilled Cajun Shrimp and Grilled Corn with Cumin Butter (page 110)

Braised Short Ribs with Chipotle-Tomato Sauce (page 115)

Sage and Shrimp White Bean Chili (page 138)

Mahogany Chicken Wings with Crumbled Blue Cheese Sauce (page 149)

Chinese Chicken Pasta Salad (page 159)

Center: Chocolate Ice Cream Roll Cake (page 210);
Inset: Rolling the cake

Grilled Chicken, Vegetable, and Aioli Platter

✓ *EASY PREPARATION*   ✓ *SOMETHING SPECIAL*

On hot summer days when it is too warm to cook inside, use your grill to make the entire dinner. This wonderful mix of colorful fresh vegetables and chicken creates a beautiful platter of foods that will please everyone. Prep the vegetables in the morning if you like and refrigerate them until you are ready to cook. These vegetables are as good at room temperature as they are cold, so grill them before you take the chicken out of the refrigerator.

✱TIP: If the **chicken begins to brown too quickly,** move it to the warming rack or a cool part of the grill, and cook with the hood closed until the chicken registers 165°F with an instant-read thermometer.

VEGETABLES

2 large red bell peppers

2 large yellow bell peppers

1 pound asparagus, trimmed

2 small fennel bulbs, ends trimmed, and sliced

1/2 cup olive oil

10 medium-sized red potatoes, steamed until tender

GRILLED CHICKEN

4 medium boneless chicken breasts with skin on (or, if the breasts are more than 10 ounces each, use only 2 and slice them in half horizontally)

1/4 cup olive oil

1/4 cup chopped fresh tarragon

1/4 cup chopped fresh thyme

1/4 cup chopped fresh rosemary

1 tablespoon salt

1 1/2 teaspoons crushed red pepper

SERVING

Herbed Aioli (next page)

6 cups arugula, rinsed and torn into bite-sized pieces (about 9 ounces)

3/4 pound fresh green beans, trimmed and steamed until just tender

1/2 cup Kalamata olives

1 pound assorted firm cheeses

6 hard-boiled eggs, quartered lengthwise

1. Make the herbed aioli.

2. Clean the grill with a wire brush. Preheat the grill to high heat for 5 to 10 minutes. Brush the peppers, asparagus, and fennel with olive oil. Grill these vegetables until tender. Add the potatoes and finish them on the grill with the other vegetables. When the peppers are cooked, peel them, seed, devein, and slice into thick pieces. Set the vegetables aside.

3. Make sure the grill is between 500° and 600°F.

4. Rinse the chicken with cold water and dry it well with paper towels. Brush the chicken with the olive oil. In a small bowl, combine the tarragon, thyme, rosemary, salt, and red pepper flakes.

5. Rub some of the herb mixture into each breast. Place on the grill, skin side down. Close the hood and grill until the skin is golden brown, then turn. Grill the chicken about 7 minutes per side. When finished, place the chicken on a platter and tent with aluminum foil. ✱

(continues)

6. To serve, line a large platter with the arugula. Arrange the platter with the chicken, grilled vegetables, green beans, olives, cheeses, quartered eggs, and the arugula. Serve with the herbed aioli or drizzle with a bit of fruity extra-virgin olive oil.

Herbed Aioli

MAKES ABOUT 1½ CUPS

This aioli is good on an assortment of grilled food like hamburgers, salmon, or even as a dipping sauce for shrimp. Its universal appeal complements the variety of food on the grilled chicken and vegetable platter. It will keep up to three days in the refrigerator.

2 tablespoons white wine vinegar

2 tablespoons sherry vinegar

¼ cup refrigerated egg product

2 tablespoons capers, drained and rinsed

2 shallot cloves, quartered

1 tablespoon chopped fresh garlic (from 3 medium cloves)

½ teaspoon salt

¼ teaspoon freshly ground pepper

1 cup extra-virgin olive oil

1 tablespoon chopped fresh chives

1 tablespoon chopped fresh tarragon

1 tablespoon chopped fresh Italian parsley

1 tablespoon chopped fresh thyme

In a food processor or blender, combine the white wine vinegar, sherry vinegar, egg product, capers, shallot, garlic, salt, and pepper. Cover and process until smooth. With the machine running, add the olive oil in a slow stream until thick and creamy, stopping to scrape the sides of the bowl if necessary. Stir in the herbs and thin with a few drops of vinegar if it is too thick. *

★ TIP: Add the oil drop by drop to the mixture to start, until the aioli begins to thicken like mayonnaise, then in a thin stream, slowly, so that the aioli won't break. It is easy to tell when a mayonnaise-like sauce breaks. It will go from thick to very liquid, and the oil will separate from the other ingredients so that the mixture looks almost like curdled milk. It is very difficult to reincorporate the oil once it breaks. It will taste fine, but look unappealing.

Brined Herb Pork Chops with Grilled Polenta

MAKES 6 SERVINGS

✓ *EASY PREPARATION*   ✓ *SOMETHING SPECIAL*

Brining actually raises the moisture content in the meat. The result is a wonderful, tender, juicy cut. The salty flavor of the chops goes very well with the hot polenta, which is crisp on the outside and mildly creamy inside. The polenta soaks up any juices from the chops so you don't lose a drop of flavor.

4 tablespoons kosher salt (¼ cup)

3 tablespoons sugar

1 cup hot water

2 cups cold water

2 tablespoons olive oil, plus up to ¼ cup more for brushing the pork chops

2 tablespoons white wine vinegar

2 teaspoons chopped fresh thyme

1 teaspoon freshly ground pepper

6 bone-in loin pork chops, at least ¾ to 1 inch thick

Grilled Polenta Rounds (next page)

1. To prepare the brine, combine the salt and sugar in a medium bowl. Pour the hot water into the bowl and whisk to dissolve the salt and sugar. Add the cold water along with the 2 tablespoons olive oil, the vinegar, thyme, and pepper. ∗

2. Place the pork chops in a large, resealable plastic bag and pour in the brine. Press the air out of the bag and seal tightly. Turn the bag to distribute the brine, place the bag in a bowl, and refrigerate for 4 hours.

3. Remove the pork chops from the bag and pat dry with paper towels. Discard the brine. Lightly brush both sides of the chops with oil. Set the chops aside at room temperature for about 20 minutes before grilling.

4. Preheat the grill for 5 to 10 minutes to indirect high heat, about 500° to 600°F.

5. Make grilled polenta rounds.

6. Brown both sides of the pork chops over the hot side of the grill and then move to the cooler side to cook through. Cook with the hood down, about 6 minutes, until the pork chops are at 160°F when tested with an instant-read thermometer. Serve with the grilled polenta rounds.

(continues)

Grilled Polenta Rounds

✓ *EASY PREPARATION*

Polenta is a wonderful side dish because it is so versatile. Polenta is ground dried cornmeal, not much different from grits, and makes a creamy cereal when cooked in liquid. You can easily stir in cheese or minced garlic for a slightly different flavor. Once cooked, it can be spread in a flat pan, chilled, and cut into shapes like wedges, squares, diamonds, or rounds. These rounds are delicious when fried in butter or olive oil, or grilled. The deliciously mild corn flavor goes with almost any meat or shellfish, and can serve as a base for creamed mushrooms, chicken, or any other saucy dish. It can be made ahead and grilled when the rest of the food is almost ready.

✱ TIP: Use a vegetable or fish grid to grill the polenta, to make sure it does not break up and fall into the coals.

3 cups water

1 teaspoon salt

2 tablespoons butter

¾ cup fine ground polenta, or fine ground yellow cornmeal

¼ teaspoon cayenne pepper

1 tablespoon olive oil

1. In a medium saucepan, combine the water, salt, and butter and bring to a boil. Gradually pour in the polenta, whisking constantly so the mixture doesn't develop lumps. Lower the heat and continue to cook, stirring frequently, until the mixture is very thick and begins to pull away from the side of the pan, about 15 minutes. Remove from the heat and beat in the cayenne.

2. Line a 9-inch pie plate with a sheet of plastic wrap, large enough for the edges to extend beyond the rim of the plate. Spread the polenta evenly over the plastic wrap and chill until firm, at least 1 hour, or as long as overnight.

3. Preheat the grill for 5 to 10 minutes to medium-high heat. Invert the pie plate to unmold the polenta onto a board or cookie sheet. Peel off the plastic wrap and cut the polenta into 6 wedges. Brush with the oil and grill over direct heat, turning once, for 10 minutes, until hot through and nicely browned and crisp on the outside. ✱

Grilled Rib-Eye Steaks with Lemon Arugula Salad

✓ *SOMETHING SPECIAL*   ✓ *EASY PREPARATION*

Rib-eyes are an excellent steak choice for grilling. They are a very tender and flavorful cut—actually from the same cut as standing rib roast—and generously marbled with fat. As an accompaniment to the richness of these steaks, I like to serve a salad of arugula, one of my favorite greens. When very fresh, arugula is delightfully crisp with a sharp peppery flavor. I just toss it with lemon juice, olive oil, salt, and pepper to have a great base for grilled meats.

6 rib-eye steaks, about 8 ounces each

1 tablespoon olive oil

Salt and freshly ground pepper, to taste

4 cups arugula, washed and well dried (about 6 ounces)

2 tablespoons extra-virgin olive oil

2 tablespoons fresh lemon juice (from 1 medium lemon)

1. Very lightly brush the steaks with the olive oil, and season them with salt and pepper to taste. Preheat the grill to medium-high heat for 5 to 10 minutes. Grill the steaks to medium-rare, 8 to 10 minutes, turning once halfway through grilling time. Remove from the grill and allow the steak to rest for about 5 minutes before serving.

2. Place the arugula in a medium bowl. Toss with the extra-virgin olive oil and lemon juice. Season with salt and pepper. Arrange the greens on a platter. Lay the steaks on the greens and serve.

SERVING SUGGESTION

Slice the steaks on an angle before arranging on the greens, and garnish with sprigs of fresh parsley.

Grilled Cajun Shrimp and Grilled Corn with Cumin Butter

✓ *SOMETHING SPECIAL*   ✓ *EASY PREPARATION*

I like to grill the shrimp in the shell and then serve it over a bed of couscous with the corn. The pasta-like taste of couscous helps to offset the spices that season the shrimp. Roasting the fresh corn deepens its flavor and the cumin butter adds a delicious balance to the sweetness.

¼ cup olive oil

2 teaspoons chopped garlic (from 2 medium cloves)

1 tablespoon fresh lemon juice (from 1 lemon)

2 teaspoons paprika

¼ teaspoon cayenne pepper

¼ teaspoon ground cumin

¼ teaspoon dried thyme

2 pounds extra-large (16–20 per pound) shrimp, in the shell

Grilled Corn with Cumin Butter (next page)

1. Heat the olive oil in a small skillet over medium-low heat. Add the garlic and cook, stirring occasionally, until soft, 2 to 3 minutes. Remove from the heat and add all the remaining ingredients except the shrimp and the Grilled Corn with Cumin Butter. Stir and cool at room temperature.

2. Using a sharp knife, split open the back of each shrimp and remove the black vein. Place the shrimp in a large resealable plastic bag and pour in the marinade. Place the bag in the refrigerator and marinate for 20 minutes. ∗

3. Preheat the grill or grill pan to high heat for 5 minutes. Make the grilled corn with cumin butter.

4. Remove the shrimp from the bag and discard the marinade. Grill until the shrimp are pink or orange, and are firm to the touch, 2 to 4 minutes, turning once halfway through grilling time. Remove from the grill and serve warm or at room temperature with the grilled corn and cumin butter, or couscous, if desired.

∗**TIP:** If you are in a hurry, **use easy-peel shrimp,** which are often available in the supermarket. The shells have already been slit and the vein has been removed. I rinse them lightly, drain well, and then add them to the marinade.

Grilled Corn with Cumin Butter

✓ *EASY PREPARATION*

Don't worry if the husks get charred and burned. The kernels will steam and be moist and tender when they're done.

6 ears of corn, in the husk *

3 tablespoons butter, at room temperature

1 teaspoon ground cumin

1 teaspoon chili powder, or more to taste

Salt and freshly ground pepper, to taste

1. Heat the grill to medium heat for 5 to 10 minutes. Carefully peel back the corn husk, but do not detach it. Remove all of the corn silk.

2. In a small bowl, combine the butter, cumin, and chili powder to make a smooth paste. Rub each ear of corn with the flavored butter and sprinkle with salt and pepper. Pull the husk back, and tie it with kitchen twine.

3. Arrange the corn on the grill. Cook, turning frequently, until the husks are well browned, about 15 minutes. Cut off the strings, remove the husks, and serve.

✱ TIP: Soak the corn to rehydrate it if you know or expect that it is several days old. Use a mixture of sugar and water, about $1/4$ cup sugar to 1 gallon water, and soak for 1 hour. Rehydrating it replaces a little of the sugars that have turned to starch. Towel dry, rub with butter, tie with twine, and grill.

Grilled London Broil with Hot Grilled Potato Salad

MAKES 8 SERVINGS

London broil is a lean piece of meat that works well on the grill. Start out over high heat to caramelize the outside, then move it to a cooler part of the grill to cook to desired doneness. It can be served on a tossed salad, used for grilled fajitas, or served with this wonderful grilled potato salad.

5 large garlic cloves, peeled

1 teaspoon salt

¼ cup dry red wine

¼ cup red wine vinegar

1 tablespoon fresh rosemary leaves

1 teaspoon honey

1½ pounds top-round London broil in one piece, about 1¼ inches thick

2 medium vine-ripened tomatoes, sliced (about 3 cups)

Hot Potato Salad (next page)

1. Mince the garlic and use the side of a large heavy knife to mash it to a paste with the salt. Add the creamy paste to a blender jar along with the red wine, vinegar, rosemary, and honey. Blend until smooth. Put the London broil in a heavy-duty resealable plastic bag, and pour in the marinade. Seal the bag, pressing out any excess air, and put in a shallow baking dish. Marinate the steak in the refrigerator, turning occasionally, for at least 4 hours and up to 24 hours.

2. Make hot potato salad.

3. Bring the steak to room temperature (this should take about 1 hour) before grilling. Preheat the grill to high indirect heat for 5 to 10 minutes. Remove the steak from the marinade, letting excess drip off. Lay the steak on the hot side of the grill and brown on both sides, 1 to 2 minutes per side. Move the steak to the cool side and cook for about 10 minutes. Transfer the steak to a cutting board and let stand 10 minutes.

4. Holding a knife at a 45-degree angle, cut the steak across the grain into thin slices. Serve with the sliced tomatoes and the hot potato salad.

Hot Potato Salad

✓ *EASY PREPARATION*

This is a quick and easy way to make potatoes on the grill. The smoky flavor of the grilled potatoes gives this warm salad a scrumptious flavor that you just don't get when they are boiled. The mustard mixture cooks right into the potatoes, making them rich and delicious. Use any type of mustard that you like.

1 cup mayonnaise

¼ cup Dijon mustard

2 teaspoons salt

1 teaspoon freshly ground pepper

3 pounds russet potatoes, well washed, unpeeled, and sliced lengthwise for long thick planks

1. Preheat the grill to high heat for 5 to 10 minutes.

2. In a large bowl, combine the mayonnaise, mustard, salt, and pepper. Add the potato slices and mix well.

3. Lay the coated slices directly on the grill. Close the hood. Grill until golden brown on each side, turning once, about 6 minutes altogether. ✳

✳ **TIP:** Make sure to **grill the potatoes with the hood closed.** The fat in the mayonnaise on the potatoes will flare up if cooked uncovered.

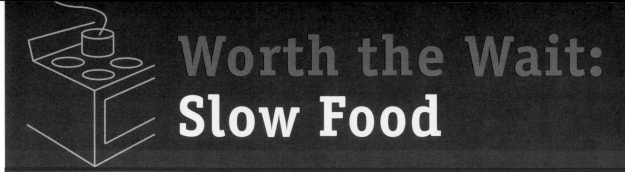

Worth the Wait:
Slow Food

We just don't cook things the way our grandmothers used to cook. We often look at cooking as a means to an end—a way of sprinting to the finish of a short race toward something else. But preparing food with care and attention to detail then letting the natural process of cooking take over, produces thoroughly pleasureable results.

What Makes Slow Food Worth the Wait?

Slow food or slow cooking for me means cooking simple dishes that don't require a lot of esoteric ingredients and time-consuming steps—dishes that some may call ordinary, peasant, or country food. This style of cooking does not include convenience foods, but there is something wonderfully hands-off about them. Stews, braised dishes that create their own sauces, and long-roasted meats like pot roast or turkey are all in this category; they are foods that often get better if allowed to sit so the flavors develop. This style of simple, hearty, seasonal cuisine has been practiced and perfected over many years in kitchens around the world.

These foods are not only enjoyable and tasty, many have made a special journey to our communal table. Many of these are classic dishes that have been brought with settlers and immigrants from their homelands, the originals often altered over the years to suit the available ingredients people found, but the essentials lovingly passed down to generations of children, grandchildren, and beyond, until they have become a part of our country's heritage.

You will be rewarded if you use your weekend to rediscover the pleasure of cooking, to revel in the pleasure of preparing and sharing a meal. Though these are definitely dishes to save for weekends when there is time for them to cook, often there are leftovers to freeze and serve again when weeknights call for something good, with only reheating needed.

Braised Short Ribs with Chipotle-Tomato Sauce

✓ SOMETHING SPECIAL   ✓ MAKE-AHEAD

As in most slow-cook dishes, the meat on these ribs becomes so meltingly tender that it literally falls off the bone. And chile lovers will really appreciate the zip in this dish. While the chiles make it hot and spicy, the wonderful flavors of the peppers aren't overwhelmingly fiery, and their unique flavor makes this an exceptional dinner.

1 dried chipotle pepper, or 2 canned chipotles, well drained *

4 large ripe tomatoes, cored, halved, seeded

4 cloves garlic

1 cup chopped onion
(from 1 medium onion)

Salt and freshly ground pepper, to taste

½ teaspoon ground cinnamon

1½ cups beef broth (or homemade stock if available)

2 tablespoons olive oil

5 pounds beef short ribs on the bone

8 ounces egg noodles

1 tablespoon butter

6 to 8 sprigs fresh cilantro, for garnish

1. Preheat the broiler for 5 minutes.

2. Stem and seed the chipotle. Broil the tomato halves, cut side down, until the skins are blistered and browned. Remove from the oven and reduce the heat to 325°F.

3. In a food processor or blender, puree the pepper, garlic, tomatoes, onion, salt, pepper, and cinnamon. Add the broth and puree for 20 seconds.

4. Heat the oil in a heavy Dutch oven with a tight-fitting lid—Le Creuset is very good here. Brown the short ribs on all sides, working in batches to avoid crowding the meat. Remove the Dutch oven from the heat, return all the meat and pour in the chipotle sauce. *

5. Cover the Dutch oven tightly and braise in the oven, turning the meat occasionally, 2 to 2½ hours, until the short ribs are very tender, removing the cover for the last 30 minutes.

6. Just before the meat is tender, boil the noodles in 6 quarts of salted water until tender, 6 to 9 minutes. Drain the noodles well and toss with the butter.

7. Remove the ribs from the sauce and keep warm. Skim the fat off the chipotle sauce. To serve, pile the short ribs in the center of a deep serving platter and pour a little of the sauce over them. Surround with the buttered noodles and garnish with freshly chopped cilantro.

Serving Suggestion

Pass the remaining chipotle sauce in a separate bowl. A bowl of sour cream might be a welcome addition, as the sauce is a bit spicy.

*TIP: Dried peppers should be toasted in a hot skillet for 3 to 4 minutes in order to soften them, release their fragrance, and reinvigorate their flavor and heat. Cooking them in boiling water for 10 minutes can also soften dried chipotles.

*TIP: When browning large quantities of meat, work in batches small enough to keep the pieces from touching each other. Set aside the browned meat on a tray before adding more to the Dutch oven. If the pieces are crowded, the temperature of the pan will decrease too much to brown the meat and it will literally stew in its own juices. The result is an unappealing gray color. Add a little more oil with each batch, if needed.

Country Pot Roast with Potatoes and Green Onions

MAKES 6 TO 8 SERVINGS

✓ EASY PREPARATION   ✓ MAKE-AHEAD

This is slow cooking at its very best—old-fashioned and time-tested. The beef and vegetables melt in your mouth after their long cooking, and the pan juices make a work-free sauce. A green salad and crusty bread complete the meal, and some good horseradish sauce is a nice match with the meat.

4 to 5 pounds boneless chuck roast, in one piece

Salt and freshly ground pepper, to taste

1 cup dry red wine or beef broth

4 large portobello mushrooms, wiped clean and thickly sliced

8 small white potatoes, scrubbed and halved

8 medium carrots, scrubbed, peeled, and halved across

5 bunches green onions, washed, ends trimmed, loose leaves removed, cut into 8-inch lengths, dark green discarded

1½ tablespoons all-purpose flour

3 tablespoons cold water

2 tablespoons chopped fresh Italian flat-leaf parsley, for garnish

1. Preheat the oven to 300°F.

2. Season the roast well with salt and pepper and place it in the bottom of a large, deep, oven-proof casserole or Dutch oven. Pour the wine or broth over the roast. Cover tightly and braise in the oven for 3 hours. Raise the heat to 350°F.

3. Remove the cover and arrange the mushroom slices, potatoes, and carrots around the roast. Cover and braise 30 minutes more. Arrange the green onions over the roast. Replace the cover and braise about 15 minutes more, until the meat and onions are very tender, and the potatoes and carrots are cooked through.

4. To serve, arrange the roast on a heated serving platter. Surround with the vegetables, cover, and keep warm. Skim the fat from the pan juices. Beat together 1½ tablespoons flour and 3 tablespoons cold water. Whisk the mixture into the hot liquid. Simmer on the stove until slightly thickened, 2 to 3 minutes. Season with salt and pepper, if necessary. Spoon a little of the sauce over the meat and vegetables. Serve the remaining sauce on the side. Garnish the roast and vegetables with parsley.

Braised Lamb Shanks with White Beans

MAKES 6 SERVINGS

✓ SOMETHING SPECIAL   ✓ MAKE-AHEAD

Lamb gives itself to slow cooking almost better than any other meat. The succulent texture and distinctive flavor of this dish charms even those who think they don't care for lamb.

2 tablespoons olive oil

6 medium lamb shanks—
about 5 pounds *

Salt and freshly ground pepper,
to taste

1 teaspoon freshly ground nutmeg

Two 14½-ounce cans diced tomatoes
with garlic and olive oil

1 cup chopped yellow onion
(from 1 medium onion)

4 teaspoons minced garlic
(from 4 medium cloves)

3 or 4 sprigs fresh rosemary

1 cup red wine or beef broth, or
homemade beef stock if available

Two 15½-ounce cans navy beans,
drained and rinsed until the foam
subsides *

½ cup beef broth or stock

2 tablespoons butter, melted

⅔ cup plain bread crumbs

1 tablespoon chopped fresh Italian
flat-leaf parsley

1. Preheat the oven to 325°F.

2. Heat the oil in a heavy Dutch oven. Season the lamb shanks with salt, pepper, and nutmeg. Brown them on all sides over medium-high heat, about 5 minutes, turning several times. Add the tomatoes, onion, garlic, and rosemary. Pour the wine or broth over all. Cover and braise in the oven for 2 to 2¼ hours, uncovering the casserole for the last 45 minutes, until the lamb is fork tender. *

3. Remove the lamb from the oven and keep warm, covered.

4. Raise the heat to 450°F. Combine the beans and ½ cup beef broth in a 1-quart baking dish and season with salt and freshly ground pepper to taste. In a small bowl, combine the butter, bread crumbs, and parsley. Spread the crumbs over the beans. Bake 15 to 20 minutes until the crumbs are golden brown and the beans are bubbling.

5. To serve, remove the rosemary sprigs and discard. Arrange the lamb shanks in a deep serving platter. Spoon the vegetables and pan juices over them. Serve hot with the savory beans alongside.

* TIP: Carefully choose the **meatiest lamb shanks** available, or the finished dish will be more bone than lamb.

* TIP: Rinse canned beans in a fine-mesh strainer under cold running water. They are packed in light brine that should be rinsed off before using the beans. When they stop foaming, all the brine and the surface starch from the beans will have been removed. I also like to do this to remove some of the added salt.

* TIP: Braising can also be done on the stove. If you like, braise the lamb, covered, on the stove over low heat for 2 hours, until the lamb is tender, turning the shanks once or twice during that time. If the lamb isn't tender by then, continue cooking 20 to 30 minutes more.

Slow-Roasted Boston Butt

✓ *EASY PREPARATION*   ✓ *MAKE-AHEAD*

Fresh pork is not only economical, but with the new leaner cuts, it is a dish everyone can feel good about enjoying. Leaner, however, doesn't always mean better. In fact, pork has now been bred so lean that it has lost much of its flavor, and has become a little tricky to cook. Slow cooking brings out the very best of pork flavor; adding a little liquid replaces the fat that has been lost in the drive to make it lean, and makes this foolproof dish so tender and moist you can cut it with a fork.

2 tablespoons olive oil or bacon grease *

4 or more pounds pork Boston butt (depending on the size available)— fresh pork shoulder, boned, rolled, and tied by the meat cutter *

Salt and freshly ground pepper, to taste

2 tablespoons dark brown sugar

1½ cups beer, ale, or stock

2 tablespoons chopped fresh Italian flat-leaf parsley, for garnish

1. Preheat the oven to 300°F.

2. Heat the oil or bacon grease on the stove in a heavy, covered, ovenproof casserole or Dutch oven over medium-high heat. Season the roast well with salt and pepper, and brown well on all sides, 6 to 8 minutes. Sprinkle with brown sugar and pour in the beer or broth. Cover the Dutch oven tightly and braise in the oven for 5 hours, until very tender and nearly falling apart.

3. Remove the string and slice the roast into thick slices. Don't worry if it falls apart.

4. Arrange the pork slices or chunks on a heated platter. Spoon some of the pan juices over the meat and pass the rest separately. Garnish the pork with parsley.

*TIP: A tablespoon or two of **bacon grease** can restore a little of the flavor that is missing from today's extremely lean pork. The next time you cook bacon, simply pour the resulting fat into a tightly covered container and store in the freezer up to several months.

*TIP: The **beer or ale** has superb tenderizing effects and improves the flavor of this dish. Most of the alcohol is evaporated during slow cooking.

*TIP: Bone-in butt can be substituted for boneless in this dish, in which case I cook it even longer, until the meat literally falls apart. I remove the bone before slicing and serving. Pile the meat high on soft onion rolls, sort of like barbecue, and serve with cole slaw and a good horseradish sauce. This is a great choice if you have late arrivals as they can just reheat it and serve themselves.

Slow-Roasted Brisket with Caramelized Onions and Carrots

✓ SOMETHING SPECIAL   ✓ EASY PREPARATION

In my grandmother's house, we always knew that on Fridays there would be brisket for dinner. Whenever I make this recipe I am transported back to the warmth of her kitchen and the favorite foods of my childhood. This naturally tough piece of meat becomes tender and flavorful as it is braised in the oven.

5 to 6 pound brisket of beef, in one piece

¼ cup all-purpose flour

2 tablespoons paprika

Salt and freshly ground pepper, to taste

2 tablespoons vegetable oil

6 large yellow onions, thinly sliced (about 12 cups)

¼ cup tomato paste

2 teaspoons finely chopped garlic (from 2 medium cloves)

2 carrots, peeled, trimmed, and quartered

3 russet potatoes, peeled and quartered

2 cups low-salt or no-salt beef broth (1 pint)

1. Preheat the oven to 375°F. Trim any excess fat from the brisket. Dust with flour and paprika and season well with salt and pepper. Heat the oil in a medium skillet, add the brisket, and brown on both sides over medium heat, about 7 minutes. Transfer the brisket to a plate. ✱

2. Add the onions to the pan and stir over medium heat. Cook, stirring from time to time, until softened and golden brown, 12 to 15 minutes. Remove the pan from the heat, place the brisket on top of the onions, and sprinkle with salt and pepper. Spread the tomato paste over the brisket. Arrange the garlic, carrots, potatoes, and broth around the brisket, cover, and bake 2 hours or until tender.

3. Slice the meat diagonally across the grain and return it to the pan. Cover and cook for an additional 40 minutes in the pan with the juices and vegetables. Serve with the carrots and potatoes. ✱

SERVING SUGGESTIONS

Make some instant polenta and serve it with the brisket and carrots, instead of the potatoes. My grandmother used to make warm brisket sandwiches with the leftovers.

✱ **TIP:** Do not trim all the fat from the brisket. Some fat is needed for the meat to become moist and flavorful. You can always trim the fat once it is cooked.

✱ **TIP:** The key to tender brisket is a combination of slow cooking and carving the brisket against or across the grain. If you aren't sure which way is against the grain, ask your butcher.

Vegetables
on the Grill

No matter what else you are grilling, always try to save a little space or a little time to grill some vegetables. The flavor is so great, even vegetable-haters might like them. You can eat them just off the grill with a little olive oil and salt; add grilled veggies to burgers; serve them alongside any kind of meat, poultry, or fish; add them to sandwiches, salads, pastas, or pizzas—the options are endless. Grill large quantities of zucchini, peppers, tomatoes, eggplants, corn, you name it, and you will not only round out a great weekend meal, you can reserve some for during the week and savor the flavor of a weekend cookout without the effort.

Vegetable Grilling Tips:

- Grilling heightens flavors by bringing out their natural sugars of foods. The dry, intense heat of the grill quickly caramelizes the exterior and seals the moisture in, so grill vegetables unpeeled. The peel

also helps hold fragile slices together, so they don't fall apart when you try to turn them.

- Brush the vegetable skin and flesh with oil before grilling, and add an herb rub for even more flavor if you like.

- Start them directly over the heat to sear them, and then move them to the cool side of the grill for finishing.

- For easy handling, use a separate vegetable grid or skewers on top of the grill itself. You might even look for the flat wooden skewers that are available now. Their shape helps keep vegetables, fruit, and smaller pieces of meat from turning around on the skewer.

By the time they're finished cooking, the vegetables are deliciously tender, slightly smoky tasting, and very tempting to see on the plate. Most vegetables only require about 15 minutes on a covered grill.

Grilled Artichoke Dip with Toasted Pita Chips

✓ *SOMETHING SPECIAL*   ✓ *MAKE-AHEAD*

A new version of a classic appetizer, this artichoke dip is fantastic when the artichokes are grilled first because they take on a delicious smoky flavor. Then grill the pita bread and slice it into wedges to go with it.

One 15-ounce can or jar water-packed artichoke hearts, well drained

One 6½-ounce jar marinated artichoke hearts, well drained

Eight 8-inch wooden skewers, soaked in water for 30 minutes before using

Up to 2 tablespoons olive oil, for brushing the artichokes before grilling

Salt and freshly ground pepper, to taste

2 ounces canned diced green chiles (½ of a 4-ounce can), or more to taste

2 tablespoons fresh garlic, mashed with the back of a knife and pounded until creamy (from 6 medium cloves)

¼ cup shredded cheddar cheese (from 1 ounce)

¼ cup mayonnaise

¼ cup sour cream

¾ cup Parmigiano-Reggiano cheese, grated (from 3 ounces)

2 teaspoons dried cumin seeds, toasted and ground *

8 pita rounds

1. Preheat the grill to high heat. Spear the artichoke hearts onto wooden skewers. *

2. Lightly brush the artichoke hearts with olive oil and season with salt and pepper. Grill over high heat until golden brown, about 6 minutes, turning once halfway through grilling time. *

3. Coarsely chop the grilled artichokes. In a medium bowl, combine the artichokes, chiles, garlic, cheddar cheese, mayonnaise, sour cream, salt, pepper, Parmigiano-Reggiano cheese, and cumin. Spoon the mixture into a fireproof dish or heavy-duty aluminum pan.

4. Preheat the grill for 5 minutes to medium indirect heat. Grill over the coolest portion of the grill with the lid closed for 20 to 25 minutes until the dip is heated through and bubbling.

5. To make the pita: Brush the pita rounds with olive oil and season with salt and pepper. Grill briefly over direct heat to warm and brown them, 1 to 2 minutes. Cut into wedges.

SERVING SUGGESTION

If you like, garnish the dip with sour cream and chopped fresh tomato. Serve with the pita wedges.

✷ TIP: To toast the seeds, heat a dry skillet over medium-high heat. Add the seeds to the hot pan and cook, tossing, for 2 to 3 minutes, until the cumin begins to release its fragrance. Grind the toasted seeds in a small coffee grinder kept only for spices. Wipe clean after each use to keep flavors and scents from transferring from one spice to another.

✷ TIP: When using any type of **wooden skewers** on the grill, soak them in water for at least 30 minutes before using them. This makes them more resistant to burning on the grill while these veggies cook.

✷ TIP: Use two skewers pushed side by side through the artichoke hearts so they will be easy to turn and will not spin around on a single skewer.

Medley of Wild Mushrooms and Fresh Thyme

MAKES 6 SERVINGS

✓ *SOMETHING SPECIAL*   ✓ *EASY PREPARATION*

These mushrooms are a great addition to any grilled meal. Allow time just before serving to make this dish—the mushrooms are at their best when they are freshly made.

Twelve 8-inch wooden skewers, soaked in water for 30 minutes before using.

2 large white onions, peeled and sliced in ½-inch slices

¼ cup olive oil

Salt and freshly ground pepper, to taste

½ pound shiitake mushrooms, brushed and stemmed

½ pound cremini mushrooms, brushed and stemmed

½ pound button mushrooms, brushed, stemmed, and thickly sliced

½ pound oyster mushrooms, brushed, stemmed, and thickly sliced

¼ cup fresh thyme leaves

1. Preheat the grill to high heat for 5 minutes.

2. Skewer the onion slices through their equators with 2 skewers at right angles so they will be easy to turn and won't fall apart on the grill. Brush them with oil and season with salt and pepper. Skewer the mushrooms, combining varieties on each skewer. Brush with olive oil, sprinkle with thyme, and season with salt and pepper. ✱

3. Grill the onions over direct high heat until golden in color, turning once, about 4 minutes a side. Grill the mushrooms until golden and beginning to soften, about 6 minutes Allow the vegetables to cool.

4. Remove the vegetables from the skewers, quarter the mushrooms, and chop the onions. Toss together in a medium bowl, and season with salt and pepper.

✱ TIP: Use any combination of the four types of mushrooms called for, depending on the quality and availability in the supermarket. If your budget is tight, you can stick to the cremini and button varieties.

Grilled Vegetable Platter

Grilled vegetables can be the inspiration for so many beautiful and unique dishes. If the grill is fired up for any reason, take the opportunity to grill whatever vegetables you have on hand to serve with the meal, or to use later in sandwiches, wraps, or salads. Potatoes, radicchio, corn, tomatoes, and eggplant slices are all excellent grilling candidates. It is no wonder why this is quickly becoming the most popular cooking method around!

1/3 cup olive oil

2 tablespoons red wine vinegar

3 tablespoons chopped fresh Italian flat-leaf parsley

Salt and freshly ground pepper, to taste

1 large red onion, cut into 1/2-inch slices

Eight 8-inch wooden skewers, soaked in water for 30 minutes before using

2 fennel bulbs, ends trimmed, and thickly sliced

2 red bell peppers, halved, seeded, quartered

8 shiitake mushrooms, stemmed

2 heads Belgian endive, halved lengthwise

12 asparagus spears, ends trimmed

1. In a small bowl, whisk together the olive oil, red wine vinegar, parsley, salt, and pepper.

2. Preheat the grill for 5 to 10 minutes to medium-high direct heat. Skewer the onion slices through their equators with 2 wooden skewers at right angles so they won't fall apart on the grill. Brush the oil mixture on the onion slices and place the skewers on the grill. Grill for about 4 minutes per side.

3. On a vegetable grid, grill the fennel for about 12 minutes. Grill the bell peppers for 10 minutes, and the mushrooms for about 6 minutes. Grill the endive for about 8 minutes and the asparagus for 4 to 6 minutes. Turn the vegetables once and remove each when just slightly soft and golden brown.

4. Serve warm on a platter with the leftover oil mixture drizzled over them.

VEGETABLES ON THE GRILL **123**

Grilled Eggplant with Fontina Cheese

✓ *SOMETHING SPECIAL*

I have always described this recipe as toasted cheese sandwiches for adults. You can use different cheeses and herbs to mix and match the flavors. For children, you could also make the more traditional cheese toasts on the grill at the same time. But why not encourage children to eat something more than traditional kid food?

½ cup extra-virgin olive oil

2 tablespoons fresh lemon juice (from 1 medium lemon)

2 tablespoons Dijon mustard

1 teaspoon chopped garlic (from 1 medium clove)

Salt and freshly ground pepper, to taste

1 large Chinese or Japanese eggplant, sliced lengthwise in ½-inch slices

2 large yellow squash, sliced lengthwise in ½-inch slices

2 large zucchini, sliced lengthwise in ½-inch slices

10 ounces fontina cheese, sliced

20 fresh sage leaves

1. In a small bowl, combine the olive oil, lemon juice, mustard, garlic, salt, and pepper.

2. Preheat the grill to medium-high heat. Brush the vegetables with the oil mixture. Arrange the vegetable slices on the grill. Grill over direct heat about 4 minutes per side, turning them once, brushing with the oil mixture, until lightly brown. ✴

3. Top half of the vegetable slices with the cheese and two leaves of the sage. Then cover with the remaining slices of vegetable. Slide to the cooler side of the grill, and grill with the lid down about 2 minutes, until the cheese melts.

✴**TIP:** To coax out the most flavor in **grilled eggplant**, make sure to season the slices with salt and pepper and then grill until golden—the seasonings are cooked into the eggplant, rather than just sitting on top as they would if seasoned later. I also brush the eggplant with balsamic vinegar as soon as it comes off of the grill to give additional flavor and sweetness.

Grilled Rosemary Tomatoes

✓ *SOMETHING SPECIAL*   ✓ *EASY PREPARATION*

Grilling tomatoes gives them tremendous flavor and sweetness. Tomatoes are fragile and can fall apart easily, so cut them thickly and be careful not to cook them too long.

¼ cup olive oil

2 tablespoons balsamic vinegar

1 tablespoon chopped shallots
(from 1 large clove)

½ teaspoon salt

¼ teaspoon freshly ground pepper

4 large vine-ripened tomatoes,
sliced in half

4 stems rosemary, cut into 2 pieces

8 green onions, tops trimmed

1. Preheat the grill to medium heat for 5 minutes. In a small bowl, mix together the oil, vinegar, shallots, salt, and pepper. Brush the tomato halves with the oil mixture. Tuck a rosemary stem into each tomato half. Grill the tomatoes with the cover down, skin side down, about 5 minutes or until the skin browns. There is no need to turn the tomatoes.

2. Brush the onions with the oil mixture. Grill until the onions are soft, about 2 minutes per side. Serve with the tomatoes. ✱

✱TIP: When grilling, remember to **turn food only once.** Foods don't brown well if they are constantly moved around; they stick to the grid if turned too quickly, and they often lose moisture if turned before the caramelization process seals it in.

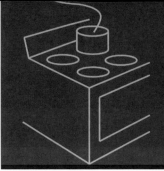

Slow-Cooked Sides

When you arrive home after a long day—even if it was a day of fun—you might be a little too weary to spend a lot of time making dinner. With all the weekend activities, it can be hard to find time to cook. Good options are often dishes you can put together fairly quickly, place in the oven, and forget about. The aromas coming from the oven are sure to get your family or friends excited about the meal that's ahead. Even if the main course is something needing last-minute attention or time on the grill, these sides cook slowly and almost take care of themselves, and are ready when your family sits down to eat.

These simple side dishes are anything but boring. You can slow roast or braise just about any vegetable in the oven. This method of cooking gently brings out all of the wonderful flavor in foods, especially many vegetables. In fact, slow cooking concentrates flavors so they are rich and intense.

Vegetable Slow Cooking Tips:

- Though most of the cooking time is totally hands-off, vegetables should be browned first, then slow cooked until tender.

- You can easily braise rather than roast the vegetables by adding a little liquid to the pan while they are cooking. The concentrated cooking liquid will serve as a sauce.

- Slow cooking works well for all types of veggies. Even dense vegetables like turnips and some squashes become incredibly tender and delicious.

Oven-Baked Polenta

✓ *EASY PREPARATION*   ✓ *MAKE-AHEAD*

Polenta doesn't need to be fussed over and stirred constantly to turn out rich and creamy. In this recipe, you'll see it can be made without all that fuss. You could add this easy side dish to the Braised Salmon with Caramelized Fennel (page 93) instead of the mashed potatoes, or add it to a menu featuring Grilled Rib-Eye Steaks (page 109), or substitute polenta for the noodles in Braised Short Ribs with Chipotle-Tomato Sauce (page 115). The polenta adds a whole new dimension.

Butter for greasing the dish, melted

2 cups polenta *

7 cups water

4 tablespoons butter

2 teaspoons salt

1. Preheat the oven to 350°F. Grease an ovenproof baking dish with melted butter. Add the polenta, water, 4 tablespoons butter, and salt. Stir. Bake uncovered for 1 hour. Stir well with a wooden spoon, then bake 15 minutes more. Cool the polenta for 5 minutes in the pan on a cooling rack.

2. Transfer the polenta to a bowl and serve hot.

✱TIP: For slow-cooking polenta, choose the coarse grind. The flavor and texture will be better than if you use finely ground, and it is closer to the Italian style.

Oven-Braised Rosemary Tomatoes

✓ *SOMETHING SPECIAL*   ✓ *EASY PREPARATION*   ✓ *MAKE-AHEAD*

Once you have several vegetable side dishes at your fingertips, you can pair them with many of your favorite main courses, creating meals with little trouble. This simple dish complements Grilled Cajun Shrimp (page 110), or Grilled Mustard London Broil (page 112), or even the Slow-Roasted Brisket (page 119). Cooking with vegetables that are in the height of their season insures flavors will be at their best.

6 medium tomatoes, cored and halved across

1 teaspoon finely chopped garlic (from 1 medium clove)

Salt and freshly ground pepper, to taste

4 to 6 fresh rosemary sprigs

¼ cup dry white wine, such as Chardonnay

2 tablespoons olive oil

1. Preheat the oven to 375°F.

2. Arrange the tomato halves, cut side up, in one layer in a glass baking dish. Sprinkle the garlic over the tomato halves, and season well with salt and pepper. Arrange the rosemary sprigs on top. Pour the wine into the dish and drizzle the tomatoes with the olive oil. ✴

3. Cover the dish with foil and braise 30 to 40 minutes, basting 2 or 3 times with the pan juices, until the tomatoes are soft but not falling apart. Remove the cover and braise 10 minutes more, until the tomatoes are bubbling hot. Serve hot.

SERVING SUGGESTION

Serve the tomatoes with hot or warm roasted meats or grilled fish.

✴ TIP: To make meal preparation even easier, the tomatoes can be prepared in advance up to this point and then covered and refrigerated several hours or overnight. Remove them from the refrigerator long enough in advance to come to room temperature, about 20 minutes, before putting the dish in the oven to cook.

Braised Beet Coins with Fresh Herbs

MAKES 6 SERVINGS

Fresh beets have a wonderful sweet flavor, much better than the familiar canned ones. Beets are easy to prepare, and will not bleed as much of their liquid if you add lemon juice, vinegar, or wine to the cooking liquid.

2 pounds small fresh beets, scrubbed clean, tops removed, and peeled (about 6 to 8 beets) *

2 tablespoons olive oil or butter

1 tablespoon chopped fresh marjoram

1 tablespoon chopped fresh oregano

1 tablespoon snipped fresh chives

2 tablespoons finely chopped Italian flat-leaf parsley, and a little more for garnish

Salt and freshly ground pepper, to taste

¾ cup chicken broth

¼ cup dry white wine

1. Cut the beets across into ¼-inch slices.

2. Heat the oil or butter in a heavy skillet over medium-high heat. Add the beets and cook, turning several times, to bring out the flavor. Sprinkle the beets with the herbs and season well with salt and pepper. Stir in the broth and wine. Cover and simmer for 25 to 30 minutes, until the beets are tender. Uncover, raise the heat, and boil until the cooking liquid is reduced to a few tablespoons of thickened reduction. (It is hard to say how long this will take as it depends on how much liquid is left after cooking, but count on only a minute or two.)

3. Serve the beets very hot with the cooking liquid spooned over them, garnished with a little more parsley.

✱ TIP: Any variety of beet on the market can be colorful **and delicious,** if you choose the freshest available. Try the candy cane or red and white striped beet, the old-fashioned deep red one, or even the lovely, sweet orange type for this recipe. The flavors will differ a bit depending on the variety, but all are equally delicious.

Roasted Baby Carrots with Lemon and Butter

✓ *EASY PREPARATION*

Carrots are one of my favorite vegetables to slow roast because of the rich flavor that is coaxed out. The natural sugar and beautiful flavors are enhanced by the dry heat of the grill or oven, and none of the taste and nutritional value is lost.

4 tablespoons butter, melted

2 tablespoons fresh lemon juice (from 1 medium lemon)

1 teaspoon grated lemon zest

½ teaspoon sugar

Salt and freshly ground pepper, to taste

1¼ pounds carrots, halved lengthwise, and cut into 3-inch pieces (7 to 8 medium carrots) *

2 bunches green onions, washed, ends trimmed, dark green parts discarded

1. Preheat the oven to 400°F. In a roasting pan or heavy skillet, add the butter, lemon juice, zest, sugar, salt, and pepper. Toss the carrots in the butter mixture, spread them out in an even layer, and roast, uncovered, for 30 minutes.

2. Add the green onions and stir the carrots. Roast until the onions are heated through, about 5 minutes. Season with salt and pepper. Taste and add more sugar if desired. Serve hot or at room temperature.

✱ TIP: In a hurry? Use bagged **baby-cut carrots** you have halved lengthwise, instead of whole large carrots.

Braised Mushrooms with Rosemary and Truffle Butter

✓ SOMETHING SPECIAL

Enjoy the decadent, intoxicating flavor of truffles without paying a fortune by roasting other mushrooms with some truffle-flavored butter. You'll love it.

Small portobello mushrooms are heartier and more flavorful than standard button mushrooms but are easier to serve whole than the large, more mature portobellos. Creminis, or Baby Bellas as they are often called, also stand up well to intense flavors, such as this truffle-scented dish. These are delicious alongside grilled chicken or steak, or even served over warm polenta.

1 tablespoon butter

1 pound small portobello, cremini, or "Baby Bella" (this is actually a marketing name) mushrooms, brushed clean and stems trimmed

1/2 cup chicken broth

Salt and freshly ground pepper, to taste

2 large sprigs fresh rosemary

2 tablespoons cold truffle butter, cut up ✱

1. Melt the plain butter in a medium-sized heavy, straight-sided, covered skillet over medium-high heat. Add the mushroom caps, turning them to coat with the butter. Pour in the chicken broth, and season well with salt and pepper. Add the rosemary. Cover, reduce the heat to medium, and braise the mushrooms gently for 10 minutes, until the mushrooms are tender. Move the mushrooms to a heated serving bowl using a slotted spoon and reserving the cooking liquid.

2. Raise the heat in the skillet to high. When the pan juices are reduced to about 1/3 cup, reduce the heat and quickly whisk in the truffle butter a couple of pieces at a time, cooking just until the sauce is thick and creamy. Be careful not to overheat and melt the butter; you want the sauce to remain about the consistency of thick cream. Remove from the heat immediately.

3. Pour the truffled herb sauce over the mushrooms and serve hot.

✱ TIP: Truffle butter is available in specialty groceries and from several web sites, or you can make your own by combining 2 tablespoons truffle shavings, from a 2-ounce can, with 1/2 cup (1 stick) softened butter. Refrigerate the flavored butter for several days before using to develop the fragrance and taste. Unused truffle butter can be frozen for a month or more.

Fall Trio of Braised Apples, Dried Cranberry, and Orange Slices

✓ SOMETHING SPECIAL   ✓ MAKE-AHEAD

Fruit dishes are a simple, refreshing, and healthful accompaniment to meat dishes, or the perfect way to end a meal. This not-too-sweet, colorful fall and winter dish goes very well with Brined Herb Pork Chops (page 107), or roast duck, for example. You know how delicious applesauce is with pork, or mint jelly with lamb—this is even better.

★TIP: For a more complex dish, **use a combination** of two or three kinds **of apples**. Combining varieties will create a more robust flavor.

6 large apples, Granny Smith or other green cooking apple (about 2 to 3 pounds) ★

½ cup dried cranberries

1 teaspoon orange zest, plus more for garnish (from 1 medium orange)

2 cups apple cider or apple juice (1 pint)

2 tablespoons fresh lemon juice (from 1 medium lemon)

2 tablespoons light brown sugar

1 teaspoon ground cardamom

1 teaspoon ground ginger

2 tablespoons butter

1 large seedless orange, peeled and thinly sliced across

1. Peel, quarter, and core the apples. Cut into 1-inch pieces.

2. In a large, deep, straight-sided skillet, combine the apple pieces, cranberries, zest, apple cider, lemon juice, brown sugar, cardamom, and ginger. Bring to a boil, reduce heat to medium-low, and simmer until the apples are just tender enough to pierce with a fork, about 15 minutes.

3. Add the butter and braise uncovered until the syrup is slightly thickened, 3 to 4 minutes.

4. Halve the orange slices and arrange them in the bottom of a glass serving bowl. Spoon the warm apple mixture over the oranges, and garnish with orange zest. You can also serve the apple mixture at room temperature. You can keep the compote in the refrigerator for several days, but slice the oranges just before serving.

SERVING SUGGESTION

The fruit may also be accompanied with slices of Brown Sugar Pound Cake (page 203), or Classic Sugar Cookies (page 196) as a quick, not-too-sweet dessert.

Chili Lovers Unite!

Chili is so versatile that one of its endless forms is bound to appeal to you. It can be rib sticking and rich, or a simple, healthful, comforting food. It can be made with lots of meat, some flavoring of meat, or no meat at all; with beans or without; fiery hot, with just a bite, or even mild. The flavor may be influenced by a wide variety of cuisines—from Mexican, to Indian, and Asian. The link among all these stewlike recipes is that they all usually have some kind of spicy kick.

Among real chili fiends and connoisseurs, a debate rages about whether there should be beans or no beans, and if you say yes to beans, are they cooked with the meat stew or separately? I add beans, and I cook everything together.

No matter how you make it, most recipes for chili are really simple. Variation in your preparation only makes each pot of chili more interesting than the last.

Tips for Making and Serving Chili:

- You can prepare it in advance and it will be ready whenever you are ready to serve it. Chili is especially good if made a day ahead, refrigerated overnight, and then reheated slowly just before serving. This gives the flavors time to blend and deepen.

- Chili is great inspiration for an easy party. Double or triple your favorite base chili or two. Put out bowls of some toppings so people can make it exactly the way they like it. Offer chopped onions, chiles, tomatoes, olives, grated cheese, and sour cream, and other extras you come up with. This make-your-own style is great for adults or for children, who love to play with their food and create their own special topping combinations.

This chapter gives you a broad variety of chili recipes. Once you have tried a few, add your own spices and flavorings to the pot for a truly unique take on chili.

Hot and Spicy Chili with Beans

✓ *SOMETHING SPECIAL*   ✓ *MAKE-AHEAD*

This is a fairly hot, rustic chili with tender chunks of beef rather than hamburger, and lots of beans. A real bowl of red, as Texans are so fond of calling chili. Serve it in deep thick bowls with crusty bread, or warm flour tortillas, and bowls of condiments for people to add to suit their fancy. This chili is especially good if made a day ahead, refrigerated overnight, and then reheated slowly just before serving—making it a great Sunday night supper.

2 tablespoons vegetable oil, more if needed

1½ pounds chuck steak, cut into ½-inch cubes

2 cups chopped yellow onions (from 2 medium onions)

1 cup stemmed seeded chopped green bell pepper (from 1 medium pepper)

1 cup stemmed seeded chopped red bell pepper (from about 1 medium pepper)

1 tablespoon finely chopped garlic (from 3 medium cloves)

2 dried ancho (or other dried red) chiles *

Two 15½-ounce cans kidney beans

Two 10-ounce cans diced tomatoes with green chiles

2 cups beef broth

3 tablespoons chili powder, or more to taste

1 tablespoon ground cumin

1 teaspoon dried oregano

Salt and freshly ground pepper, to taste

¼ cup chopped fresh cilantro

1 cup seeded chopped tomato, for garnish (from 1 large tomato)

⅓ cup sliced green onions, for garnish (from about 5 thin onions, or 1 bunch)

1 cup shredded extra-sharp cheddar cheese, for garnish (from 4 ounces)

1. Heat the oil in a heavy 4-quart kettle or soup pot over high heat. Brown the beef cubes in small batches, setting each batch aside until all is cooked.

2. Add the yellow onions and bell peppers to the kettle with a little more oil, if necessary. Cook over medium heat, stirring, until the vegetables are tender, about 6 to 8 minutes.

3. Add the garlic and ancho chiles. Stir in the reserved meat, beans, tomatoes, broth, chili powder, cumin, and oregano. Season well with salt and pepper.

4. Cover partially and simmer over low heat for 2 hours or longer if needed, until the meat is very tender, stirring from time to time. Stir in the cilantro and cook 15 more minutes.

5. Serve very hot, in thick deep bowls, with tomato, green onions, and cheddar cheese on the side.

∗ TIP: To get the most flavor out of dried chiles, heat a small skillet over high heat for 3 minutes. Add the dried chiles and heat, tossing, until they soften, become flexible, and give off their fragrance. Remove from the heat, let cool, then stem, halve, seed, and chop the chiles.

Turkey and Black Bean Chili

✓ *SOMETHING SPECIAL*   ✓ *MAKE-AHEAD*

This chili is so hearty and tasty you won't miss the beef. Dark meat turkey works well here for rich flavor and tenderness. Black beans add a distinctive flavor and look to turkey chili. A note for all those holiday cooks: This is a nice way to use up leftover turkey.

2 turkey thighs or 4 turkey legs, skinned, or 5 cups cooked leftover turkey, preferably dark meat ∗

6 cups chicken broth (1½ quarts)

3 tablespoons olive oil

2 cups coarsely chopped onions (from about 2 medium onions)

2 tablespoons finely chopped garlic (from 6 medium cloves)

1 jalapeño chile, stemmed, seeded, ribs removed, finely chopped

Three 15-ounce cans black beans, drained and rinsed until the foam subsides

1 cup fresh or frozen corn kernels (white corn is especially good, though any color is fine)

One 28-ounce can diced tomatoes (not crushed), with juice

3 tablespoons chili powder, more or less to taste

1 teaspoon ground cumin

Salt and freshly ground pepper, to taste

½ cup chopped fresh cilantro

1 cup reduced-fat sour cream, for garnish (½ pint)

1 cup shredded Monterey Jack cheese, for garnish (from 4 ounces)

8-inch flour tortillas (optional)

1. In a Dutch oven or heavy deep pot with a cover, combine the turkey pieces and chicken broth. Cover and simmer over medium heat for 30 to 40 minutes, until very tender. Set aside the turkey to cool, and reduce the broth over high heat to 4 cups, about 15 minutes.

2. Remove the cooled turkey meat from the bone and pull into pieces. (Skip steps 1 and 2 if using leftover turkey.)

3. Clean the Dutch oven and then heat the olive oil in it over medium-high heat. Add the onions and cook, stirring, until transparent, about 5 minutes. Add the garlic and jalapeño. Cook 2 minutes more. Stir in the reserved broth, turkey, beans, corn, tomatoes, chili powder, and cumin. ∗

4. Cover and simmer for 1 hour. Season well with salt and pepper and stir in the cilantro. Simmer 10 minutes more.

5. Serve very hot in flat soup bowls, with sour cream and grated cheese on the side. If using the flour tortillas, heat them briefly in a microwave or toaster oven before serving.

∗**TIP:** Turkey leg and thigh meat is best for long-cooking dishes. It holds its texture better, and adds a great deal more flavor to the dish than white meat would.

∗**TIP:** Substitute 4 cups chicken broth for the reserved turkey cooking liquid if you are using leftover turkey and not simmering the legs.

Chicken and White Bean Chili

I am a real chili lover—traditional and innovative versions alike. The flavors of chicken and spices here are cleaner and simpler than those in beef chilis, perfect for a lighter meal. Serve this with flour tortillas and a green salad for a quick meal.

TIP: Substitute 3 cans of **Great Northern beans** if you are in a hurry. Just rinse them under running cold water until the foam dissipates completely.

1 pound dried large white beans (Great Northern) *

6 cups chicken broth or homemade stock (1½ quarts)

2 teaspoons finely chopped garlic (from 2 medium cloves)

2 cups finely chopped onions (from 2 medium onions)

2 tablespoons olive oil

Two 4-ounce cans chopped green chiles (whatever heat you prefer: hot, medium, or mild)

2 teaspoons ground cumin

1½ teaspoons dried oregano

⅛ teaspoon ground cloves

¼ teaspoon cayenne pepper

Salt and freshly ground pepper, to taste

4 cups diced cooked chicken breast

1. In a large bowl, cover the dried beans with water and soak overnight in the refrigerator. Drain the beans and rinse.

2. In a 4-quart kettle or soup pot, combine the rinsed beans, broth or stock, garlic, and half the chopped onions, and bring to a boil. Reduce the heat to simmer and cook until the beans are soft, about 2 hours, adding more broth if the beans begin to dry out on the surface.

3. Heat the oil in a medium heavy skillet over medium-high heat. Add the remaining onion and cook, stirring, until transparent, 5 to 6 minutes. Add the chiles, cumin, oregano, cloves, and cayenne, and mix thoroughly. Stir into the bean mixture. Season with salt and pepper. Add the cooked chicken and continue to simmer for 45 minutes.

SERVING SUGGESTION

Serve in heavy, deep bowls garnished with shredded Jack cheese, chopped tomatoes, cilantro, green onions, sour cream, and olives.

Cumin-Spiced Steak Chili

✓ *SOMETHING SPECIAL*　　✓ *MAKE-AHEAD*

Round steak has an exceptional flavor featured in this dish. Often cheaper cuts like round steak, chuck steak, or even stewing beef, have far more beef flavor than more expensive, often leaner, cuts. Since they are less tender, they take well to low-temperature, slow cooking. For a low-fat choice, you can make this chili using turkey or chicken instead of beef.

★TIP: Brown the meat in a single layer, in batches. The steak needs to brown and caramelize on at least two sides before going into the stockpot for better flavor. Too much meat in the skillet at one time reduces the temperature too much and the meat will steam in its own juices rather than brown.

1 pound smoked bacon, cut into 3/8-inch pieces

3 pounds round steak, cut into 1/4-inch cubes

Two 28-ounce cans whole tomatoes

One 15-ounce can tomato sauce

One 6-ounce can tomato paste

Two 4-ounce cans diced green chiles (whatever heat you prefer: hot, medium, or mild)

2 cups chopped onions (from 2 medium onions)

2 tablespoons olive oil

2 cups halved seeded and chopped green bell pepper (from 2 medium peppers)

1 cup finely chopped fresh curly-leaf parsley

2 teaspoons ground coriander

2 teaspoons finely chopped fresh garlic (from 2 medium cloves)

8 teaspoons ground cumin

1 teaspoon cayenne pepper

1 teaspoon dried oregano

1/4 teaspoon paprika

2 teaspoons salt

1 teaspoon freshly ground pepper

1 tablespoon fresh lemon juice (from 1 medium lemon)

2 tablespoons mild chili powder, or more to taste

1 cup sour cream or plain yogurt, for garnish (1/2 pint)

1 cup shredded cheddar or Monterey Jack cheese, for garnish (from 4 ounces)

1. Brown the bacon in a large heavy skillet on medium-high heat, drain on paper towels, and set aside. In the same skillet, brown the round steak cubes in batches in the bacon grease. ★

2. In a large stockpot, add the bacon, steak, tomatoes, tomato sauce, tomato paste, and green chiles. Heat to simmering. In the skillet used for the bacon and steak, cook the onions in the olive oil, stirring from time to time, until transparent, 5 to 8 minutes. Add the onions to the stockpot. Add the bell peppers to the same skillet and cook, stirring from time to time, until transparent, 5 to 8 minutes. Add to the stockpot. Stir the parsley, coriander, garlic, cumin, cayenne, oregano, paprika, salt, pepper, lemon juice, and chili powder into the stockpot.

3. Simmer the chili over low heat, stirring occasionally, up to 1 hour or in a slow cooker up to 4 hours.

4. Serve in heavy, deep china bowls and garnish with sour cream or plain yogurt, and shredded cheese.

Sage and Shrimp White Bean Chili

✓ *SOMETHING SPECIAL*   ✓ *EASY PREPARATION*

Almost a bean stew, this fragrant chili is a delicious change of pace. If you are making this chili ahead of time, refrigerate or freeze it before adding the shrimp. Reheat and add the raw shrimp just minutes before serving, or they will be overcooked and tough by the time the chili is hot enough to eat.

1 tablespoon olive oil

1½ cups chopped onions
(from 2 medium onions)

1 tablespoon finely chopped garlic
(from 3 medium cloves)

4 tomatillos, husk removed,
chopped ✱

1 tablespoon ground cumin

5 tablespoons chopped fresh sage
(⅓ cup)

Three 15½-ounce cans navy, Great
Northern, or cannellini beans,
drained and rinsed until the foam
subsides

2½ cups chicken broth

½ teaspoon crushed red pepper,
or more to taste

Salt and freshly ground pepper,
to taste

1 pound small (36–45 per pound)
raw shrimp, peeled and deveined

2 tablespoons chopped fresh Italian
flat-leaf parsley

1 cup sour cream, for garnish
(½ pint)

1. Heat the oil in a large kettle over medium-high heat. Add the onions and cook, stirring, until transparent, 5 to 6 minutes. Add the garlic and tomatillos. Cook, stirring, for 2 minutes. Stir in the cumin and sage and cook 1 minute more.

2. Add the beans and chicken broth to the vegetables. Stir in the crushed red pepper.

3. Simmer for 30 minutes. Season well with salt and pepper. Just before serving, add the shrimp and parsley; stir to mix. Simmer just until the shrimp are pink, 2 to 3 minutes—do not overcook.

4. Serve very hot in bowls, as soon as the shrimp are cooked, topped with a small dollop of sour cream.

✱ **TIP:** Tomatillos look like little, shiny, green tomatoes encased in a papery husk. They have a lovely lemony flavor. Whether eaten raw or cooked, tomatillos add a delicious fruity flavor to all kinds of dishes. To prepare them, peel off the husk, wash well to remove the sticky sap, stem, and slice or dice as needed.

Five-Bean Chili

✓ MAKE-AHEAD

This fairly mild vegetarian chili is delicious as a main course or can be served as a side dish along with barbecued ribs, chicken, or beef. The yeasty taste of the beer brings out the complex flavors from the different beans.

3 tablespoons vegetable oil

3 cups chopped onions (from 2 large or 3 medium onions)

1 cup stemmed seeded and chopped green bell pepper (from 1 medium pepper)

2 jalapeño peppers, stemmed, seeded, and finely chopped ✶

2 teaspoons chopped garlic (from 2 medium cloves)

One 4-ounce can chopped green chiles

Three 14½-ounce cans chili-style diced tomatoes

2 tablespoons chili powder— as hot as you like

3 cups beer (two 12-ounce cans)

Salt and freshly ground pepper, to taste

One 15-ounce can pinto beans, drained and rinsed until the foam subsides

One 16-ounce can kidney beans, drained and rinsed until the foam subsides

One 15½-ounce can Great Northern beans, drained and rinsed until the foam subsides

One 15-ounce can black beans, drained and rinsed until the foam subsides

1 cup frozen baby lima beans

1 cup chicken broth

¼ cup chopped fresh cilantro

1 cup sour cream, for garnish (½ pint)

1 cup seeded chopped tomato, for garnish (from 1 large tomato)

1 cup chopped Vidalia or other sweet onion, for garnish (from 1 medium onion)

2 cups shredded Monterey Jack cheese, for garnish (8 ounces)

1. In a 4-quart kettle or soup pot, heat the oil over medium-high heat. Add the onions and bell pepper and cook, stirring, for 5 minutes. Add the jalapeños, garlic, and green chiles and cook 2 minutes more. Add the tomatoes, chili powder, beer, salt, and pepper. Cook 2 minutes.

2. Stir in the beans and broth and simmer, uncovered, until the mixture is very thick and the flavors have mellowed, 1 hour. Stir in the cilantro and cook 10 to 15 minutes more.

3. Serve very hot, either in bowls or alongside the main course, with sour cream, chopped tomato, chopped onion, and shredded Monterey Jack, or your favorite condiments passed separately.

✶ **TIP:** When working with chiles or hot peppers, remember these tips:

Protect your hands. Put on latex gloves before handling them. Don't touch your face or skin until you remove the gloves and have washed your hands thoroughly.

The hottest parts of the pepper are the ribs and seeds. Remove them or leave them in—depending on how spicy you like your food.

Dairy products, like milk, sour cream, or yogurt, cut the heat in peppers; water or drinks only spread it around your mouth. Capsaicin, the heat-bearing enzyme in the peppers, is not soluble in water. After working with hot peppers, I generally wipe hands and cutting surfaces first with milk, then with soap and water, so the heat isn't transferred to other ingredients.

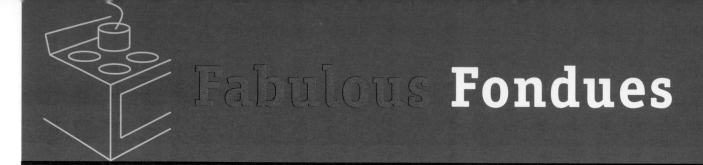

Fabulous Fondues

Fondue has reemerged in the last few years since its heyday 30 to 40 years ago. It's a fun way to cook and eat, especially with your family or friends—everyone's huddled around the fondue pot, which is bound to foster conversation (similar to the camaraderie around a campfire).

Fondue is a rustic dish from the mountainous districts of France and Switzerland of cheese melted in wine and served with bread. Fondue is about more than cheese; there is meat fondue cooked in hot oil, or Asian ones that cook meat, poultry, seafoods, and vegetables in broth. Chocolate fondue is one of the best desserts around, served with fruit or pound cake.

Why Should You Fondue?

Because fondue uses special equipment, it may seem fussy or even like a gourmet style of eating. But fondue is essentially the dipping of food in a simmering liquid. It's easy for the cook because each person makes his or her own food. For the family or a party, you can fill some platters with a large selection of prepared food, cubed bread, and interesting sauces, and let everyone help themselves.

My family loves fondue. We always have fondue when we are on vacation at our lake house. We have one pot for a simple cheese fondue, while another pot is oil for meat fondue. One day we started to fry the bread and vegetables in the oil and it has remained a favorite idea ever since. We serve several sauces on the side, and they can be as complex or simple as we like. You can do the same. We usually pair a light mixed green salad with the fondue.

And fondue doesn't just have to be for adults. Kids will love cooking with sticks and "playing" with their food as they hold it in the simmering liquid (or watching the cheese drip from bread). Watch the younger children near the hot pot, though, and advise them to wait until the food cools down a little before putting it in their mouths.

Fondue Tips:

- Usually cheese fondue is brought to the table in a pottery or ceramic dish. Meat and seafood fondues are best in metal pots.

- Some fondue pots—such as the one for Mongolian hot pot, which is a meat fondue where the meat is sliced rather than cubed and the cooking medium is beef broth instead of hot oil—have a chimney that runs up through the cooking liquid. This dissipates some of the heat away from the liquid so it doesn't boil over.

- Denatured alcohol, either solid jelly like Sterno® or liquid, is the favored heat source, though candle lamps are good for chocolate.

- Cut foods for dipping about the size equivalent to two bites. Too small and you risk losing it in the cooking liquid, too large and it takes too long to cook.

- Everyone should have his or her own fondue fork. They are usually color coded or individually marked so you can remember whose is whose and keep track of how your food is cooking.

- Never put the fork in your mouth—it is going right back in the fondue pot! The cooked food or bread should be pulled off the fork onto the plate and eaten from there.

Cheese and Mushroom Fondue

✓ SOMETHING SPECIAL

Brie may seem like an unlikely choice for melting, but it produces a smooth, creamy, full-bodied fondue. In addition, I like to use a blend of the best mushrooms I can get for this fondue. You can usually find at least three or four different types of mushrooms in the grocery store—just combine any types that look good. Button mushrooms are available everywhere, but minimize their use because their high water content will cause the cheese in the fondue to coagulate and the mixture will break. Dippers for this fondue can include sturdy chunks of crusty bread, vegetables, even cubes of cooked chicken or beef.

FONDUE

2 tablespoons butter

4 ounces oyster mushrooms, stemmed, finely chopped

4 ounces cremini mushrooms, stemmed, finely chopped

8 ounces fresh shiitake mushrooms, stemmed, finely chopped

2 tablespoons shallots, finely chopped (from about 4 medium cloves)

1 cup dry white wine

1 pound ripe Brie cheese, well chilled, rind trimmed, cut into 1/2-inch pieces (about 3 cups) *

Salt and freshly ground pepper, to taste

DIPPERS

Bite-sized pieces of cooked meat

Steamed and quartered small red-skinned potatoes

Lightly steamed asparagus or green beans

Bite-sized pieces of French bread or foccacia

1. Melt the butter in a heavy large saucepan over medium heat. Add the mushrooms, stir, and cook until tender, about 6 minutes. Add the shallots, stir, and cook 1 minute. Increase the heat to high and boil until all the liquid evaporates and the mushrooms begin to color a little, about 3 minutes. *

2. Add the wine to the cooked mushrooms. Bring to a simmer over medium heat. Stir in the cheese in three batches, stirring with a wooden spoon after each addition until the cheese melts before adding more. Continue stirring until the mixture is smooth, and just begins to bubble or simmer (do not boil). Season to taste with salt and pepper. *

3. Transfer the fondue to a warmed pottery fondue pot. Set over the heat source, such as Sterno® or alcohol. Serve with your favorite cooked meat, cooked potatoes, steamed asparagus or green beans (or your favorite cooked vegetables), and French bread, foccacia, or other bread cubes to dip.

*TIP: Select your cheese carefully. Look for imported cheese that is well matured, with a clean white rind and a center that gives a little when you press it gently with your thumb. Avoid any cheeses that have dark spots on the rind.

*TIP: This dish can be made to this point up to 8 hours ahead. Cover and chill.

*TIP: To avoid lumpy fondue, use diced cheese instead of grated. Cubes melt more slowly and smoothly than thin grated pieces.

Meat Broth Shabu Shabu

✓ *SOMETHING SPECIAL*

One of the lightest versions of fondue or hot pot cooking is the Japanese dish shabu shabu—so called to represent the sound made when ingredients are simmering in the broth. The meat and vegetables are cooked in the broth and served with delicious Asian sauces. In addition to the two we suggest, a good commercial plum sauce is always a fine dipping sauce.

Teriyaki Sauce (next page)

Chutney Curry Sauce (next page)

DIPPERS

2 pounds high-quality beef, such as sirloin or tenderloin, cut into thin slices

8 ounces shiitake mushrooms, cleaned and stemmed

8 ounces snow peas

8 ounces baby bok choy, cut into small pieces

10 ounces extra-firm tofu, drained and cut into cubes

8 green onions, each cut on the diagonal into 2-inch pieces

FONDUE

3 quarts low-salt beef broth

1. Make the teriyaki and chutney curry sauces.

2. Arrange the meat and vegetables attractively on a platter.

3. Fill a metal fondue pot with the beef broth. Bring the broth to a boil on the stove and then set it over the Sterno or alcohol burner. ✳

4. Each diner picks up a piece of meat or vegetable from the serving platter with a metal skewer and cooks it in the simmering broth until the red meat becomes pink, or cooked to the degree desired. The tofu breaks easily, so be careful when adding it to the pot. Serve with the teriyaki sauce and chutney curry sauce, for dipping the cooked meat and vegetables in.

✳ TIP: If serving a **meat fondue**, heat the broth at the stove and then move it to the table warmer. This will insure that the broth is hot enough to cook the meat. If it cools, warm it again at the stove.

Teriyaki Sauce

This is a light soy-based sauce for dipping meat, chicken, and vegetables.

½ cup soy sauce

¼ cup dry Sherry

1 teaspoon finely chopped fresh garlic (from 1 medium clove)

1 tablespoon brown sugar

1 teaspoon grated fresh ginger

Combine all of the ingredients in a small bowl and mix well. Chill and serve as a dipping sauce with the fondue.

Chutney Curry Sauce

Our fondue table always includes this curry sauce. It is a perfect accompaniment for chicken or beef.

1 cup mayonnaise

2 tablespoons mango chutney

2 teaspoons curry powder

2 teaspoons grated lime zest (from 1 large lime)

¼ cup fresh lime juice (from 2 large or 3 medium limes)

½ teaspoon salt

Combine all of the ingredients in a small bowl, beating to mix well. Chill and serve as a dipping sauce with the fondue.

Fillet of Beef Fondue with a Trio of Sauces

MAKES 8 SERVINGS

✓ SOMETHING SPECIAL   ✓ EASY PREPARATION

This may be the ultimate in meat fondues. The meltingly tender fillet needs little cooking in the oil, and the rich meat flavor paired with the different sauces makes this a fondue for a special evening. All meat fondues can be made by simply heating oil on the stove in your enamel-coated cast-iron fondue pot. Meats, vegetables, and bread can all be fried in the oil on metal skewers, and served with various sauces.

Roasted Garlic Herb Butter (below)

Horseradish Cream (next page)

Dijon Cream Sauce (next page)

FONDUE

4 cups peanut oil *

DIPPERS

2 pounds fillet of beef, trimmed and cut into 1/2-inch cubes

4 cups cubed bread

1 cup green beans

1 cup halved seeded and sliced red bell pepper (from about 1/2 medium pepper)

1 cup peeled and thickly sliced carrot (from about 1 large carrot)

1. Make roasted garlic herb butter, horseradish cream, and Dijon cream sauce.

2. Heat the oil in a heavy metal fondue pot on top of the stove at medium heat until the temperature reaches 375°F. Place over the Sterno or alcohol burner.

3. Use metal skewers to spear and cook the meat, bread, and vegetables in the oil. Serve with the roasted garlic herb butter, horseradish cream, and Dijon cream sauce, for dipping the cooked meat, bread, or vegetables in. *

★ TIP: The best oil for fondue frying is peanut oil because it can withstand being heated to 375°F without smoking. You should check it with a thermometer or by placing a piece of bread into the oil. If the bread browns quickly then the oil is hot enough.

★ TIP: To reduce the splattering of the oil, add 1 teaspoon salt to 3 cups of oil used. Always blot the moisture from the meat—water and juice always spit in hot oil.

Roasted Garlic Herb Butter

MAKES ABOUT 1 1/4 CUPS

Melted butter sauce is commonly served with meat; here it acts as a dip for the food cooked in the fondue.

1/2 cup (1 stick) butter, at room temperature

1 head of roasted garlic, cloves removed and chopped *

2 tablespoons chopped fresh thyme

3 tablespoons finely chopped fresh Italian flat-leaf parsley

1/2 teaspoon salt

1/2 teaspoon freshly ground pepper

2 tablespoons very finely chopped shallots (from 4 medium cloves)

1 teaspoon fresh lemon juice (from 1 medium lemon)

1 tablespoon Dijon mustard

1. In a bowl, beat the butter until smooth. Then add the garlic and the remaining ingredients, beating well to incorporate everything.

2. Form the butter into a log about 4 inches long. Wrap in plastic

wrap, and chill until firm. You can freeze this for up to 6 months. The butter can be cut into slices 1/3 inch thick and used to top grilled meats or fish, or melted to use as a sauce as it is here.

3. To serve with the fondue, melt the butter in a small bowl in the microwave. Keep it warm over a candle warmer.

★ TIP: To roast a head of garlic: Preheat the oven to 325°F. Trim the top of the head of garlic to expose the cloves. Place the head on a piece of foil large enough to wrap it in. Drizzle the garlic with olive oil and wrap it in the foil. Place the bundle in the oven and bake for 1 hour or until the cloves are fork tender. Cool and remove the cloves from the head.

Horseradish Cream

Frequently paired with beef, this dipping sauce is smooth and creamy with a zesty bite of horseradish. Use it along with the mustard sauce following, or add a bowl of your favorite cocktail sauce for variety to create your own menu.

1 tablespoon chopped fresh
horseradish

¾ cup sour cream

1 tablespoon finely chopped shallots
(from 2 medium cloves)

Combine all of the ingredients in a small bowl and mix well. Chill and serve.

Dijon Cream Sauce

This sauce came about by accident. We lightly whipped some heavy cream to come up with an impromptu crème fraîche, we added mustard, and we loved it. You will too with the beef or even another time with fish.

1 cup heavy whipping cream
(½ pint)

2 tablespoons Dijon mustard

1 teaspoon salt

¼ teaspoon freshly ground pepper

1. In the chilled bowl of a mixer, beat the whipping cream with chilled beaters until it is lightly thickened. It should be at the point where the cream will just hold the mark of the beaters when whipped without sinking. It will be about as thick as ketchup.

2. Fold in the mustard, salt, and pepper. Use immediately.

Spiced Tomato Fondue with Fish, Chicken, or Vegetables

✓ SOMETHING SPECIAL

Like cheese or chocolate fondue, tomato sauce is great for dipping. The refreshing tomato flavor is wonderful on cold winter evenings when you want something with more taste than cheese. I make this dish with white fish, chicken, or vegetables, even chunks of cheddar cheese.

FONDUE

2 tablespoons butter

¼ cup finely chopped shallots (from 8 medium cloves)

3 cups drained Italian canned tomatoes, chopped

¼ cup heavy cream

1 teaspoon chopped fresh tarragon

Salt and freshly ground pepper, to taste

DIPPERS

6 to 8 cups cubed, cooked shrimp or fish, such as haddock, cod, tilapia, even calamari

Pieces of roasted, poached, or broiled chicken

Vegetables, especially cooked potatoes

Chunks of crusty bread

1. Heat the butter in a small skillet over medium heat. Add the shallots and cook for 2 minutes without browning. Add the tomatoes and cook, covered, over medium-high heat for 4 or 5 minutes until the mixture reduces and thickens. When it has thickened, fold in the cream and the tarragon. Season well with salt and pepper.

2. Transfer the fondue to a warmed pottery fondue pot. Set over the heat source, such as Sterno or alcohol. Serve warm with the fish, chicken, or vegetables and bread to dip. ∗

∗**TIP:** To prevent spills, always turn the fondue pot handle away from the diners and away from the edge of the table.

Chocolate Citrus Fondue

✓ *SOMETHING SPECIAL* ✓ *EASY PREPARATION* ✓ *MAKE-AHEAD*

This should be served with pieces of fruit and cake—an assortment of fruit, like strawberries, bananas, or apples, and squares of pound cake are perfect. But why be restrictive when dealing with chocolate? You can dip just about anything compatible with the deep chocolate flavor of this fondue. Try frying small mint leaves in hot canola oil until they are crisp to serve along with it.

FONDUE

4 ounces bittersweet chocolate
(4 squares)

4 ounces semisweet chocolate
(4 squares)

1 cup heavy whipping cream
(½ pint)

⅓ cup Grand Marnier

⅓ cup sugar

2 teaspoons orange zest
(from 1 medium orange)

DIPPERS

Pound cake or angel food cake,
cut into cubes

An assortment of fruit, cut into
bite-sized pieces, like strawberries,
bananas, or apples

1. Chop the chocolate into small chunks.

2. In a heavy saucepan over medium heat, warm the cream, Grand Marnier, and sugar, without bringing to a boil. Remove from the heat and quickly add the chocolate. Whisk until the chocolate is melted. Stir in the orange zest.

3. Transfer the fondue to a warmed metal fondue pot. Set over the heat source, such as Sterno or alcohol. Serve warm. ✱

✱TIP: This fondue can be reheated over a double boiler or in a pottery dish on fifty percent power in the microwave. It will keep in the refrigerator for 1 month.

Summer Picnic Foods

The foods of summer are fresh, simple foods. If it's warm outside, it's time for refreshing salads, hearty sandwiches, and fun finger foods. It's time for picnics—whether a simple meal on the grass in your backyard, a special spread for a concert in the park, or a feast for a family reunion. Eating in the fresh air stimulates the appetite, seems to make everything taste better, and makes any meal fun.

The Right Foods for Picnics

Primary inspiration for any warm-weather meal is the availability of ingredients at their peak. The ingredients I use in the summer reflect all of the wonderful things I can find in the grocery store or farmer's markets at this time of year. The stores and markets are abundantly stocked with beautiful foods—stacks of fresh corn on the cob; smooth, ripe red tomatoes; fragrant, blushed peaches—all inspiring the cook to create dishes that come together with minimal effort.

Getting It All Out the Door

The aim in summer, especially for picnics, is minimal cooking, which heats up the kitchen. I like to use the grill, or make dishes requiring no cooking at all, using simple recipes that can be prepared without standing over the hot stove or heating up the oven.

Whether your picnic food will be eaten outside on the deck or patio, or enjoyed by the lake or the shore, summer foods need to travel well. They are every bit as good hot as they are at room temperature or even cold. I don't want to worry about reheating when I get to my destination, though last-minute grilling is fun and the aromas will entice everyone from wherever they may be straight to the table.

I want the food to be ready when I'm ready! On long summer days, lunch or dinner can be delayed by the ball game going overtime, the kids spending longer in the water than you expected, or the gang arriving late. But with these hearty summer picnic recipes, your meal can be served quickly whenever you need it to be ready.

Tips for Transporting Food in Summer Heat:

- A good cooler or two is a must. Gel ice packs that can be kept frozen, ready for use at a moment's notice, are handy along with them. Freeze juice boxes as well and pack them with the food. They will be icy cold when they are wanted and will help keep food well chilled.

- Wrap foods well in plastic wrap or foil and pack them carefully in the cooler, surrounded by the ice packs.

- If transporting raw chicken, fish, or meat to cook on site, pack it—well wrapped—in a separate cooler or insulated bag so it doesn't come in contact with already prepared food.

- Some ingredients for salads or other dishes can be carried in separate containers to be arranged on serving plates or mixed in bowls at the site. This prevents greens and other fragile foods from getting soggy or from being overwhelmed by dressings rather than being enhanced by them.

- Return salads and other dishes with perishable ingredients like mayonnaise to the cooler with the ice packs after 45 minutes to an hour outside. Bring them out again later if you like, for second or third helpings.

Mahogany Chicken Wings with Crumbled Blue Cheese Sauce

✓ *EASY PREPARATION*

These chicken wings are good hot or cold, so you can serve them right away, or make them up to two days ahead and serve straight from the fridge. Celery and carrot sticks are easy sides for the wings. Pack everything in an insulated bag and they are ready to go anywhere.

¾ cup cider vinegar

1 tablespoon olive oil

2 tablespoon Worcestershire sauce

¼ cup mild chili powder

1 teaspoon dried red pepper flakes or crushed red pepper

1 teaspoon salt

1 teaspoon freshly ground pepper

1 tablespoon Tabasco sauce

4 pounds chicken wings, rinsed and patted dry

Crumbled Blue Cheese Sauce (next page)

1. To make the marinade, stir together the vinegar, oil, Worcestershire sauce, chili powder, red pepper flakes, salt, pepper, and Tabasco sauce. Place the chicken wings in a large heavy-duty resealable plastic bag. Add the marinade, press out the air, and seal the bag tightly. Massage the bag to distribute the marinade. Place in a large bowl and refrigerate for at least 4 hours, turning and massaging every 30 minutes. Marinate the wings for up to 24 hours.

2. Make crumbled blue cheese sauce.

3. Preheat the grill for 5 to 10 minutes to medium-high indirect heat. Remove the wings from the marinade and pat them dry. Arrange the wings on the grill, meat side down, directly over the heat. Close the hood on the grill. Check the wings from time to time and turn them after about 5 minutes, as soon as they are mahogany brown on the meat side. Brown on the bone side and then move them to the cool side of the grill. ✱

4. Grill the wings under the closed hood for about 20 minutes or until the juices run clear and the meat is no longer pink. Remove the wings from the grill, tent with foil, and allow them to rest 10 minutes before serving with the crumbled blue cheese sauce. ✱

✱**TIP:** When the chicken wings hit the grill, the **oil in the marinade will briefly flare up** so be prepared to step back and use caution.

✱**TIP:** Keep the grill at 450°F over the fire. Use this **direct heat** to quickly **brown the meat.** Be sure to also have a cool spot on the grill away from the fire. This cool side can be used to cook with indirect heat at about 350°F. With the hood closed, it creates the perfect oven for the wings to bake in once they have been browned.

(continues)

Crumbled Blue Cheese Sauce

Use this as a dipping sauce for chicken wings, or for vegetables. It is so delicious you will most likely never use bottled again.

1 cup sour cream

1 cup mayonnaise

2 teaspoons minced fresh garlic (from 2 medium cloves)

1 tablespoon Worcestershire sauce

2 cups crumbled blue cheese (from 8 ounces)

Salt and freshly ground pepper, to taste

Milk, for thinning sauce (optional)

1. In a medium bowl, whisk together the sour cream, mayonnaise, garlic, and Worcestershire sauce. Carefully stir in the blue cheese with a spoon. Season to taste with salt and pepper. If the sauce is too thick, add enough milk to make the consistency of pancake batter.

2. Cover and refrigerate. This sauce will keep 2 to 3 days in a covered container.

Muffoletta

✓ SOMETHING SPECIAL   ✓ NO COOKING NEEDED   ✓ MAKE-AHEAD

Made famous in New Orleans, this overfilled, highly flavorful sandwich originally may have come from Sicily. A classic muffoletta is filled with cold cuts, but this vegetarian version is as delicious as the original. Some people like to warm this sandwich in the oven, others serve it right after it is made—it's your choice.

1½ cups Olive Salad (next page), or store-bought *

2 small zucchini, sliced lengthwise into ¼-inch slices

2 green bell peppers, stemmed, seeded, quartered

1 tablespoon olive oil

¼ teaspoon dried oregano

Salt and freshly ground pepper, to taste

Four 4- to 6-inch Italian-style sesame seed rolls, split horizontally

¼ pound very thinly sliced provolone cheese

¼ pound very thinly sliced Emmentaler cheese

1. Make the olive salad.

2. Heat a grill pan on medium-high heat for 5 minutes. Brush the zucchini and bell peppers with oil and sprinkle with the oregano, salt, and pepper. Grill, turning the vegetables once, until lightly charred on both sides, 4 to 5 minutes total. Remove from the heat and cool.

3. To make the sandwiches: Spread the bottom half of each roll with ¼ to ⅓ cup olive salad, letting some of the oil soak into the bread. *

4. Top each sandwich with one-quarter of the grilled zucchini and bell pepper, then one-quarter of the provolone and Emmentaler. Close the sandwich, pressing down on the top, so the juices are forced to seep into the bread. Wrap each one tightly in plastic wrap or foil until ready to eat.

VARIATION

Make this a classic muffoletta by substituting thin slices of mortadella and salami (available at a quality deli) for the grilled vegetables.

★TIP: A good olive salad is the key to a delicious muffoletta. If you are short on time, Boscoli—among others—makes a wonderful salad in a jar, and it is available in the olive section of some supermarkets and specialty stores, or by mail.

★TIP: If you like a **less bready sandwich**, pull some of the soft inside from the rolls to hollow them out a little.

(continues)

Olive Salad

✓ *NO COOKING NEEDED*   ✓ *MAKE-AHEAD*

I also enjoy this salad served as a relish with cold roast meats, such as pork, lamb, or beef.

One 16-ounce jar Italian pickled vegetables or "giardiniera," drained and very coarsely chopped

2 tablespoons rinsed and drained pickled cocktail onions, very coarsely chopped

1 teaspoon rinsed and drained whole capers, chopped

½ cup drained salad olives, very coarsely chopped

2 tablespoons pitted halved Kalamata olives

¼ cup drained pickled mushroom caps, very coarsely chopped

2 tablespoons drained sliced pickled pepperoncini, very coarsely chopped— hot or mild, to taste

1 cup olive oil

1 teaspoon red wine vinegar

3 tablespoons chopped fresh Italian flat-leaf parsley

Salt and freshly ground pepper, to taste

1. Stir together all the vegetables in a medium glass bowl. Stir in the olive oil, vinegar, and parsley. Season with salt and pepper.

2. Pack the salad into a quart glass jar or plastic container with a tight-fitting lid. Refrigerate at least overnight or for several days. This salad will keep refrigerated for a week.

Cedar-Planked Salmon

✓ *SOMETHING SPECIAL*   ✓ *EASY PREPARATION*

Hands down, this is my favorite fish-on-the-grill dish. I like to serve the salmon with greens tossed in olive oil. Soak the planks before you leave home and seal them in a large resealable plastic bag with a little extra water. Light the grill when you get to the picnic site, and when you begin to think about eating, it will be ready for cooking. Brush the salmon with the oil and lemon, put it on the heated cedar plank, and just sit back until the salmon is cooked. If you are serving with a salad, toss the greens with the dressing just before serving.

*TIP: Buy **virgin cedar planks specially made for food preparation**—usually sold in cookware stores. Planks bought from a lumberyard may have been treated with chemicals.

Two 10-inch cedar grilling planks, soaked in water for at least 3 hours *****

2 salmon fillets, 9 inches in length (about 2 pounds each), trimmed of the belly meat and the skin

2 tablespoons olive oil

2 tablespoons lemon juice (from 1 medium lemon)

Salt and freshly ground pepper, to taste

Lemon wedges for garnish

1. Immerse the cedar planks in water. Soak at least 3 hours or up to 1 day.

2. Brush the salmon fillets with olive oil and lemon juice and season with salt and pepper. Preheat the grill to medium-high heat.

3. Lay the planks on the grill and lower the cover. After about 10 minutes, when the planks begin to smoke—you will see the smoke seeping out of the grill—lay the salmon on the hot planks. Cover the grill. Grill 25 to 30 minutes or until the salmon is just opaque in the center and the flesh flakes easily with a fork. Resist the temptation to open the cover. The planks will smoke, but if they have been soaked long enough, they will not burn. There is no need to turn the fish.

4. Serve hot, garnished with lemon wedges.

Grilled Balsamic Lamb Chops and Grilled Ratatouille

Cooking expert and friend, John Ash, calls these small lamb chops "lambcicles" because you pick them up by the thin bone and eat the top of each them. I love these with a little bit of couscous and grilled vegetables. They're a good picnic choice as they can be eaten out of hand, just like fried chicken.

✱ TIP: Cook the vegetables only until they are lightly browned. Cooking them until they are dark will cause them to taste bitter.

LAMB

½ cup olive oil, plus more for brushing lamb before grilling

1½ teaspoons fresh thyme

1 teaspoon chopped fresh garlic (from 1 medium clove)

¼ cup balsamic vinegar

1 tablespoon honey

1 teaspoon salt

½ teaspoon freshly ground pepper

16 rib lamb chops, each about 1 inch thick, trimmed of most of the fat

Salt and freshly ground pepper, to taste

RATATOUILLE

2 small Japanese eggplants, cut into lengthwise planks ¼ inch thick

1 small yellow onion, sliced across ¼ inch thick

1 zucchini, sliced ¼ inch thick

1 yellow squash, sliced ¼ inch thick

Olive oil, for brushing vegetables

Salt and freshly ground pepper, to taste

2 cups diced tomatoes (from 2 large tomatoes)

¼ cup basil leaves, thinly sliced

Up to 2 tablespoons extra-virgin olive oil, for drizzling

1. Preheat the grill to medium-high heat.

2. In a small bowl, whisk together the olive oil, thyme, garlic, vinegar, honey, salt, and pepper.

3. Place the lamb chops in a shallow dish or a large resealable plastic bag in one even layer. Reserve ¼ cup of the marinade to brush on the lamb chops while grilling. Pour the remaining marinade over the lamb chops, turning them over to ensure they are well coated. Cover with plastic wrap, and marinate for 30 minutes or up to 2 hours in the refrigerator, allowing them to come to room temperature for the last 30 minutes.

4. Meanwhile, brush the slices of the eggplant, onion, zucchini, and squash with olive oil and season with salt and pepper. Grill the vegetables over direct heat until tender, 4 to 6 minutes, turning once halfway through grilling time. ✱

5. Cut the vegetables into ¼-inch cubes, and place in a large bowl. Add the diced tomatoes and basil, and season with salt and freshly ground pepper and a little extra-virgin olive oil. Serve the ratatouille hot, warm, or at room temperature. This can all be done at home if you are taking your picnic on the road.

6. Remove the lamb chops from the marinade and pat dry. Lightly brush with olive oil and season with salt and pepper. Grill the lamb over direct heat until medium-rare, about 5 minutes, turning halfway through grilling time. Serve hot with the ratatouille.

Hoisin-Glazed Duck with Spicy Eggplant

MAKES 6 SERVINGS

The sweet flavor of the duck is balanced beautifully with the spiciness of the eggplant in this dish. The duck can be made at home, as it is here, or in a heavy skillet on the grill if you are going to take it on a picnic. Or you can cook it at home, wrap to keep warm, and then slice on site. Some people are afraid of cooking duck, but as you can see from this recipe, there's really nothing to it.

Spicy Eggplant with Garlic Sauce
(next page)

2 boneless duck breasts,
approximately 1 pound each *

Salt and freshly ground pepper,
to taste

1/3 cup gently packed, finely chopped
shallots (from about 10 medium
cloves)

1 tablespoon grated fresh ginger

1 tablespoon rice wine vinegar

1 tablespoon honey

1/3 cup hoisin sauce

1. Make the spicy eggplant with garlic sauce.

2. Gently score the skin side of the duck breasts in crosshatch pattern, being careful not to cut through the flesh of the meat. Season the duck breasts with salt and pepper.

3. Heat a skillet over medium heat for 2 minutes. When hot, add the duck breast to the skillet, skin side down. Cook for approximately 5 minutes, rendering the fat from the skin. Be sure to turn on your exhaust fan as the pan may smoke a bit.

4. Using tongs, transfer the duck breasts to a plate and carefully pour off the accumulated fat into a heatproof container. Replace the duck breasts, meat side down, and cook for 1 minute. Return the breasts to the skin side and continue rendering and caramelizing, 4 to 5 minutes more. Again, remove accumulated fat and turn the duck breasts over to cook on the meat side to desired doneness, 3 to 4 more minutes for medium-rare.

5. Carefully remove the duck from the pan, place on a platter, and tent with aluminum foil to keep warm. Let the duck breasts

rest for several minutes. Pour out all but 1 tablespoon of the fat into a heatproof container.

6. Add the chopped shallots and ginger to the hot skillet. Cook over medium heat until slightly softened, about 3 minutes. Add the rice wine vinegar and stir with a wooden spoon to remove any browned bits on the bottom of the pan. Add the honey and hoisin sauce to the pan. Cook until a thick glaze forms, about 1 minute. Brush some of the glaze on the skin side on the duck breasts.

7. Slice the duck breasts on a slight diagonal across the grain and place several slices on each plate. Brush the warm glaze over the duck slices and serve with the spicy eggplant with garlic sauce. *

(continues)

✳ TIP: Duck breasts (or magrets) are available at specialty butchers or from several web sites.

✳ TIP: Hoisin sauce is available in Asian markets, and in the Asian section of most supermarkets. Soy-based, tangy, and spicy sweet, hoisin sauce is a great addition to marinades, basting sauces, or as a dip for all kinds of foods.

Spicy Eggplant with Garlic Sauce

✓ *SOMETHING SPECIAL*

This eggplant dish can be served with grilled meats or as a meatless entrée over couscous. Japanese or even Chinese eggplant can be substituted for the globe if you can find them.

2 small globe eggplant

1 tablespoon salt

1½ teaspoons finely chopped garlic (from 2 medium cloves)

1 teaspoon crushed red pepper

2 tablespoons soy sauce

1 tablespoon balsamic vinegar

3 tablespoons olive oil, plus more for brushing the eggplant

1. Preheat the broiler and adjust the rack to 4 inches from the heat source.

2. Slice the eggplant into lengthwise planks, ¼ inch thick. Salt the planks on both sides, and place them on a rack set on a cookie sheet to drain for 30 minutes.

3. In a small bowl, combine the garlic, red pepper, soy sauce, vinegar, and oil.

4. Pat the eggplant dry, brush with olive oil and arrange in one layer on an oiled cookie sheet. Broil until the eggplant is softened and lightly browned on one side, about 5 minutes. Turn the eggplant slices over, brush with olive oil, and broil until softened and lightly browned, 5 minutes more.

5. Transfer the eggplant to a platter, brush with the garlic and pepper sauce, and allow it to cool.

6. Transport the eggplant to the picnic in a tightly sealed plastic container. Serve at room temperature with the duck.

Great American Potluck

My grandparents used to have big potlucks on their farm in Colorado. Everyone from the surrounding farms would bring a salad, main dish, side dish, or dessert—whatever dish they were most proud of. Each was a special dish, which would feed at least 20.

Potlucks like that still happen all the time but they have also come a long way—even straight into the city. No matter where you live, having a potluck now means entertaining is possible for all of us because the work and the cost is shared among all the guests.

When you entertain, how many times has someone said to you, "Can I bring something?" Taking your guests up on this offer adds variety to the meal and takes the pressure off of you. And the recipes can be as homespun or gourmet as you like, whether you bring or serve your favorite casserole or a fabulous chocolate tart.

Potluck Tips:

- The food should travel easily—it shouldn't be something that will spill or fall apart when moved—and be good both hot and at room temperature. You never know if there will be burner or oven space available where you're going.

- Make recipes that can be finished ahead so you aren't making the food the hour before you go to the party—except for some dishes that you might want to pack up right out of the oven so they will still be hot when you arrive at the dinner.

- Wrap hot foods in spillproof containers then in layers of newspapers and then in a heavy blanket—or better yet, if you do a lot of potlucking, invest in an insulated wrappers or containers especially made for carrying hot dishes to picnics and potlucks.

- Save final touches, like tossing the salad, placing delicate vegetables in a serving dish, or adding the final garnish, until after you get to your party. The food will look and taste fresher.

- Finally, make sure that your dish can safely sit out for a while. Foods that are heavy in mayonnaise, for example, can spoil on the buffet, if left out for more than 45 minutes to an hour.

Asian Slaw

✓ *EASY PREPARATION*   ✓ *MAKE-AHEAD*   ✓ *TAKE-ALONG*

This is a refreshing, flavorful fusion of a classic slaw and a Thai salad. The crunch of the juicy, crisp jicama replaces the green papaya often found in Thai salads, but the flavor and heat here are very much the same. Because this salad is best when the dressing has time to mix with the slaw, it is ideal for a potluck.

4 cups cored finely shredded napa cabbage (from about 1/2 medium head cabbage)

1 cup shredded carrots (from about 2 medium carrots)

1 cup very thinly sliced Vidalia onion (from 1/2 large onion)

1 cup very thinly sliced stemmed and seeded green bell pepper (from about 1/2 large pepper)

1 cup shredded jicama (from about 1/2 of a 1-pound tuber) *

1 jalapeño pepper, stemmed, seeded, and very thinly sliced

1 tablespoon very thinly sliced garlic (from about 3 medium cloves)

2 teaspoons freshly grated ginger

1 teaspoon ground cumin

1/4 cup rice vinegar

1/2 teaspoon soy sauce

1/2 cup olive oil

1 tablespoon Asian hot oil

Salt and freshly ground pepper, to taste

2 tablespoons chopped fresh cilantro

1. In a large bowl, toss together the cabbage, carrots, onion, bell pepper, jicama, jalapeño, and garlic.

2. In a smaller bowl, combine the ginger, cumin, vinegar, soy sauce, oils, salt, and pepper. Stir in the cilantro.

3. Toss the dressing with the cabbage mix, cover, and refrigerate at least 2 hours or up to 24 hours.

✻ TIP: Jicama is an unassuming looking knobby brown potato-like tuber popular in nearly every tropical country in the world. Once peeled, the crisp flesh can be sliced or cut into any shape that will suit the recipe, and can be eaten either raw or cooked. Unlike potatoes, the creamy white flesh will not darken when cut, so it can be prepared ahead of time. Add it to salads, stir fries, and stews, or use in any dish that calls for potatoes.

Chinese Chicken Pasta Salad

✓ *MAKE-AHEAD*   ✓ *TAKE-ALONG*

A great new version of an old favorite, this salad is full of the goodness of fresh vegetables and pasta. Served lightly chilled or at room temperature, it is a perfect take-along dish, brightening up any potluck occasion. Using high-quality soy sauce and sesame oil makes a better-tasting dressing. You will receive many compliments and lots of requests for this recipe.

SALAD

8 ounces penne pasta

1 cup cleaned and grated carrots (from 2 medium carrots)

1/3 cup sesame seeds, toasted

5 cups cubed poached or deli roast chicken

1 cup halved seeded and chopped red bell pepper (from 1 medium pepper)

1 cup halved seeded and chopped green bell pepper (from 1 medium pepper)

1 cup halved seeded and chopped yellow bell pepper (from 1 medium pepper)

1/2 cup trimmed and chopped green onions (from about 8 to 10 thin onions or 2 bunches)

DRESSING

1 1/2 cups rice wine vinegar

1 1/2 cups olive oil

1/3 cup superior light soy sauce

1 tablespoon dark Asian sesame oil

2 teaspoons finely chopped garlic (from 2 medium cloves)

2 teaspoons grated fresh ginger

1 teaspoon freshly ground pepper

1/2 teaspoon dried red pepper flakes

1/2 cup chopped fresh cilantro

1. Bring a large pot of salted water to a boil and add the pasta. Cook until al dente, and drain in a colander. Bring another pot of water to a boil, add the carrots, and blanch until tender, about 5 minutes. Drain the carrots in a colander and run cold water over them to stop the cooking.

2. In a large bowl, combine the sesame seeds, chicken, bell peppers, onions, and drained, cooled carrots.

3. In a small bowl, mix together all of the dressing ingredients, and stir to combine with a fork. Add the drained pasta to the large bowl with the vegetables, and then pour the dressing over the salad. Toss lightly and serve at room temperature. *

* TIP: Chop the vegetables and cook the pasta up to 3 days before you need the final salad; store them separately. Toss the ingredients together the day of the party, but leave the cilantro out until just before you are ready to serve.

Chicken Enchiladas with Tomatillo Sauce

✓ SOMETHING SPECIAL   ✓ MAKE-AHEAD   ✓ TAKE-ALONG

Take a hot dish full of these enchiladas wrapped in an insulated container to your next potluck occasion and watch it disappear. This dish is good any time of the year. Make it up to two days ahead, and freeze some extra sauce so that it will be ready for the next time you crave these.

TOMATILLO SAUCE

6 tomatillos, husked, stemmed, well washed, and roasted

1 cup chopped white onion (from 1 medium onion)

1 serrano chile, stemmed, seeded, and finely chopped

2 teaspoons chopped garlic (from 2 medium cloves)

2 cups chicken stock or low-salt broth (1 pint)

1/2 cup toasted pumpkin seeds (about 2 ounces)

6 poblano chiles, roasted, peeled, and seeded

1/2 cup chopped fresh cilantro

1 leaf of romaine lettuce

1/2 teaspoon salt

1 tablespoon peanut oil

FILLING

1/2 cup half and half

8 ounces cream cheese, softened

2 cups grilled shredded chicken

3/4 cup finely chopped white onion (from about 1 small onion)

1/2 teaspoon salt

1 tablespoon butter

Twelve 8-inch corn tortillas, heated

3/4 cup grated cheddar cheese (from 3 ounces)

3/4 cup grated Monterey Jack cheese (from 3 ounces)

1. In a small saucepan, combine the tomatillos, onion, serrano chile, garlic, and stock. Bring this mixture to a boil over medium-high heat. Cover the pan and simmer for 10 minutes. Reserve the liquid.

2. Place the pumpkin seeds and 4 tablespoons of the tomatillo cooking liquid in a food processor and chop until fine. Add the tomatillo mixture, poblano chiles, cilantro, lettuce, and salt to the food processor. Puree until the mixture is smooth.

3. Heat the oil in a medium skillet over high heat. Add the pureed mixture, lower the heat and stir over medium heat until thickened, about 5 minutes. *

4. Beat the half and half and cream cheese in a medium bowl, until smooth and fluffy. Fold the chicken, onion, and salt into the cream cheese mixture. *

5. Preheat the oven to 350°F. Spoon a thin layer of the tomatillo sauce on the bottom of a 9- × 13-inch baking dish. To assemble the enchiladas, spread a thin layer of the sauce on the tortilla. Spoon 1/4 cup of the chicken mixture down the center of the tortilla. Roll the tortilla and place it seam side down in the baking dish. Repeat with the remaining tortillas. Spoon the remaining sauce over the finished tortillas. *

6. Cover the dish with foil and bake for 20 minutes or until hot. Remove the foil and sprinkle the enchiladas with the cheddar and Monterey Jack cheese. Bake about 10 minutes more, until the cheese melts and the sauce is bubbling.

∗ TIP: The tomatillo sauce can be made ahead and frozen in an airtight freezer container or resealable freezer bag for up to 3 months.

∗ TIP: Try grilling the poblano chiles and tomatillos instead of roasting them. This will add a delicious smokiness and rich flavor to the dish.

∗ TIP: At this point the dish can be covered and refrigerated for up to 24 hours. Remove from the refrigerator and bring to room temperature before baking.

Stuffed Pork Loin with Lemon, Feta, and Herbs

MAKES 4 SERVINGS

✓ *SOMETHING SPECIAL*   ✓ *TAKE-ALONG*

Pork loin is great for a potluck because you can roast and slice it, then serve it hot or cold. This cut of pork makes the perfect accompaniment to any other potluck side dishes and salads. Bring along a bowl of Olive Salad (page 152) to serve separately.

3 tablespoons olive oil

2 cups fresh spinach leaves, cleaned and the stems removed (about 3 ounces)

Salt

1/3 cup seeded and sliced red bell pepper (from 1/2 medium pepper)

1/3 cup seeded and sliced yellow bell pepper (from 1/2 medium pepper)

2 teaspoons finely chopped garlic (from 2 medium cloves)

1 cup crumbled feta cheese (from 4 ounces)

2 tablespoons bread crumbs

1/2 teaspoon dried oregano

1 teaspoon lemon zest (from 1 medium lemon)

Salt and freshly ground pepper, to taste

11/2- to 2-pound boneless pork loin

1. Preheat the oven to 350°F.

2. Heat 1 tablespoon of the olive oil in a large skillet over low heat. Add the spinach and season with a pinch of salt. Cook until just wilted, about 2 minutes, turning often with tongs. Transfer the spinach to a strainer and allow it to cool. Add 1 tablespoon of olive oil to the pan and heat over medium heat. Add the bell peppers, season with a pinch of salt, and cook until softened, about 5 minutes. Stir in the garlic and cook until fragrant, about 1 minute more. Remove from the heat and allow the vegetables to cool.

3. Remove the spinach from the strainer and squeeze out any excess water with your hands. Chop the spinach and place it in a medium bowl. Add the crumbled feta cheese, bread crumbs, oregano, and lemon zest. Mix

well with a wooden spoon and season with salt and pepper, as desired.

4. Butterfly the loin of pork and season it with salt and pepper. ∗

5. Place the cooled spinach mixture in the center of the loin and top with the peppers. Roll the meat tightly, jelly roll style. Tie the meat every 2 inches with kitchen twine.

6. Heat the last tablespoon of olive oil in a medium ovenproof skillet over medium-high heat. Brown the pork loin on all sides. Roast the pork loin in the preheated oven for 25 minutes or until it reaches 160° to 170°F on an instant-read thermometer. Remove from the oven and tent with aluminum foil to keep warm. Let pork loin rest at least 10 minutes before slicing. ∗

∗ TIP: To butterfly the pork loin, place it fat side down on the cutting board. Cut lengthwise down through the middle, about two-thirds of the way through, and open the roast like a book. Then make another cut on the left side and the right, opening up each side so you end up with one flattened piece of meat about one-third the thickness of the original roast. If this process seems beyond you, ask your supermarket meat cutter to butterfly the roast for you.

∗ TIP: This **pork roast can be** stuffed, seared, cooled, then **frozen**. When you are ready to serve it, just thaw in the refrigerator and roast as directed.

Baked Tomato Penne

✓ *MAKE-AHEAD*   ✓ *TAKE-ALONG*

A tray of baked pasta is a real crowd favorite. It holds heat well, so you can heat it at home, wrap it in foil, and serve it up to two hours later.

2 tablespoons olive oil, plus more for greasing the baking dish

1 cup finely chopped white onion (from about 1 medium onion)

1 tablespoon chopped fresh garlic (from 3 medium cloves)

1 pound Italian sausage, removed from the casing and crumbled

¼ cup dry red wine

3 cups whole Italian canned tomatoes, chopped with the juice

¼ cup chopped fresh oregano

Salt and freshly ground pepper, to taste

1 cup ricotta cheese (about ½ pint)

1 cup grated Parmigiano-Reggiano cheese (from 4 ounces)

½ cup finely chopped fresh Italian flat-leaf parsley

1 pound penne pasta

3 cups cubed fresh mozzarella (from about 8 ounces)

1. Preheat the oven to 400°F. Lightly oil a 9- × 13-inch baking dish.

2. Heat the olive oil in a large skillet over medium-high heat. Add the onion, stir, and cook until soft, 4 to 5 minutes. Add the garlic and the sausage, stir, and cook until the sausage is browned, about 6 minutes more. If the sausage renders a lot of fat, pour it off before you continue.

3. Add the red wine to the pan and boil until about 1 tablespoon of the liquid remains. Add the tomatoes and their juice and simmer uncovered until the mixture thickens. Add the oregano and season with salt and pepper.

4. In a large bowl, mix the ricotta, half of the Parmigiano-Reggiano, and the parsley. Season with salt and pepper.

5. Meanwhile, cook the penne in a large pot of boiling salted water until al dente. Drain the pasta well and toss with the cheese mixture. Add the sausage mixture and toss again. Toss in the mozzarella and pour into the prepared dish. Sprinkle with the remaining Parmigiano-Reggiano and bake, uncovered, about 20 minutes, until lightly browned. ✱

✱ TIP: Make several casseroles at once and freeze them to have something handy for your next potluck or for a few dinners during the week (divide them into containers in the portions you'll need before freezing).

Apple Cranberry Pecan Pie

✓ *SOMETHING SPECIAL*　　✓ *MAKE-AHEAD*　　✓ *TAKE-ALONG*

If you like to dress up old reliable recipes, this new take on apple pie is for you. The tang of cranberries and the tasty crunch of toasted pecan pieces are a great addition to America's favorite.

✱ TIP: If the crust begins to brown too quickly, lay a sheet of foil gently on the surface of the pie to prevent burning.

Pastry dough for a 2-crust pie, homemade, frozen, or refrigerated

2 pounds apples, try a combination of Granny Smith, Golden Delicious, and/or Fuji (about 8 large apples)

2 tablespoons butter

2/3 cup dried cranberries

1/2 cup sugar

1 teaspoon ground cinnamon, or more to taste

Pinch salt

1/4 cup flour

3/4 cup toasted pecan pieces (3 ounces)

2 tablespoons spiced rum (optional)

1. Preheat the oven to 425°F.

2. Roll half the pastry to fit a 9-inch pie plate. Line the pie plate, leaving the additional pastry hanging over the edge.

3. Peel, quarter, and core the apples. Slice thinly.

4. Melt the butter in a large heavy skillet. Add the apples and cranberries. Sprinkle with sugar and cinnamon and cook over medium-high heat, stirring, until the apples are softened—but not falling apart—and the cranberries are plumped, about 20 minutes. Remove from the heat. Sprinkle the apples with salt and flour and stir to mix well. Stir in the pecans. Add rum, if using, and cool the mixture for 5 to 10 minutes.

5. Pour the apple mixture into the bottom crust.

6. Cover with the second crust, folding under the overlap, and forming an edge with your fingers. Cut slits in the surface to allow steam to escape.

7. Bake for 50 to 60 minutes, until the crust is well browned and the filling is bubbling. ✱

SERVING SUGGESTION

A scoop of vanilla, butter pecan, or rum raisin ice cream on top of a warm wedge of pie makes an extra-special dessert.

Layered Brownie Tart

✓ *SOMETHING SPECIAL*   ✓ *MAKE-AHEAD*   ✓ *TAKE-ALONG*

This chocolate tart has a brownielike texture with the elegance of a tart presentation; it makes the perfect potluck dessert, because it is easily divided into servings. And who doesn't like chocolate? Serve it with a lightly sweetened whipped cream or a vanilla sorbet that you take along in an insulated freezer bag.

PASTRY CRUST

1⅔ cups all-purpose flour

¼ cup sugar

¼ teaspoon salt

1 ounce unsweetened chocolate, finely chopped (1 square)

⅔ cup cold unsalted butter (1¼ sticks), cubed

2 cold egg yolks

1 teaspoon vanilla extract

4 teaspoons ice water

BROWNIE FILLING

6 ounces bittersweet chocolate (6 squares)

½ cup unsalted butter (1 stick), at room temperature, cubed

1½ cups sugar

3 large eggs, at room temperature, lightly beaten with a fork

2 teaspoons vanilla

¾ cup all-purpose flour

CHOCOLATE GLAZE

½ cup semisweet chocolate chips, melted, warm

4 tablespoons unsalted butter, at room temperature, cubed

2 teaspoons vegetable oil

1. Sift the flour, sugar, and salt into a mixing bowl. Add the chocolate. Cut the chilled butter into the dry ingredients using a pastry cutter, two knives, or with a food processor.

2. In a small bowl, combine the egg yolks, vanilla, and ice water. Mix the liquids into the flour with a wooden spoon until it begins to hold together in a dough. Using your hands, gently knead the dough just until the dough is well blended. Be careful not to overwork the dough or it will become tough. Press the dough into the bottom of a 10½-inch springform pan with a removable bottom.

3. Preheat the oven to 350°F.

4. Melt the bittersweet chocolate in a double boiler. Stir in the butter. Transfer the mixture to a large bowl and add the sugar. Stir to combine the ingredients, and to cool the mixture. Add the beaten eggs to the slightly cooled chocolate mixture and mix in the vanilla. Gradually add the flour, folding until just combined—the batter will be fairly thick. Pour the batter into the lined springform pan. Bake about 45 minutes, until a toothpick inserted in the center comes out clean. Cool on a wire rack.

5. Melt the chocolate chips in a glass dish in the microwave on high for 1 minute. Stir and microwave in 20-second increments until melted and hot. Add the butter and oil to the warm melted chocolate. Cool slightly and pour onto the cooled tart, spreading the glaze evenly with a small spatula. Cover the tart and refrigerate for several hours, to let the glaze set. Run a knife around the edges before removing the outside of the springform pan.

6. Cut into wedges and serve.

Cooking for the Week Ahead

Let's face it—your weeknights are often too busy to allow you to plan and shop each day for your meals. Waiting for Monday to plan meals for the week usually requires simple meals or repeating repertoire favorites because you don't have to think too much about them. On weekends, taking advantage of the time to arrange your own schedule and think more creatively will lead to more varied and fun meals, and to less work and stress during the week. Sunday afternoon and early evening can be perfect for shopping and cooking for the week to come.

Prep Now, Cook Later Tips:

- Plan a really good shopping list, beginning with either the dishes you want to serve, or the ingredients you want to incorporate. Expand the list beyond the food you routinely buy, like bananas and bread, to include some fun things like a roast, baby carrots, or fresh pineapple.

- Casseroles, large roasts, as well as big pots of soup, stew, or chili are perfect for make-ahead meals. Not only are they great the first evening, but there can be plenty left to freeze, or serve again in a day or two. (Check out the soups and chilis chapters, pages 54, 60, and 133, for more choices.)

- Doing some prep work before the groceries make it to the refrigerator is another way to lighten the load of weekday cooking. Once you have the week's food on hand, you can slice, dice, chop, and cook today what you will enjoy later in the week when there is less time to prepare.

- Vegetables (except mushrooms, which will need to be wiped at the last minute or they will spoil) can be cleaned, sliced, and trimmed so everything is ready to use.

- Roasting a chicken in the oven will give you meat for that night plus possibly some leftover for another meal later in the week, like fajitas a night or two later.

- You can also do twice the work on a day when you are cooking ahead to have a ready-made home-cooked meal later. Try making one pan of lasagne for tonight, and freezing one for a month from now.

The recipes that follow are ideal for preparing in advance for the week ahead, and are meant to inspire you to think about your own recipes this way.

Oven-Braised Chardonnay Chicken

MAKES 4 TO 6 SERVINGS

✓ *EASY PREPARATION* ✓ *MAKE-AHEAD*

Poached chicken is a lovely old-fashioned dish. While the color remains delicately pale, this modern version becomes a one-dish meal with more complex flavors than the simple original. It can be cooked one day, then warmed and served the next. Or, enjoy some that night with some leftover another night. For an even heartier dish, add one seasoned chicken sausage for each serving to the pot to create a sort of rustic one-pot meal.

3½-pound chicken, cut into 8 pieces, discarding the back

1 cup sliced Vidalia onion (from about ½ large onion)

2 cups baby carrots (about 8 ounces)

8 ounces button mushrooms, brushed clean, stems trimmed

2 cups Chardonnay wine (1 pint)

½ cup chicken broth

1 teaspoon fresh thyme leaves

¼ cup chopped fresh curly parsley, plus more for garnish

Salt and freshly ground pepper, to taste

4 to 6 Aidells or other seasoned chicken sausages (optional)

2 tablespoons flour

2 tablespoons butter, softened

1. Preheat the oven to 375°F.

2. Arrange the chicken pieces in a heavy oven- and burner-proof Dutch oven, such as Le Creuset, or a deep pot with a lid. Add the onion, carrots, and mushrooms. Pour in the wine and broth and sprinkle with the thyme and parsley. Season well with salt and pepper.

3. Cover and cook in the oven for 1 hour. Add the sausages, if you are using them. Poach for 20 to 30 minutes more.

4. Remove the chicken and sausages to a heated serving platter. Remove the vegetables with a slotted spoon and arrange around the chicken. Tent with foil to keep warm.

5. In a small bowl, stir together the flour and butter to make a smooth paste. ✶

6. Place the Dutch oven on top of the stove and bring the pan juices to a boil. Skim off any fat. Beat the butter mixture into the boiling broth with a whisk, 1 teaspoon at a time, just until the sauce is thickened and shiny. It may not take all the butter to thicken it. Reduce the heat and simmer 2 minutes more. ✶

7. To serve, arrange the chicken and vegetables in a large deep bowl and pour the sauce over them. Garnish with parsley.

SERVING SUGGESTION

A side dish of buttered noodles with Parmigiano-Reggiano cheese grated on top would go well with this, along with crusty French bread for dipping.

✶**TIP:** This flour and butter paste is called a **beurre manié** (or kneaded butter). It will thicken sauces, and it is a great trick to use at the last minute if gravies or other hot sauces have not thickened enough. It has the added benefit of making the sauce attractively smooth and glossy.

✶**TIP:** This dish can be **refrigerated** up to 2 days and then reheated when you are ready to serve.

Herb Roasted Chicken with New Potatoes

✓ MAKE-AHEAD

With just a little preparation, you can pop this chicken into the oven for nearly effortless roasting. It fills the kitchen with the aromas of the delicious meal to come, and the whole family will gather for dinner without needing to be called twice. Serve it with butter-cooked carrots or green beans, and a green salad. The leftover chicken can be set aside and used later in the week in a pasta dish or stir-fry or it can be frozen for up to two weeks.

3½ pound whole chicken

2 medium lemons, halved

2 tablespoons chopped fresh rosemary, plus 4 whole sprigs

2 tablespoons chopped fresh garlic (from about 6 medium cloves)

4 Yukon Gold or new potatoes, peeled and cut into 2-inch cubes

3 tablespoons butter

3 tablespoons olive oil

Salt and freshly ground pepper, to taste

½ cup chicken broth

1. Preheat the oven to 350°F. Rinse the chicken and pat it dry. Rub inside and out with a lemon half. Combine the chopped fresh rosemary and garlic to form a paste.

2. Place the chicken in a roasting pan and surround it with the potatoes. Melt the butter in a small pan and add the oil. Brush the mixture evenly over the chicken and potatoes and then sprinkle with the garlic and rosemary mixture.

3. Place the lemons and 2 of the rosemary sprigs in the cavity of the chicken. Season the entire chicken and potatoes lightly with salt and pepper.

4. Roast the prepared chicken for 30 minutes. Add the broth to the pan and baste the chicken with the pan juices. Season to taste with salt and pepper. Roast 30 minutes longer, until the chicken is tender, or until an instant-read thermometer placed in the thickest part of the thigh registers 160°F.

5. Transfer the chicken to a warmed platter and surround with the potatoes. Garnish with the 2 remaining rosemary sprigs. Serve the pan juices in a bowl on the side. ∗

∗ TIP: Allow the chicken to rest at least 10 minutes before carving to redistribute the juices. The meat will be juicier and the juices won't end up on the cutting board or platter—or the floor—and the chicken will be easier to carve.

Roasted Lamb Shoulder with Lemony Brown Rice

✓ *SOMETHING SPECIAL*   ✓ *MAKE-AHEAD*

The rub on this succulent lamb roast has a slightly exotic Indian flavor. Paired with the fragrant brown rice, it makes a wonderful change-of-pace dinner choice. Once cooked, the remaining lamb can be used for a quick curry dish, a platter of cold lamb with salad for a fast busy meal, or even chopped and added to soup.

1 tablespoon dried oregano

1 tablespoon ground coriander

1 teaspoon ground cumin

2 teaspoons finely chopped garlic (from 2 medium cloves)

2 tablespoons very finely chopped fresh curly parsley

Salt and freshly ground pepper, to taste

1 tablespoon fresh lime juice (from 1 medium lime)

3-pound lamb shoulder, boned, and rolled *

Lemony Brown Rice (next page)

Bottled mint sauce

* TIP: Substitute the loin half of a lamb leg if you cannot find lamb shoulder. Simply ask the butcher to remove the bone and roll and tie it.

1. Preheat the oven to 425°F.

2. In a small bowl, combine the oregano, coriander, cumin, garlic, parsley, salt, and pepper. Spread the herbs on a sheet of waxed paper.

3. Rub the lime juice over the surface of the lamb. Roll the roast in the herbs and spices, pressing them firmly into the surface.

4. Place the roast in a small, heavy roasting pan. Roast at 425°F for 10 minutes. Reduce the heat to 325°F and roast 40 to 50 minutes more, until an instant-read thermometer reaches 160°F for medium (less if you like your lamb very pink) when inserted into the center of the roast. Remove the roast from the oven and tent with foil to keep warm. Set aside for 10 to 15 minutes before slicing.

5. While the roast is cooking, make the lemony brown rice.

6. To serve, slice the roast thinly and accompany it with steaming rice. Spoon any pan juices over the lamb slices and pass some mint sauce on the side.

Lemony Brown Rice

Brown rice has a toasty, nutty flavor that goes well with the vibrant taste of this roast lamb—and the fragrant lemon overtones make it especially good.

1 tablespoon butter

1 cup brown rice

Salt and freshly ground pepper, to taste

2 cups chicken broth

1 teaspoon fresh lemon juice (from 1 large lemon)

2 tablespoons grated fresh lemon zest (from 1 large lemon)

1. Melt the butter in a heavy 2-quart saucepan with a lid. Cook the rice, stirring, for 3 minutes, tossing to coat all the grains with butter. Season well with salt and pepper. Stir in the chicken broth, lemon juice, and ⅔ of the zest. Bring to a boil, lower the heat and simmer, uncovered, 40 minutes or until all the broth is absorbed.

2. Remove the pan from the heat. Cover with a towel and top with the lid. Let the rice stand for 10 minutes.

3. Add the remaining lemon zest, fluff the rice with a fork, and serve while still hot.

Sugar-Roasted Root Vegetables

✓ *SOMETHING SPECIAL*   ✓ *EASY PREPARATION*

Serve these with almost any plain broiled chicken, chops, or roasts, such as Brined Herb Pork Chops (page 107), Slow-Roasted Boston Butt (page 118), or Roasted Lamb Shoulder (page 168). You can parboil these vegetables up to a day in advance. Leave the skins on the vegetables so that when they are roasted they will take on a beautiful golden color.

½ **pound red potatoes, scrubbed and sliced very thin**

½ **pound carrots, scrubbed and sliced very thin**

½ **pound parsnips, scrubbed and sliced very thin**

2 **tablespoons butter**

2 **tablespoons brown sugar**

1 **tablespoon heavy cream**

Salt and freshly ground pepper, to taste

Chopped fresh Italian flat-leaf parsley, for garnish

1. Bring a large pot of water to a boil. Salt the water and add the potatoes. Bring back to a boil and reduce the heat, slightly. Parboil for 5 minutes, and drain them well. Repeat this process with the carrots and the parsnips. ✱

2. Preheat the oven to 400°F. Melt the butter in a small skillet over medium-high heat. Add the brown sugar and whisk until the mix is smooth. Continue cooking for 2 minutes and then add the cream. Whisk again and then remove the mixture from the heat.

3. Toss the vegetables together in a 9- × 13-inch baking dish. Toss the brown sugar mixture with the vegetables and season with salt and pepper. Roast them for 20 to 30 minutes, until they are golden. Sprinkle with the parsley and serve on a platter.

✱ TIP: Parboiling is much the same as blanching, but the vegetables are boiled a bit longer when they are parboiled. This process is used when the vegetable or other food will be cooked again by another process, such as roasting. Parboiling can speed up the second cooking, or it can reduce a strong flavor.

Trio of Bell Peppers with Balsamic Vinegar

MAKES 6 SERVINGS

✓ *EASY PREPARATION*   ✓ *NO COOKING NEEDED*   ✓ *MAKE-AHEAD*

This is a quick, light side dish that will go with just about any meat or fish course. Use aged balsamic vinegar, which is mellower than other vinegars and adds a richer flavor to the dressing. You can slice the peppers up to three days in advance, and then just toss and serve when you are ready during the week.

1 cup halved seeded and chopped
green bell pepper (from 1 medium
pepper)

1 cup halved seeded and chopped red
bell pepper (from 1 medium pepper)

1 cup halved seeded and chopped
yellow bell pepper (from 1 medium
pepper)

2 tablespoons extra-virgin olive oil

2 tablespoons balsamic vinegar

Salt and freshly ground pepper,
to taste

In a medium bowl, toss the bell peppers with the olive oil and balsamic vinegar. Season with salt and pepper. Serve.

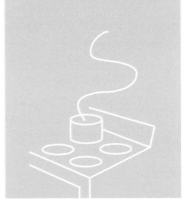

Braised Fresh Pineapple Chutney with Fresh Coconut

MAKES ABOUT 5 CUPS

✓ *SOMETHING SPECIAL*   ✓ *MAKE-AHEAD*

Fresh pineapple chutney or relish is very popular in India and Thailand where it is served with curries. Like many popular dishes, there are myriad versions—this is just one. Make it several days in advance so the flavors have time to merge. Serve with Roasted Lamb Shoulder (page 168) or with any cold meat or poultry.

2 tablespoons butter

1 cup sliced Vidalia or other sweet onion (from ½ large onion)

2 jalapeño peppers, stemmed, seeded, and very finely chopped

½ teaspoon finely chopped garlic (from 1 small clove)

1 whole pineapple, peeled, cored, and cut into ½-inch pieces

2 tablespoons crystallized ginger, finely chopped *

1 teaspoon ground cumin

½ teaspoon cayenne pepper

1 teaspoon ground coriander

½ teaspoon dry mustard

1 teaspoon hot curry powder

⅔ cup packed light brown sugar

¼ cup cider vinegar

2 tablespoons lime juice (from 1 large lime)

1 cup golden raisins

½ cup freshly shredded coconut or frozen unsweetened shredded coconut *

1. Heat the butter in a large, deep, straight-sided skillet. Add the onion, jalapeño, and garlic. Cook, stirring, until tender, about 5 minutes. Stir in the pineapple. Cook 3 minutes, stirring once or twice.

2. In a small bowl, mix together the ginger, cumin, cayenne, coriander, mustard, and curry powder. Stir into the skillet with the pineapple. Add the sugar, vinegar, lime juice, and raisins.

3. Simmer over low heat until the pineapple is very soft and the chutney is thick, 30 to 40 minutes. Remove from the heat, stir in the coconut, and cool completely.

4. Once cooled, the chutney can be served at once, or packed in jars and refrigerated up to 2 weeks.

＊TIP: Crystallized ginger is available in jars in the spice section of all major supermarkets.

＊TIP: Don't be intimidated by whole fresh coconut. It's not impossible to open it; just use caution. Puncture the three dark spots or "eyes" at one end with a screwdriver and hammer. Drain the liquid (refrigerate or discard). Place the coconut on a rack and bake in a 325°F preheated oven for about 20 minutes. Let the coconut cool for 10 minutes, then crack it with a hammer so that the shell breaks into several pieces. Remove the shell from the coconut, peel off the brown skin with a paring knife or vegetable peeler, and cut the meat into chunks. Shred with a hand shredder, Microplane, or with the shredding disk of a food processor.

Or, instead of preparing fresh coconut, you can substitute unsweetened flaked coconut from the freezer section of your supermarket.

Creamy Mint Peas

✓ *SOMETHING SPECIAL*

If fresh peas are in the market, take advantage of their very short season in the late spring and summer. Bring them home as quickly as you can after they have been picked, then shell them, or invite your children to help. The delicious sweetness of fresh peas is a treat you will want to enjoy whenever possible. When fresh peas are not available, petit frozen peas are fine. This dish goes extremely well with lamb or poultry. You can prepare the peas, refrigerate, and reheat in the microwave the next day.

✱ TIP: If you have **extra peas**, add them to salads and side dishes.

2 cups low-salt chicken broth

4 sprigs flat-leaf parsley

2 bay leaves

3 sprigs fresh mint, plus 2 tablespoons finely chopped, for garnish

1 teaspoon sugar

4 cups petit peas (from about 4 pounds in the pod), or, if fresh are not available, use frozen ✱

4 tablespoons butter

2 tablespoons heavy cream

Salt and freshly ground pepper, to taste

1. Pour the broth into a medium skillet and bring it to a boil over medium heat. Meanwhile gather the parsley, bay leaves, and mint sprigs and tie them together with kitchen string. Add the bundle to the broth along with the sugar and peas. Simmer, uncovered, for 3 minutes.

2. Pour off all the remaining broth except for ½ cup, add the butter and cream, and season with salt and pepper. Cook, stirring frequently, until heated through; the time will vary if the peas are very fresh, so check after about 10 minutes; frozen peas take 4 to 6 minutes. Discard the herb bundle, transfer to a bowl, and sprinkle with the chopped mint to serve.

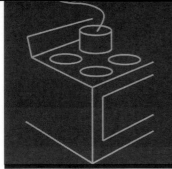

An Ice Cream Social

The smooth, rich, creamy deliciousness of ice cream is just about impossible to resist. It doesn't have to come from a tub or a truck, though; it's quite easy and satisfying to make your own.

Children have a special affinity for ice cream and because they love it, they will often love to help make it. Have them help make the mix, work the freezer, or set out the toppings for a sundae buffet.

With these recipes, you will be able to enjoy many different ice cream desserts, at home. With a little planning, a summer Saturday or Sunday can be the perfect time to bring the whole family together or to invite your friends over for ice cream. Topped with a mound of whipped cream, nuts, and cherries on the top, these treats will make you feel like a kid again.

Equipment

There are many kinds of ice-cream makers on the market—choose the one that best suits your needs from the following.

- Fully automatic electric freezers—just pour in the base, turn it on, and enjoy the end result. These are very expensive, more than $500, but are wonderful to use.

- Electric machines with removable bowls that must be frozen in the freezer section of the refrigerator. Pour in the base, turn it on, and the machine will do the rest. These are available for $50 or more.

- Manual machines with removable bowls that must be frozen in the freezer section of the refrigerator. Pour in the base, cover, and turn by hand until the ice cream is made. These are available for less than $20.

- Granitas and ices can be made in ice cube trays.

Ingredients

The main reason for making ice cream at home, aside from the pleasure it gives the entire family, is that you can tailor the recipes and make them with your favorite ingredients. There are no big secrets to making ice cream. It is essentially a sweet mixture of milk, cream, sugar, and, sometimes, egg yolks. The butterfat content of the ice cream depends on the amount of cream and whole milk that is used. Eggs add richness; sugar or honey are the sweeteners.

An ice cream base has only a few ingredients, and all you have to do is add your choice of flavorings or fruit to it and you have ice cream. Whatever recipe you use, pay careful attention to measuring the ingredients precisely. Any changes that you make almost always affect the taste or texture of the final product.

Vanilla is by far the most popular flavor of ice cream in the world. Almost 75% of all the ice cream consumed is vanilla; chocolate is second. A departure from the ordinary can be fun too—experimenting with different flavors is what makes creating your own ice cream so much fun. You can simply stir in fun items like chopped chocolate, candy, or fruit, or add flavors to the base like flavor extracts or fruit syrups.

One thing to remember is to always use a high-butterfat base when making a fruit ice cream. Cut up the fresh fruit, add some sugar or lemon juice, and then refrigerate it in a bowl for about 30 minutes. The addition of the sugar will lower the freezing point of the fruit and prevent it from icing up. The sugar and lemon juice will extract the juices from the fruit and flavor the ice cream.

Sometimes all ice cream needs to give it pizzazz is a special sauce. You'll find my three favorites here: caramel, hot fudge, and raspberry.

Basic Vanilla Bean Base

✓ *SOMETHING SPECIAL*   ✓ *MAKE-AHEAD*

A basic base can take you a long way. Once you have this technique and recipe down, you can make many different kinds of ice cream.

1 vanilla bean

2 cups whole milk (1 pint)

¾ cup sugar

⅛ teaspoon salt

6 large egg yolks, lightly beaten with a fork

2 cups heavy cream, chilled (1 pint)

1. Using a small sharp knife, cut the vanilla bean in half, lengthwise. Using the back of the knife blade, scrape the seeds from the pod and put them in a medium saucepan. Add the milk, and bring the mixture to a simmer over medium heat. Cover, remove from the heat, and let the mixture stand for 30 minutes. ∗

2. Return the pan to the heat and bring it to a simmer. Meanwhile, in a medium bowl, whisk the sugar, salt, and yolks together. Gradually add the hot milk to the bowl, whisking it constantly. Return the mixture to the same saucepan and cook over medium-low heat, stirring constantly, until the custard thickens and coats the back of a spoon. Be careful not to boil this mixture, or the egg yolks will curdle and the mixture will be spoiled.

3. Remove the custard from the heat and slowly mix in the cream. Pour the mixture through a fine-mesh strainer set over a clean bowl. Cover and refrigerate about 1 hour, until cold. Transfer the cooled mixture to the ice-cream maker and proceed according to the manufacturer's instructions. Place in the freezer, freeze the mixture until firm, and then serve. This will keep for up to 3 days in the freezer.

∗TIP: Using the seeds from **whole vanilla beans** to flavor the milk in this base gives the finished ice cream a rich vanilla flavor without the addition of the alcohol found in vanilla extract. The leftover bean pod can be added to a tin or jar filled with sugar in order to give the sugar a light, pleasant vanilla flavor. Used in place of plain sugar in baking or on cereals it's a whole new taste. Don't compromise on quality: buy the best, pure extract or whole beans you can find. There is no reason to ever use artificial vanilla flavoring.

Sugared-Almond Ice Cream

✓ *SOMETHING SPECIAL*   ✓ *MAKE-AHEAD*

This is one of my favorite ice creams. For added elegance, if you can find dried lavender, add one-half teaspoon of dried lavender to the milk while you heat it. Strain off the lavender after the milk has cooled slightly, then add the milk to the yolk mixture. ✱

1¼ cups sugar

½ cup slivered almonds

2 cups whole milk (1 pint)

4 large egg yolks, lightly beaten with a fork

⅛ teaspoon salt

2 cups heavy cream, chilled (1 pint)

1 teaspoon pure vanilla extract

½ teaspoon almond extract

1. In a small skillet, heat ½ cup of the sugar over medium heat until it begins to melt. Add the almonds and cook them until the sugar begins to brown, 4 to 5 minutes. Pour them out into a Pyrex® dish and separate the almonds with a fork. Allow them to cool. These can be made a week ahead, and stored in an airtight container.

2. Bring the milk to a simmer in a medium saucepan over medium heat. Remove from the heat and set it aside. In a medium bowl, whisk the egg yolks with the remaining ¾ cup of sugar and the salt until they are pale yellow. Gradually, whisk in the hot milk. Pour the mixture back into the pan and cook over medium-low heat, whisking constantly, until

the mixture thickens and coats the back of a spoon—take care that the mixture doesn't boil, or the eggs will curdle and the mixture will be spoiled. Remove the custard from the heat and stir in the cream, vanilla, and almond extract. ✱

3. Chill the mixture, covered with plastic wrap, for 1 hour, then pour it into an ice-cream maker and freeze according to the manufacturer's directions. When the ice cream is about 5 minutes from being frozen—and is the consistency of soft frozen custard—add the almonds, then complete the freezing. Store in the freezer compartment of the refrigerator for up to 3 days.

✱ TIP: Be sure to use food-quality **lavender**, not the processed lavender used in sachets and potpourris.

✱ TIP: Coat the back of a **spoon means** when the liquid forms a film on the spoon just thick enough to hold its form when you run a fingertip down the back of the bowl of the spoon. The mark made by your finger remains "clean."

Peach Ice Cream

✓ *MAKE-AHEAD*

Be sure to make this recipe in the summer when fresh peaches are in season. You can also make this recipe with an equal amount of fresh strawberries or blueberries.

Basic Vanilla Bean Base, unfrozen (page 175)

3 cups peeled, stoned, and sliced fresh peaches (from about 6 medium peaches)

¾ cup sugar

2 tablespoons fresh lemon juice (from 1 medium lemon)

1. Make basic vanilla bean base.

2. In the food processor or blender, combine the peaches, sugar, and lemon juice. Blend until smooth. Transfer to a strainer set over a bowl and allow the juices from the peaches to drain. This should strain for about 1 hour. Stir the fruit puree into the basic vanilla bean base. Add 1 cup of the strained juice. Pour the mixture into an ice-cream maker and freeze according to the manufacturer's directions. Store in the freezer compartment of the refrigerator for up to 3 days.

SERVING SUGGESTION

Serve it in ice cream bowls made from scooped-out lemons.

Enticingly Rich Chocolate Sorbet

✓ *SOMETHING SPECIAL*   ✓ *MAKE-AHEAD*

I have made this for a crowd and they couldn't believe it was sorbet. It tastes so rich they thought it had been made with cream or milk. Try serving it with meringue on the top for a light dessert.

1 cup sugar

¾ **cup good quality unsweetened Dutch-processed cocoa**

2 cups water (1 pint)

3 ounces bittersweet chocolate, chopped (3 squares)

2 tablespoons light corn syrup

1. Combine the sugar and cocoa in a medium saucepan. Gradually add the water and bring to a boil. Whisk constantly until smooth, about 4 minutes. Reduce the heat to low, and add the chocolate and corn syrup. Stir just until the chocolate melts. Pour the mixture into a medium bowl and refrigerate the mixture about 1½ hours, until chilled through. *

2. Transfer the chilled sorbet mixture to an ice-cream freezer and process according to the manufacturer's instructions. Transfer the mixture to a freezer container and cover. Freeze overnight to allow the flavors to develop.

*TIP: The trick to great sorbets is the proper balance of water to sugar. Add more corn syrup, about 1 teaspoon at a time, to the mixture if it doesn't turn out as creamy as you want it to be.

Raspberry Sorbet

✓ *SOMETHING SPECIAL*   ✓ *MAKE-AHEAD*

An Italian meringue base of egg whites beaten with hot sugar syrup until they are stiff makes this sorbet very smooth in texture. To make strawberry sorbet, substitute frozen strawberries for the raspberries.

∗ TIP: If sugar crystals form on the side of the pan when you're preparing the simple syrup, brush down the sides with a pastry brush dipped in ice water.

ITALIAN MERINGUE

3/4 cup sugar

1/3 cup water

3 large egg whites, at room temperature (about 1/2 cup)

1/8 teaspoon cream of tartar

1/8 teaspoon salt

RASPBERRY FLAVORING

Two 10-ounce packages frozen raspberries packed in syrup, partially defrosted

1/3 cup fresh lemon juice (from 3 medium lemons)

2 tablespoons Framboise— raspberry liqueur

1. Combine the sugar and water in a small saucepan. Swirl the saucepan slowly over medium-high heat until the mixture begins to boil. Do not stir the mixture. Continue to swirl the pan until the sugar melts and the syrup becomes clear. Cover the pan and reduce the heat to low. ∗

2. In a large bowl, using an electric mixer on medium-low, beat the egg whites until foamy. Add the cream of tartar and salt. Increase the mixer speed to high and beat until soft peaks form.

3. Remove the cover from the saucepan and boil the syrup rapidly over medium heat for 1 minute. The mixture should register 280°F on a candy thermometer. Immediately remove from the heat.

4. With the mixer on medium speed, carefully pour the hot sugar syrup in a steady stream directly into the middle of the egg whites, beating all the time with the electric mixer. Once all the syrup has been added, increase the speed to high and beat the egg whites until the meringue will hold stiff peaks and is very shiny.

5. In a food processor or blender, combine the raspberries, lemon juice, and Framboise. Strain the mixture through a fine mesh strainer. Transfer the mixture to a large bowl and thoroughly fold in the meringue. Transfer the mixture to an ice-cream freezer and freeze according to the manufacturer's directions. To serve, spoon the mixture into chilled glasses and decorate with fresh raspberries and mint leaves.

Classic Caramel Sauce

MAKES 1½ CUPS

✓ *MAKE-AHEAD*   ✓ *TAKE-ALONG*

Once you have made your own caramel sauce, you will only go back to store-bought when time is short. (But you will long for your homemade version.) The difference in taste is amazing. Heat the sugar slowly. It will melt and turn a beautiful amber color. Use a heavy-bottomed saucepan to prevent it from burning.

¾ cup sugar

¼ cup light corn syrup

½ cup heavy cream

½ teaspoon pure vanilla extract

⅛ teaspoon salt

1. Combine the sugar and the corn syrup in a deep, heavy medium saucepan. Cook over medium heat, watching carefully, until the sugar completely melts, and begins to turn golden brown. This will take 4 to 6 minutes.

2. Remove the pan from the heat and carefully stir in the cream, vanilla, and salt. (The mixture may foam up a bit—just keep stirring, but do not add the cream to the sugar mixture while it is still on the heat.) Serve the sauce warm. This will keep in the refrigerator for up to 3 weeks.

Homemade Hot Fudge Sauce

✓ *MAKE-AHEAD*   ✓ *TAKE-ALONG*

This is a delicious creamy hot fudge sauce that can be reheated easily in a saucepan over low heat. So make it ahead, then reheat and serve.

2 ounces bittersweet chocolate (2 squares)

1 tablespoon unsalted butter

⅓ cup whole milk, scalded *

¾ cup sugar

2 tablespoons unsweetened cocoa

3 tablespoons light corn syrup

⅛ teaspoon salt

1 teaspoon pure vanilla extract

1. Combine the chocolate and butter in a medium saucepan over medium heat. Cook until the mixture has melted. Stir until smooth. Slowly add the heated milk. Add the sugar, cocoa, corn syrup, and salt. Stir until well blended.

2. Cook over medium-low heat, stirring frequently, until the mixture reaches a low boil, and simmer for 5 minutes, stirring, until thick and creamy. Remove the pan from the heat and stir in the vanilla. Serve this hot. This will keep in the refrigerator for 3 weeks.

* TIP: **Scalding milk** is sometimes thought to be overkill now that all of our milk is thoroughly pasteurized and homogenized. However, adding hot milk to the chocolate makes it melt more smoothly, and if you are watching for the scald temperature, you will not have milk boiling all over the stove. To scald milk, heat it in a saucepan just until bubbles begin to form around the edge of the liquid. Remove from the heat.

Raspberry Sauce

✓ *SOMETHING SPECIAL*   ✓ *MAKE-AHEAD*   ✓ *TAKE-ALONG*

Use this sauce to dress up any dessert, or pour over ice cream and serve with fresh raspberries. It is especially good when spooned over chocolate ice cream.

2½ cups raspberries, fresh or frozen and thawed

½ cup sugar

¼ cup Framboise—raspberry liqueur

Place the raspberries, sugar, and liqueur in a blender and puree until smooth. If you want a seedless puree, then pass it through a fine mesh strainer. This can be stored in an airtight container in the refrigerator for 2 days.

Ice Cream Cookie Bowls

✓ *SOMETHING SPECIAL*　　✓ *MAKE-AHEAD*　　✓ *TAKE-ALONG*

Sweet tooths everywhere get an extra kick when they can eat the bowl their dessert is served in. These crisp cookies are molded while they are still hot. They can be shaped into bowls or saucers for the ice cream. This versatile recipe can also be used to make delicate cookies in different shapes. The only crucial factor is timing: they must be molded while they are still warm.

★ TIP: Use a saucer or bowl as a guide and **trace the rounds** on the parchment with a pencil. The outlines will help you make identically sized cookies.

½ cup unsalted butter (1 stick), softened, plus more for greasing custard cups

1 cup confectioners' sugar

1 teaspoon pure vanilla extract

½ cup egg whites, lightly beaten until well mixed and frothy (from 3 or 4 large eggs)

²⁄₃ cup all-purpose flour

1 to 2 tablespoons cocoa

1. Preheat the oven to 350°F. Invert 6 custard cups on a work surface and lightly grease the sides and bottoms. Line 2 baking sheets with parchment paper to bake the cookies on.

2. Combine the softened butter with the confectioners' sugar in a medium bowl. Beat until smooth and creamy. Beat in the vanilla. Add the egg whites a little at a time, until combined. Stir in the flour until a smooth paste is formed.

3. Remove ¼ cup of the paste and put it in a small bowl. Mix in the cocoa. The vanilla and cocoa pastes can be made ahead and refrigerated at this point. You must bring them to room temperature before you use them.

4. Using a rubber scraper, spread a thin circle of vanilla paste about 4 inches in diameter onto the prepared baking sheet. Three circles should fit on each sheet. Put the cocoa paste in a pastry bag and pipe a decorative pattern on the circles. ★

5. Bake the cookies for about 5 minutes, or until slightly golden on top and barely browned on the edges. Remove the baking sheet from the oven and, while the cookies are still hot, carefully remove the cookies with a wide spatula, and invert them onto the custard cups, pressing lightly to form a cookie cup. Repeat with the remaining vanilla and cocoa pastes. Let the cups cool completely before removing from the molds. If the cookies become too stiff to form over the cups, return them to the oven for 30 seconds and try again. You must work fairly fast as they will form better cups while still very warm.

6. Store up to 3 days in a deep, airtight container with a square of waxed paper between each.

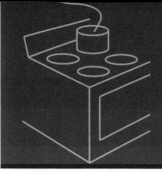

Desserts to Delight

Desserts are more than just sweet indulgences. Something sweet, even a simple, satisfying warm fruit dish like Grilled Nectarine Cobbler (page 188), is a beautiful finish to a hearty weekend meal. Chocolate never fails to please and you'll be able to serve it in multiple ways with these recipes—in mousse, in brownies, in cookies, and more. Variations for desserts are endless, and so are options for including your family and friends in the fun.

Dessert Tips:

- Desserts can often take on any of the seasonal flavors that you want. Give bread pudding or other classic recipes a seasonal spin by simply adding raisins, or sliced peaches, or a cup of blueberries.

- On weekends, plan at least one homemade dessert and see if you can get every family member to take turns making his or her favorite to share.

- Desserts flavored with certain spirits are a special treat when you are entertaining. Although not for family night dinners, these desserts can be simple to make but have great impact for your guests.

For most of us, we develop a sweet tooth when we are young and we never outgrow it. Nothing pleases everyone at the office more than when you bring a plate of fresh-baked brownies or cookies to work. The smiles that greet the gift of these tasty treats are priceless. A few lusciously chocolate bites have the power to balance the challenges of work demands in a hectic life.

Chocolate Mousse in Chocolate Swirl Cups

✓ *SOMETHING SPECIAL*   ✓ *MAKE-AHEAD*

The contrast of the delicate creamy flavor of white chocolate with the profound taste of bittersweet is a chocoholic's delight. Here's a dessert cup of white and dark chocolate filled with a luxurious chocolate mousse. Keep the cups cold as you work with them (and until serving) to prevent breakage.

CHOCOLATE CUPS

12 ounces good-quality white chocolate, chopped (12 squares)

10 ounces bittersweet chocolate, chopped (10 squares)

12 small balloons blown up and tied off, lightly oiled on the outside

MOUSSE

7 ounces bittersweet chocolate, chopped (7 squares)

1 ounce unsweetened chocolate, chopped (1 square)

3 tablespoons unsalted butter

1/3 cup sugar

2 tablespoons water

1 tablespoon light corn syrup

2 teaspoons orange zest (from 1 large orange)

1 cup large egg whites (from about 7 large eggs)

1/8 teaspoon cream of tartar

4 cups chilled heavy cream (1 quart)

1 teaspoon pure vanilla extract

Confectioners' sugar for serving

1 cup berries, any kind, or a mixture, for serving

Fresh mint leaves

1. To melt the chocolates, stir the bittersweet chocolate in the top of a double boiler over simmering water until melted and smooth. Spread the bittersweet chocolate over a sheet of parchment. Stir the white chocolate in the top of a clean double boiler over barely simmering water until melted and smooth. Drizzle the white chocolate over the dark chocolate.

2. To form the cups: Take a balloon and gently set it into the middle of the chocolate. Gently press the balloon forward, then back. Now move the balloon left, then right. You should start to see a tulip shape forming on the balloon. Slowly move the balloon on the diagonal, to the left forward then back. Now to the right on the diagonal, forward, then back. Lift the balloon and place it carefully upright on a cookie sheet that has been covered with parchment. Be careful not to dip the balloon too high in the chocolate or you will not be able to fill it with mousse. The cup should be about the size of a teacup. Repeat with all of the balloons. Place the cookie sheet in the refrigerator.

3. After the balloons have been in the refrigerator about 7 minutes, check if the chocolate is firm. Once it is firm, carefully pop the balloons at the stem by cutting a small slit in the top where the balloon is tied. Place the sheet back in the refrigerator. Do not pull the balloons out until the chocolate is very firm, about 2 hours more. Carefully remove the balloons and return the shells to the refrigerator.

4. For the mousse: Combine both chocolates and the butter in small saucepan. Stir over low heat until smooth. Cool slightly.

5. In a heavy small saucepan, combine the sugar, water, corn syrup, and zest. Stir over low heat until the sugar dissolves. Increase the heat; boil until a candy thermometer registers 238°F (tilting the pan, if necessary, to submerge the bulb of the thermometer), about 4 minutes. Brush down the sides of the pan with a wet pastry brush to keep the mixture from sticking.

6. Meanwhile, using an electric mixer on high, beat the egg whites and cream of tartar in the large bowl until soft peaks form. Remove the bowl and beater from the mixer and add the boiling syrup to the whites. With a wooden spoon, mix quickly by hand, so none of the syrup sticks to the sides of the bowl. Place the beater back on the mixer and beat until firm peaks form and meringue is completely cool and very shiny, about 5 minutes. Gradually fold the lukewarm chocolate mixture into the cooled meringue.

7. Beat the cream and vanilla in a small bowl until firm peaks form. Gently fold into the chocolate mixture. Chill about 1 hour, until cold. (The mousse filling can be made 1 day ahead. Cover separately; keep chilled.)

8. When you are ready to serve, pipe or spoon the mousse into the cups, swirling the top. Dust the cups with confectioners' sugar and garnish with berries and mint. Serve at once.

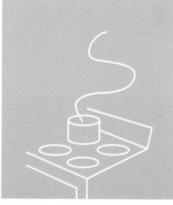

Chocolate Chip Mousse Brownies

✓ *SOMETHING SPECIAL*   ✓ *MAKE-AHEAD*

When I first moved to Reno, Nevada, I had the toughest time making great brownies because of the high elevation, until I created this recipe, which has become a family favorite. These brownies have a cake-like bottom layer, topped by an airy light and creamy layer, a combination that works well at all altitudes.

BATTER

½ cup margarine, at room temperature (Fleischmann's® preferred) *

2 cups semisweet chocolate chips (12 ounces)

1²/₃ cups sugar

1¹/₃ cups all-purpose flour

1 teaspoon pure vanilla extract

½ teaspoon baking powder

½ teaspoon salt

3 large eggs, at room temperature

TOPPING

¾ cup heavy cream

1 cup semisweet chocolate chips (6 ounces)

3 large eggs, at room temperature

¹/₃ cup sugar

¼ teaspoon salt

1. Make the batter: Preheat the oven to 350°F. Grease a 9- × 13-inch glass baking dish. Melt the margarine and the chocolate chips in a medium saucepan over medium-low heat. Pour the mixture into a large bowl. Add the sugar, flour, vanilla, baking powder, salt, and eggs, beating just until well mixed. Spread the mixture in the pan.

2. Make the topping: In a small saucepan, warm the heavy cream over medium heat until it starts to simmer, but don't let it boil. Add the chocolate chips and stir until the chocolate is melted. Cool this mixture slightly.

3. In the bowl of an electric mixer, combine the eggs, sugar, and salt. Mix at medium speed until foamy. Add the chocolate mixture and stir until combined. Pour this over the batter in the pan.

4. Bake for 45 minutes or until a toothpick inserted in the middle comes out surrounded with gooey crumbs. Cool on a wire cooling rack and then cut into 2-inch squares.

✻TIP: While **butter** and stick **margarine** are interchangeable in sauces and savory dishes, baking and pastry recipes that have been developed specifically with either butter or margarine frequently will not work if you substitute. Margarine has different shortening power, which will affect the texture of the finished dish.

Grilled Nectarine Cobbler

✓ *SOMETHING SPECIAL*   ✓ *EASY PREPARATION*

We all need a dessert recipe that we can throw together in a hurry, but with wonderful results. This delicious fruit crisp fills that need. Fruit is beautiful grilled—the caramelization of the sugars in the fruit emphasizes the unique flavor of each variety.

1 cup all-purpose flour

1/3 cup firmly packed brown sugar

1/4 cup granulated sugar

1/2 teaspoon ground cinnamon

1 tablespoon grated orange zest
(from 1 medium orange)

5 tablespoons unsalted butter

1/2 cup pecan halves, toasted
(2 ounces)

2 tablespoons fresh orange juice
(from 1 medium orange)

8 whole nectarines, sliced in half
with the pit removed

1. In a large bowl, combine the flour, brown sugar, granulated sugar, cinnamon, and zest. Cut the butter into the mixture. When the mixture resembles oatmeal, add the pecans and set aside.

2. Preheat the grill to medium-high heat. Drizzle the orange juice over the nectarine halves. Place some of the pecan mixture in each of the nectarine halves. Place the halves on the grill and close the hood. Cook for 12 to 15 minutes until the toppings brown and the nectarines begin to soften. ✱

SERVING SUGGESTION

Accompany this cobbler with ice cream or lightly sweetened whipped cream for an added treat.

VARIATION

Ripe fresh peaches can be substituted for the nectarines.

✱ TIP: For even **more grilled flavor** in the nectarines, start them cut side down on the grill before filling them. Once they are lightly browned, turn them over, place the topping in the half, and bake over indirect heat until done.

Grilled Bread Pudding with Dried Fruit

✓ *SOMETHING SPECIAL*   ✓ *MAKE-AHEAD*

Whenever I am grilling for dinner, I love to make dessert on the grill, too. You can make this classic dessert and put it on the grill as soon as you sit down to eat the main course and it will be ready when you are. Bread pudding isn't the only dessert that can be grilled. Place a cookie sheet over indirect heat and make cookies or bake a tray of brownies. Bake a fresh fruit cobbler. Whatever you want to make on the grill, when you know the exact temperature, anything is possible.

5 eggs

1 cup sugar

1 teaspoon pure vanilla extract

½ teaspoon ground cinnamon

¼ teaspoon ground nutmeg

2½ cups whole milk

½ cup dried cherries

2 teaspoons orange zest
(from 1 medium orange)

1 cup assorted dried fruit bits,
such as apples, apricots, pears,
dates, cranberries, blueberries, etc.

Six 1-inch-thick slices French bread,
cubed (about 4 to 6 cups)

1. In a medium bowl, beat the eggs until thick and yellow. Add the sugar, vanilla, cinnamon, and nutmeg. Beat until well blended. Add the milk, and then stir in the dried cherries, zest, and dried fruit. Add the bread cubes and toss until mixed well. Cover and allow to stand about 10 minutes to absorb all of the liquid.

2. Preheat the grill to medium indirect heat. Transfer the mixture into a greased 8- × 8-inch metal disposable aluminum pan or 8 individual ones.

3. Grill in a closed grill at about 375°F on the indirect heat side for about 40 minutes. The bread pudding should be firm and puffy. *

SERVING SUGGESTION

Top each serving of warm bread pudding with a scoop of vanilla ice cream or a dollop of whipped cream.

＊TIP: To grill-bake dessert, set an oven **thermometer** on the grill so you know exactly what the temperature is. Set up one side on the grill with heat under it and one side that is cool. The cool, or indirect, side is the side that you bake on.

Citrus Moscato Zabaglione

✓ *SOMETHING SPECIAL*   ✓ *MAKE-AHEAD*

Zabaglione or the French sabayon, a creamy sweet custard sauce, is delicious on its own, simply spooned out of wine glasses, but it becomes something very special when combined with fruit. This is one of my favorite desserts because it can be made with so many different flavored wines, including Chardonnay. Choose seasonal fruit and berries as the base.

8 egg yolks

½ cup sugar

¾ cup Muscat or Moscato Bianco wine ✻

1 teaspoon orange zest (from 1 medium orange)

1. In a large bowl, beat the egg yolks and the sugar with a balloon whisk or hand-held electric mixer, until the mixture is thick and pale yellow. Set the mixture in the top of a double boiler with simmering water under it. Add the wine slowly, beating all the while to incorporate air. Continue to cook and beat constantly until the mixture has doubled in volume to become a foamy cream, and is just barely hot to the touch. ✻

2. Fold in the orange zest and serve spooned over fruit.

SERVING SUGGESTION

Place fresh fruit such as orange slices, apples, apricots, or berries in a wine or martini glass. Spoon the zabaglione in the glass over the fruit and serve with a delicate cookie as a garnish.

✻**TIP:** Muscat or Moscato Bianco is a sweet dessert wine made from Muscat grapes.

✻**TIP:** For even more volume, use a large metal bowl over a stockpot of gently boiling water instead of a double boiler. With the added space you will be able to whisk more air into the zabaglione, which will make it lighter and foamier.

Cabernet Sorbet With Chocolate Cookies

✓ *SOMETHING SPECIAL*   ✓ *MAKE-AHEAD*

The fresh flavor of this wine sorbet is almost like biting into a bunch of cabernet grapes, a taste sensation unlike any other. The glorious purple color and deep wine taste make it a treat for both the eye and the palate, and chocolate is the perfect accompaniment.

Chocolate Cookies (next page)

1 cup sugar

1 cup water

2 cups Cabernet wine

2 tablespoons lemon juice (from 1 medium lemon)

4 small sprigs fresh mint, for garnish

1. Prepare the chocolate cookies. Then, in a saucepan, combine the sugar, water, and ½ cup of the Cabernet wine over medium-high heat. Bring to a boil, stirring to dissolve the sugar. Boil until the syrup thickens slightly, 2 minutes more. Remove from the heat and cool completely.

2. Combine the wine syrup with the remaining wine and the lemon juice. Pour the mixture into an ice-cream maker and freeze according to the manufacturer's instructions.

3. Serve the sorbet in wine glasses, garnished with fresh mint, and pass the chocolate cookies on the side.

VARIATION

Undiluted grape juice can be substituted for wine in this sorbet if you prefer. It will be slightly sweeter than the sorbet made with Cabernet.

(continues)

Chocolate Cookies

✓ *SOMETHING SPECIAL*   ✓ *MAKE-AHEAD*

The surface of these cookies will be cracked and slightly puffed with a crunchy sugar coating. These delicious ragged-edge cookies are perfect with our Cabernet Sorbet, complementing each other as only chocolate and red wine can.

2 cups semisweet chocolate chips (about 12 ounces)

1½ cups all-purpose flour

¾ teaspoon baking powder

½ teaspoon baking soda

Pinch salt

5 tablespoons butter, softened

⅓ cup sugar, plus ½ cup more for coating the cookies

1 teaspoon pure vanilla extract

1 egg, lightly beaten with a fork

2 tablespoons strong coffee

1. Preheat the oven to 350°F.

2. Place the chocolate chips in a microwave-safe bowl. Microwave on high for 60 seconds. Stir the chocolate. If it hasn't melted completely, microwave on medium in 10- to 20-second increments, stirring after each, until the chocolate is melted and smooth. The chocolate may also be melted in the top of a double boiler set over simmering water.

3. In a small bowl, stir together the flour, baking powder, baking soda, and salt.

4. In a larger bowl, beat together the butter and ⅓ cup sugar until light and fluffy. Beat in the vanilla. Beat in the egg and coffee. Stir in

the cooled chocolate. Stir in the flour mixture. The dough will be very soft.

5. Dip your hands in flour and roll the dough by tablespoonfuls into balls. Fill a flat bowl with the ½ cup sugar. Roll the dough balls in the sugar and place on a lightly greased cookie sheet. Dip the bottom of a glass in sugar and flatten the cookies.

6. Bake 10 to 12 minutes, until the surface is cracked.

7. Cool the cookies completely on a rack. Store them up to 1 week in a tightly closed can or jar—but not in a plastic container, as they will become soggy in plastic.

Muscat-Poached Pears with Candied Orange Slices

✓ *EASY PREPARATION*   ✓ *MAKE-AHEAD*

This very easy, but elegant, make-ahead dessert will be the perfect ending to your next celebration dinner. The candied orange slices are not difficult, but require time in between the steps, so make them the day before.

Candied Orange Slices (next page)

4 large Bosc pears, peeled, halved, and cored ✱

3 cups Muscat wine, or white grape juice

1 tablespoon orange zest cut in strips with a zester, not grated on a Microplane (from 1 medium orange)

4 sprigs fresh mint, for garnish

1. Make the candied orange slices at least one, but up to several days ahead.

2. In a large saucepan, combine the pear halves, wine, and zest. Simmer over low heat, just until the pears are tender but not falling apart when pierced with a cake tester, about 20 minutes. Cover, remove from the heat, and cool the pears completely in the syrup.

3. To serve: Place 3 candied orange slice halves in each of 4 compote or dessert dishes. Arrange 2 pear halves on top. Spoon some of the Muscat syrup over all. Garnish with 1 orange slice cut in half, and top with a sprig of fresh mint.

✱ TIP: Pears are an especially good fruit for **poaching** as they absorb both the flavor and color of the poaching liquid. Red and white wines are both good poaching liquids, but you will need to add sugar to sweeten the mixture. The advantage of using sweet wine is that you do not need to add anything else. Peeled peaches and apricots are also fine for poaching, but they are not as resilient as pears.

(continues)

Candied Orange Slices

✓ *SOMETHING SPECIAL*   ✓ *MAKE-AHEAD*

After making the candied orange, reserve the sugar syrup for pancakes, or for drizzling over pound cake or vanilla ice cream.

2 large seedless oranges, well washed

About 2½ cups water

1¼ cups sugar

1. Cut the oranges across into ¼-inch slices. In a large heavy saucepan, cover the oranges with the water and simmer gently, just until the rind is barely tender when pierced with a knife, 6 to 8 minutes. Drain, reserving the cooking water. Spread the fruit in one layer on a rack set over a cloth towel. Dry for 30 minutes.

2. In the same saucepan, combine 1¼ cups of the reserved cooking water and ¾ cup of the sugar. Cook over low heat just until the sugar is melted. Add the fruit and simmer for 5 minutes. Remove from the heat and cool the oranges completely in the syrup. Return the orange slices to the rack for 30 minutes.

3. Add the remaining ½ cup sugar to the syrup and simmer just until the sugar dissolves. Return the fruit to the saucepan and simmer 5 minutes more.

Remove from the heat and cool the fruit in the syrup again. When cool, spread the slices in one layer on the rack, and dry overnight.

VARIATION

Dry the orange slices on the rack set over a rimmed baking sheet in a 150°F oven for 6 hours. Cool completely. Dip one-half of each slice in melted chocolate, chill, and serve as a candy, alongside cups of strong black coffee.

Cookie Temptations

Baking cookies can recall some of your first cooking memories. And bringing your children into the kitchen with you helps you continue the legacy. I love to bake with my son, Matthew. It takes more time to bake with him because he wants to learn every step, or to make special shapes out of the dough, but the time spent is well worth it—and weekends are the perfect time for indulging in the satisfying pleasure of baking cookies. We have a lot of fun together mixing the dough, rolling it out, and decorating the cookies. Whether the final cookies are perfect or not, children get a lot of satisfaction showing off what they have accomplished.

Crisp, soft, or chewy, decorated or not, cookies all have special meanings to us. Who doesn't appreciate a cookie or two (or five. . .) to make us feel better? I think cookies work better than chicken soup to chase the blues away and are worth the effort if I can lift the spirits of not only myself but my family and friends.

Among the tried-and-true recipes in this chapter are my favorite Classic Sugar Cookies (page 196)—which you can vary endlessly simply by cutting different shapes or using special decorative sugars and icings—and my grandmother's Chocolate Chip and Cinnamon Rugelach (page 201). For something a little different, try light crisp almond-flavored Amaretti (page 199) or jazz up rich and delicious shortbread with crunchy toffee. You can't miss with any of these recipes.

Classic Sugar Cookies

✓ *MAKE-AHEAD*   ✓ *TAKE-ALONG*

My favorite after-school ritual when I was a kid was munching on freshly made sugar cookies right off the cooling rack. This recipe is a close re-creation of that childhood favorite. You may find you are making these often, as they don't last very long, especially if you cut them into fun shapes.

1 cup butter (2 sticks), softened

1 cup sugar

1 egg, lightly beaten with a fork

2 tablespoons whole milk

1 tablespoon pure vanilla extract

2½ cups all-purpose flour

½ teaspoon baking powder

1. Preheat the oven to 375°F. In a large bowl, beat together the butter and sugar until light and fluffy. Beat in the egg and milk. Beat in the vanilla.

2. In a smaller bowl, combine the flour and baking powder with a fork. Stir into the butter mixture and gather the dough together into a ball. Divide the dough into 4 parts and shape each into a round flat cake. Cover with plastic wrap and refrigerate for 2 hours.

3. On a silicone baking pad, such as Silpat, roll 1 portion of the dough into a ⅛- to ¼-inch-thick round. Keep remaining rounds refrigerated until ready to cook. Cut with a 2- or 3-inch cookie or biscuit cutter, dipping it in flour each time to prevent it sticking to the dough. Using your fingers and the tip of a knife, remove the excess dough from around the cookies, and set it aside. Set the mat with the cookies on a baking sheet.

4. Bake for 8 to 10 minutes until golden brown around the edges. While the cookies are still warm, remove them from the mat with a wide spatula and cool completely on a rack.

5. Repeat with the remaining 3 dough rounds. With 2 silicone mats, you can prepare a second pan of cookies while one bakes. Gather the excess dough into another round and refrigerate, covered, or freeze to bake at another time.

VARIATION

Cut into special shapes with cookie cutters. Decorate, if you like, with colored sugar before baking, or with colored icings once they are cooled.

Toffee Shortbread

✓ *MAKE-AHEAD*　✓ *TAKE-ALONG*

Shortbread, a Scottish staple, is a crisp, ultra-rich butter pastry that is the perfect accompaniment for a steaming cup of coffee or milky tea. Cut these into scallop-edged rounds with a fluted cookie or biscuit cutter and put them in a decorative box, along with a variety of your favorite cookies, for a great gift.

1½ cups all-purpose flour

⅓ cup firmly packed brown sugar

2½ tablespoons cornstarch

⅛ teaspoon salt

½ cup (1 stick) unsalted butter, chilled and cubed

¾ teaspoon pure vanilla extract

2 large egg yolks

2 tablespoons cold water

½ cup pecan pieces, toasted and finely chopped (from 2 ounces)

⅓ cup finely chopped English toffee

2 tablespoons granulated sugar

1. In a large bowl, combine the flour, brown sugar, cornstarch, and salt. Add the butter and cut it into the dry ingredients with a pastry cutter, until the mixture resembles oatmeal flakes. Make a well in the center of the flour mixture and add the vanilla, egg yolks, and cold water.

2. Mix in the liquids with a wooden spoon until the dough is just formed and fairly stiff. Add the pecans and the toffee, and combine with your hands just until all ingredients are well mixed. Be careful not to overwork the dough. Form the dough into a disk, wrap it in plastic, and chill for 1 hour.

3. Preheat the oven to 350°F. Place the dough between 2 pieces of plastic wrap. Roll out the dough to ¼-inch thickness. Remove the top piece of plastic wrap. Using a 2-inch fluted round cutter, cut the cookies, and place on a parch-ment-lined cookie sheet. Gently combine the dough scraps into a disk, cover with plastic, and roll out to ¼-inch thickness. Cut cookies out of the remaining dough and place on a parchment-lined cookie sheet. Chill the raw cookies for 10 minutes before baking.

4. Lightly sprinkle the cookies with granulated sugar. Bake in the preheated oven about 20 minutes, until they are light golden brown. Do not overbake. Cool the cookies on the sheet for 5 minutes. Transfer the cookies to a wire cooling rack to cool completely. Store them in an airtight container.

VARIATION

Substitute ¼ cup finely chopped candied ginger for the toffee if you prefer your cookies with a little spicy bite.

Pecan Nut Tassies

MAKES 2 DOZEN COOKIES

✓ *SOMETHING SPECIAL*   ✓ *MAKE-AHEAD*   ✓ *TAKE-ALONG*

These bite-sized morsels are one of my favorite cookies to make during the holidays. They will remind you of a pecan pie, only in little packages. Substitute other nuts for the pecans, such as walnuts or macadamia nuts, or, if you would like a plainer cake, eliminate the nuts from the filling altogether. Then they will resemble tiny brown sugar pies. Whatever you choose, these will please your holiday crowd every time!

¼ cup cream cheese, at room temperature (2 ounces)

½ cup (1 stick) unsalted butter, plus 1 tablespoon, at room temperature

1 cup all-purpose flour

1 large egg, at room temperature

¾ cup firmly packed dark brown sugar

1 teaspoon pure vanilla extract

⅛ teaspoon salt

⅔ cup pecan pieces, toasted (from about 2½ ounces)

1. To make the pastry, combine the cream cheese and ½ cup of the butter in the bowl of an electric mixer. Mix at high speed until the mixture is light and fluffy. Reduce the speed to low and add the flour. Mix until just incorporated.

2. Form the dough into two 6-inch logs and wrap them in plastic wrap. Refrigerate them at least 1½ hours, until firm.

3. Preheat the oven to 325°F. Unwrap the dough and cut each log into twelve ½-inch-thick pieces. Press each piece into a miniature muffin cup so that the dough lines the bottom and sides. Press the edges up just beyond the rim. *

4. In a medium bowl, combine the egg, brown sugar, 1 tablespoon butter, vanilla, and salt. Mix in one-half of the pecans. Spoon the mixture into the lined muffin cups. Fill the cups almost to the top. Use the remaining pecans to top the cookies.

5. Bake about 25 minutes, until the filling is puffed and set, and the crust begins to turn golden.

6. Cool the cookies completely in the tins on a wire cooling rack. Carefully remove the cookies from the tins, loosening gently with a sharp paring knife if they stick. Store in an airtight container in the refrigerator for up to 3 days.

*TIP: Miniature muffin tins with 1½-inch cups come in 12- or 24-cup sizes, and are often available in your supermarket bakeware section, or at kitchen stores.

Amaretti

✓ *SOMETHING SPECIAL*   ✓ *MAKE-AHEAD*   ✓ *TAKE-ALONG*

I first had these cookies when I was in Italy. There they are often served, wrapped in pairs in tissue paper, with strong coffee and sometimes even with a glass of red wine, or as a digestif after dinner. A little bit like a macaroon—light and airy, with just a hint of almond flavor—they nearly melt in your mouth. Making amaretti cookies at home isn't difficult, but it is definitely not a busy-night task. Plan on making this a weekend project and enlist anyone who's home to join in. This dough will seem wet, but it will bake up perfectly to create a wonderful chewy cookie.

4 cups blanched almonds, finely ground in a food processor along with ¼ cup sugar

1¼ cups sugar

2 teaspoons pure vanilla extract

2 tablespoons Amaretto liqueur

3 large egg whites, at room temperature

1. Preheat the oven to 300°F. Grease and flour a baking sheet. In a medium bowl, use a wooden spoon to combine the almond and sugar mixture, sugar, vanilla, and Amaretto. Stir in the egg whites, one at a time, to make a paste.

2. Dampen your hands with water and form the dough into 1-inch balls. Place them on a baking sheet lined with parchment or a silicone mat. ✱

3. Bake in the preheated oven for 20 to 30 minutes, until lightly golden brown. Cool completely on a wire cooling rack. Store up to 1 week in an airtight container.

✱**TIP:** Because they are dishwasher safe, the durable, nonstick surface of **silicone mats, used on cookie sheets instead of parchment,** is great for baking, candy making, or anything that can be messy. They are sold at most gourmet supply stores and can withstand heat up to 650°F. There is another mat, capable of temperatures up to 900°F, that can be used for pizza baking, but they are still basically nonstick baking surfaces.

Caramel Turtle Bars

✓ *SOMETHING SPECIAL*   ✓ *MAKE-AHEAD*   ✓ *TAKE-ALONG*

Turtle candies, those thick chocolate-covered caramels studded with pecan halves, are a favorite around our house. These bars make you think of the luscious little candy patties, but they are even more delicious. You might want to freeze some as soon as they are cool or they might all disappear before your eyes.

2 cups all-purpose flour

½ cup (1 stick) butter, softened, plus ¾ cup (1½ sticks)

1 pinch salt

1 cup firmly packed light brown sugar, plus ⅔ cup

1½ cups toasted pecan halves (from 6 ounces)

1 teaspoon pure vanilla extract

1 cup semisweet chocolate chips (6 ounces)

1. Preheat the oven to 375°F. In a medium bowl, combine the flour, 1 stick of the butter, salt, and 1 cup of the brown sugar, stirring until smooth. Press the dough evenly into a 9- × 13-inch ungreased baking pan. The mixture appears dry and crumbly, but just go ahead and press it firmly into the pan. Arrange the pecan halves on top.

2. In a small saucepan over medium-high heat, combine the remaining ¾ cup butter and ⅔ cup brown sugar and stir until the sugar is melted. Bring to a boil and cook until slightly thickened, 1 minute. Remove from the heat. With a wooden spoon, beat in the vanilla until the mixture is smooth. Pour the caramel into the pan over the pecans.

3. Bake 18 to 20 minutes, until the caramel is bubbling and the edges of the crust are lightly browned. Watch carefully so the cookies do not burn. Remove from the oven and sprinkle the chocolate chips over the top. Return to the oven for 2 minutes, until the chips melt. Remove the pan from the oven and, with a small spatula, spread the melted chocolate evenly over the caramel.

4. Cool completely in the pan. When cooled, cut into 1- × 2-inch bars.

Chocolate Chip and Cinnamon Rugelach

✓ *MAKE-AHEAD*   ✓ *TAKE-ALONG*

My grandmother had a very small repertoire of recipes that she used to make, and these rugelach cookies were always at her house when I came to visit. This traditional cookie combines a rich cream cheese dough rolled around a spicy filling that can contain fruit, nuts, chocolate, cinnamon, whatever is at hand. They keep well for several days in an airtight container, and can be frozen for up to two weeks.

★TIP: Refrigerate the dough disk between sheets of plastic wrap if the pastry becomes too soft and sticky as you roll it out. Finish rolling it out and then chill the pastry again. It will be easier to cut if it is cold. Keeping the pastry chilled will also result in a flakier cookie.

PASTRY

1 cup (2 sticks) unsalted butter, at room temperature

One 8-ounce bar cream cheese, at room temperature

1/2 teaspoon salt

2 1/4 cups all-purpose flour

FILLING

1/2 cup sugar

3 teaspoons ground cinnamon

3 tablespoons unsalted butter, melted

3/4 cup miniature semisweet chocolate chips (about 4 ounces)

TOPPING

1 egg white, beaten with a fork until light and foamy

1 teaspoon water

1/2 cup sugar

1 1/2 teaspoons ground cinnamon

1. To make the pastry, combine the butter and cream cheese in the bowl of an electric mixer on high speed. Beat until smooth.

Mix in the salt. Add the flour and mix well, but don't overbeat. Bring the pastry together into a flat round. Cut into 4 equal pieces. Flatten each piece into a disk and wrap separately in waxed paper. Refrigerate overnight.

2. Preheat the oven to 375°F. Lightly butter three cookie sheets. Take 1 of the disks out of the refrigerator. Place it on a floured sheet of plastic wrap, flour the disk, and top with more plastic wrap. Roll the disk out to a round 1/8 inch thick. Loosen the plastic wrap and remove the top sheet. Repeat with the other 3 disks. ★

3. To make the filling, combine the sugar and cinnamon in a small bowl. Brush the pastry with melted butter, and immediately sprinkle the mixture over the buttered pastry. Top with one-fourth of the chocolate chips.

Using a rolling pin, gently roll over the filling to help the chips adhere to the pastry. Cut the round of pastry through its center into 12 wedges. Starting at the wide end, roll up each wedge into a horn shape. Transfer the cookies to a cookie sheet. Arrange them point-sides down, spaced 1 inch apart. Repeat with the remaining disks of pastry and filling ingredients.

4. To make the topping, beat the egg white with the water in a small bowl. Combine the sugar and cinnamon in a separate bowl. Brush the cookies with the egg white and water mixture, and sprinkle the cinnamon-sugar mixture over the cookies. Bake about 15 minutes, until golden brown. Transfer the hot cookies to wire racks to cool completely. Store in an airtight container at room temperature for up to 5 days.

Bake the Cake

You don't need to become a master baker to make a great cake. You just need a few fail-safe recipes to make any birthday, holiday, get-together, or weekend family night special. (And just think how happy your kids will be with a slice of homemade cake with their lunch during the week.)

Baking a cake can be true culinary magic. Like nothing else that you can do in the kitchen, it is the transformation before your eyes of a few simple ingredients into something profound. Kids love watching or helping out because it's a tasty version of science-in-action.

The Secrets to Baking

It is the relative need for precision in the cake-baking preparation that separates baking from savory cooking. The proper measurements, temperatures, mixing times, pans, and oven preparation do need to be addressed. Although it is different from the more casual or creative work needed for cooking, don't let it scare you off. The results are terrific, and the whole family will share your pleasure in the final product. Whether your favorite is an old-fashioned coconut lemon-filled delight, the rich, deeply buttery flavor of a pound cake, or the lighter, more diet-friendly angel food cake topped with fresh fruit, you will find a great version here. I call these cakes my "Basic Six" because one of them fits for just about any occasion—deliciously.

Cake Tips:

- Have all ingredients at room temperature.

- Assemble all the equipment before you begin.

- Be sure your oven temperature is correct. Use an oven thermometer to be certain.

- Grease and flour baking pans as directed, or use nonstick spray.

- Fill layer pans equally. Tap filled pans against the countertop to force out air bubbles and settle the batter—except for angel food cake.

- Let the cake cool in the pan for about ten minutes (except for the angel food cake, which should be cooled completely in the pan)—then turn it upside down on a rack, remove the pan, and let it cool completely.

- Use a clean, soft brush to remove crumbs before icing the completely cooled cake.

- Store in covered containers, in the refrigerator if keeping for more than a few hours.

You can count on one 8- or 10-inch cake making 12 to 16 servings, depending on the size of the cut.

Brown Sugar Pound Cake

✓ *MAKE-AHEAD*   ✓ *TAKE-ALONG*

If you grew up in the South 50 years ago, you knew this traditional cake was reserved for special occasions and special people. To me, as a child, it seemed there were never enough special occasions, and slices of this treasure were few and far between. Make it yourself, today, and see how delicious it still is.

1 cup butter (2 sticks), softened, plus 2 tablespoons to grease the cake pan (2¼ sticks in all)

2 tablespoons granulated sugar

2½ cups all-purpose flour

¼ teaspoon salt

1 teaspoon baking powder

1¾ cups firmly packed light brown sugar

4 large eggs

2 teaspoons pure vanilla extract

⅔ cup sour cream

1. Preheat the oven to 325°F. Very generously butter a tube pan with a removable bottom. Dust evenly with granulated sugar.

2. In a large bowl, stir together the flour, salt, and baking powder.

3. In the bowl of an electric mixer, cream the 1 cup of butter and brown sugar on medium speed until light and fluffy. Beat in the eggs, 1 at a time, until well mixed. Beat in the vanilla. On low speed, blend in the sour cream alternately with the dry ingredients, until barely mixed after each addition.

4. Spoon the batter into the prepared pan. Bake 1 hour and 10 to 15 minutes, until a cake tester comes out clean. ✱

5. Cool the cake in the pan for 10 minutes. Loosen the edges, turn the cake out onto a rack, and cool completely. ✱

✱ **TIP:** To test whether a cake is done, insert a wooden skewer or metal cake tester into the middle of the cake. When it is removed, the skewer should be clean, or have only a few moist crumbs clinging to it—there should be no uncooked batter adhering to the surface.

✱ **TIP:** The flavor of this cake deepens and matures if it is made a day or two in advance and stored, well covered, at room temperature before cutting.

Almond Bundt Cake

✓ *SOMETHING SPECIAL*　　✓ *MAKE-AHEAD*　　✓ *TAKE-ALONG*

You'll love how quickly and easily you can make this cake; it may just become your favorite "company is coming" cake or cake for the office. Bundt pans are deep, have a 12- to 14-cup capacity, and a characteristic fluted pattern. They are available everywhere now and are not expensive, especially the lightweight Teflon-coated pans.

1 cup (2 sticks) unsalted butter, at room temperature

1 cup sour cream, at room temperature (1/2 pint)

1 teaspoon pure vanilla extract

3 cups all-purpose flour, sifted

1/2 teaspoon salt

3 teaspoons baking powder

1 teaspoon baking soda

1 1/2 cups sugar

1 1/2 teaspoons ground cinnamon

3 large eggs, at room temperature

1 cup chopped almonds with skins on (from 4 ounces)

1. Preheat the oven to 350°F. Generously grease and flour a 10-inch Bundt pan.

2. In the bowl of an electric mixer, combine the butter, sour cream, and vanilla. With the flat beater, mix on medium speed until the ingredients are combined, about 1 minute.

3. Sift the flour, salt, baking powder, baking soda, sugar, and cinnamon onto a piece of parchment paper or waxed paper. Add to the butter mixture, and beat for another 2 minutes. ✱

4. Add the eggs, 1 at a time, with the mixer on low speed. Finish by gently folding in the nuts.

5. Pour the batter into the prepared pan, and bake for 1 hour or until a wooden skewer or cake tester inserted into the middle of the cake comes out clean. Cool the cake in the pan for 15 minutes. Remove the cake from the pan and cool it completely on a wire cooling rack.

✱ **TIP:** By **sifting** the dry ingredients onto a piece of waxed paper or parchment, you will be able to add the dry ingredients to the mixer without spilling them. Pour the mixture into the butter mixture, no spooning, no mess.

Coconut Cake with Lemon Curd Filling

✓ *SOMETHING SPECIAL*   ✓ *MAKE-AHEAD*   ✓ *TAKE-ALONG*

Baking a cake from scratch for a special occasion is a perfect weekend family project. Many a county-fair blue ribbon has been won by some variation of this old-fashioned beauty. Easier to make than some, this cake retains all the lure of the prize-winning versions. Try your skills at shredding your own fresh coconut for an extra special treat.

2¼ cups sifted cake flour, plus more for flouring pans *

2 teaspoons baking powder

Pinch salt

¾ cup butter (1½ sticks), softened, plus more for greasing pans

1½ cups sugar

3 eggs, separated

1½ teaspoons pure vanilla extract

1 cup whole milk

2 cups flaked or shredded, unsweetened coconut (for preparing fresh coconut, see Tip on page 172)

Cream Cheese Frosting (next page)

1 cup lemon curd (from one 10-ounce jar)

1. Preheat the oven to 350°F. Generously butter and flour two 9-inch cake tins and line the bottoms with parchment or waxed paper.

2. In a medium bowl, sift together the flour, baking powder, and salt.

3. In the bowl of an electric mixer on medium speed, beat together the butter and sugar until light and fluffy. Beat in the egg yolks, 1 at a time, until well mixed. Beat in the vanilla. On low speed, add the flour mixture alternately with the milk, beginning and ending with the flour. Remove the bowl from the mixer and stir in 1 cup of the coconut.

4. In a clean bowl, with clean beaters, beat the egg whites until soft peaks form. *

5. Combine about one-quarter of the egg whites with the cake batter to lighten it a little. Very carefully fold the remaining egg whites into the batter until it is light and airy.

6. Pour the batter evenly into the prepared cake pans. Tap them

lightly on the counter to settle the batter. Bake 20 to 25 minutes, or until a tester inserted in the center comes out clean. Loosen the edges of the cake with a sharp knife and turn the layers out onto a rack. Cool completely.

7. While the cake is baking, make the cream cheese frosting.

8. To build the cake: Turn 1 layer upside down on the cake plate. Spread thickly with 1 cup of the lemon curd. Top with the second layer, right side up. Frost the sides and top with the cream cheese frosting. Spread the remaining 1 cup of coconut evenly over the top of the cake, pressing it into the soft frosting. Refrigerate several hours to set the frosting.

(continues)

*TIP: **Cake flour** is sold in boxes in the baking section of your supermarket. If you don't have any cake flour on hand, here is a simple substitute: For each cup of flour, add 2 tablespoons cornstarch and sift all together two or three times until fully combined.

*TIP: **Egg whites** have reached the **soft peak stage** when you can lift the beater out of the egg whites, turn the beater upside down, and the egg whites will fold over gracefully, sort of like the curl on a soft custard cone.

Cream Cheese Frosting

½ cup (1 stick) butter, softened

One 8-ounce package cream cheese, softened

4 cups confectioners' sugar

2 tablespoons fresh lemon juice (from 1 medium lemon)

1½ teaspoons pure vanilla extract

In the bowl of an electric mixer on medium speed, beat together the butter and cream cheese until light and fluffy. On low speed, add the sugar, lemon juice, and vanilla. Beat on high until smooth and creamy, about 3 minutes.

Mrs. Sarrett's Chocolate Cake

✓ *SOMETHING SPECIAL*　　✓ *MAKE-AHEAD*　　✓ *TAKE-ALONG*

When I was young, I lived in Evansville, Indiana. We were lucky to have a dear friend by the name of Helen Sarrett who made the most beautiful chocolate cake. Every one of my birthdays was celebrated with this chocolate cake. It rose high and light, was very moist, and had just enough chocolate to hit the spot. Fortunately, I was able to get her recipe, and now we can make it at home.

1½ tablespoons lemon juice (from 1 medium lemon)

1½ cups whole milk

2 cups sugar

½ cup unsweetened processed cocoa, sifted

½ cup (1 stick) unsalted butter, at room temperature

2 large eggs, at room temperature

2 cups all-purpose flour

1 teaspoon baking soda

½ teaspoon salt

1 teaspoon pure vanilla extract

Chocolate Cream Frosting (next page)

1. Position the rack in the center of the oven and preheat to 375°F. Butter and flour two 10-inch cake pans with 2-inch-high sides. Line each with a round of parchment paper or waxed paper.

2. Combine the lemon juice and milk to make the sour milk. Allow this to stand for at least 10 minutes at room temperature.

3. In a small bowl, combine 1 cup of the sugar, the cocoa, and ½ cup of the sour milk. Set aside.

4. In the bowl of an electric mixer on medium speed, beat the remaining 1 cup of sugar and the butter until light and fluffy. Beat in the eggs 1 at a time.

5. Sift together the flour, baking soda, and salt. Add the remaining 1 cup sour milk to the butter mixture, alternately with the dry ingredients, in three additions. Beat until smooth. Beat in the cocoa mixture and the vanilla.

6. Pour the batter into the prepared cake pans. Wipe any drips that fall onto the edges of the cake pans. Place the cake pans on the center rack, being careful that they do not touch each other. Bake the layers about 40 minutes, until a tester inserted into the center comes out clean. Cool

the layers completely in the pans on cooling racks.

7. While the cake is baking, make the chocolate cream frosting.

8. To build the cake: Place 1 cake layer upside down on a platter. Spread ½ cup of the chocolate cream frosting over the top. Cover with the other cake layer, top up. Spread the remaining frosting over the sides and top of the cake in decorative swirls. This cake can be prepared 1 day ahead. Cover with a cake dome and store at cool room temperature.

(continues)

Chocolate Cream Frosting

This frosting is versatile and easy to put together. Plan to combine the frosting while the layers are baking, so it will be at spreading consistency when you are ready to frost the cake. Place a damp paper towel over the frosting bowl while you are waiting to frost the cake.

1 cup (2 sticks) unsalted butter

½ cup cocoa

4 cups confectioners' sugar

½ cup whipping cream

1 teaspoon pure vanilla extract

Melt the butter in a small saucepan over low heat or in a microwavable bowl for 1 minute in the microwave. Add the cocoa and stir until smooth. Transfer to a large bowl. Cool. Add the sugar, cream, and vanilla. Beat with an electric mixer until smooth and shiny. If necessary, refrigerate the frosting until firm enough to spread.

Angel Food Cake

✓ *MAKE-AHEAD*   ✓ *TAKE-ALONG*

This dieter's dream dessert—at about 150 calories per slice—goes in and out of fashion like hemlines, but always tastes delicious. Top a slice of this sponge cake with lightly sweetened fruit, or even a drizzle of chocolate syrup, and you have an elegant, but easy, ending for any meal.

1 cup cake flour (see Tip page 205)

¼ teaspoon salt

1½ cups superfine granulated sugar

12 egg whites, at room temperature ∗

1 teaspoon pure vanilla extract

1. Preheat the oven to 350°F.

2. In a large bowl, sift together the flour, salt, and half the sugar.

3. In the bowl of an electric mixer on medium-high speed, beat the egg whites and vanilla until soft peaks form. With the mixer on medium speed, gradually add the remaining the sugar, ¼ cup at a time. Beat until the whites are stiff and shiny, 4 to 5 minutes all together.

4. Remove the bowl from the mixer and sprinkle the flour mixture over the egg whites, ¼ cup at a time. Fold the flour into the egg white mixture very gently after each addition, just until there are no visible signs of the flour. Do not overmix or the cake will not be as high and tender.

5. Gently spoon the batter into an ungreased tube pan with a removable bottom. ∗

6. Bake 35 to 45 minutes, until the surface springs back when touched, and a wooden skewer or metal cake tester inserted at the center between the side and the inner tube of the pan comes out clean. Cool the cake completely, upside down in the pan. ∗

7. Run a knife gently around the edges, and turn the cake out onto a plate.

∗**TIP:** Save the egg yolks for sauces or other cakes. Egg yolks will keep in the refrigerator for 1 week in a tightly closed refrigerator container. Spoon a tablespoon or two of vegetable oil over the surface of the yolks for added protection.

∗**TIP:** The **secret to a great angel food cake** is no grease. Everything, from the mixing bowls, to the beaters, to the cake tin, should be scrupulously washed, rinsed, and dried before using, because grease makes the egg whites deflate.

∗**TIP:** If the **tube pan** does not have "legs" on the rim to hold it above the work surface when turned upside down, slip the hole in the middle of the pan over a filled soda or wine bottle to keep it suspended in the air. This will allow the cake to cool evenly, with no weight on it while it is hot.

Chocolate Ice Cream Roll Cake

✓ SOMETHING SPECIAL

This begins with a classic egg-rich chocolate sponge cake. It becomes a "wow" dessert when filled with your favorite flavor of ice cream, rolled, and then cut into slices. Each slice presents a pretty spiral of ice cream and cake.

8 large eggs, separated, at room temperature

1 cup sugar

⅓ cup sifted unsweetened cocoa, plus extra for dusting

3 tablespoons all-purpose flour

1 quart best-quality ice cream of choice

1. Position a rack in the middle of the oven and preheat to 350°F. Line an 11½- × 17-inch jellyroll pan with parchment paper.

2. Combine the egg yolks and ½ cup of the sugar in the bowl of an electric mixer. Beat on high speed until thick and pale. Remove the bowl from the stand and, with a rubber spatula, gently fold in the cocoa and flour.

3. In another electric mixer bowl, with clean beaters, beat the egg whites on low speed until foamy. When the whites are foamy,

increase the speed and slowly add the remaining ½ cup sugar beating until soft peaks form. Using a rubber spatula, add one-third of the whites to the cocoa mixture. This will help the mixture stay fluffy. Stir until just combined, and the batter is lightened. Add in one-third more of the whites and carefully fold them into the batter. Finish with the remaining whites and fold them in until they are just combined. ✱

4. Spread the batter in the pan and smooth the top. Bake about 9 to 12 minutes, until the top looks and feels spongy. Cool in the pan on a wire cooling rack.

5. Run a knife around the cake's edges to loosen it from the pan. Dust the top with cocoa. Place plastic wrap over the top to extend slightly beyond the pan edges.

Place a baking sheet upside down on top and invert the pan. Lift off the pan and peel off the parchment paper.

6. Beat the ice cream with an electric mixer until soft and spreadable, about 1 minute. Spread the softened ice cream onto the cake, leaving a 1-inch border all around. With the help of the plastic wrap and starting from a long side, roll up to form a long, firm roll. Wrap the roll in plastic wrap and then aluminum foil and freeze for 4 hours or up to 1 month. To serve, unwrap and cut it into slices.

SERVING SUGGESTION

Serve with Homemade Hot Fudge Sauce (page 181).

✱ **TIP:** When **beating egg whites**, start the mixer slowly, gradually increasing speed as the whites begin to foam. Add the sugar slowly so that you don't weigh down the whites. When they are done they will be shiny and take the shape of soft-serve ice cream, no firmer.

Index

Metric Conversion Guide

Weight

U.S. Units	Canadian Metric	Australian Metric
1 ounce	30 grams	30 grams
2 ounces	55 grams	60 grams
3 ounces	85 grams	90 grams
4 ounces (1/4 pound)	115 grams	125 grams
8 ounces (1/2 pound)	225 grams	225 grams
16 ounces (1 pound)	455 grams	500 grams (1/2 kilogram)

Volume

U.S. Units	Canadian Metric	Australian Metric
1/4 teaspoon	1 mL	1 ml
1/2 teaspoon	2 mL	2 ml
1 teaspoon	5 mL	5 ml
1 tablespoon	15 mL	20 ml
1/4 cup	50 mL	60 ml
1/3 cup	75 mL	80 ml
1/2 cup	125 mL	125 ml
2/3 cup	150 mL	170 ml
3/4 cup	175 mL	190 ml
1 cup	250 mL	250 ml
1 quart	1 liter	1 liter
2 quarts	2 liters	2 liters
3 quarts	3 liters	3 liters
4 quarts	4 liters	4 liters

Note: The recipes in this cookbook have not been developed or tested using metric measures.

Temperatures

Fahrenheit	Celsius
32°	0°
212°	100°
250°	120°
275°	140°
300°	150°
325°	160°
350°	180°
375°	190°
400°	200°
425°	220°
450°	230°
475°	240°
500°	260°

Measurements

Inches	Centimeters
1	2.5
2	5.0
3	7.5
4	10.0
5	12.5
6	15.0
7	17.5
8	20.5
9	23.0
10	25.5
11	28.0
12	30.5